Reframing Teacher Education: Dimensions of a Constructivist Approach

Edited by

Julie D. Rainer

Association of
Teacher Educators

KENDALL/HUNT PUBLISHING COMPANY
4050 Westmark Drive   Dubuque, Iowa 52002

Contents

Preface

Reframing Teacher Education: Dimensions of a Constructivist Approach is the product of a three-year project (ATE Commission on Constructivist Teacher Education) during which ten individuals, in collaboration, explored constructivist theory from teacher educators' perspectives. While we take great pride in our product, it is the process of professional development that engaged our minds, and our hearts. That process involved sharing our scholarship and experience, generating a common understanding and vision, negotiating strong beliefs and philosophical stances, studying and clarifying conceptions of constructivism, sharing our work in process with experts in the field, critiquing and encouraging each others' writing, all the while rethinking our ideas as necessary. We wanted to honor our beliefs by living them. No wonder it took us three years! Indeed constructivist teacher education seems like life-long work. While different authors take primary responsibility for exploring each dimension, it was not the kind of process where each person worked in isolation (like often occurs in our schools of education). Our collaboration is characterized by rigor, respect and relationships.

Our charge was to define constructivist teacher education and suggest principles and practices to guide teacher educators as they interpret theory and develop their own practice. Our study builds on Richardson's (1997) definition of constructivist teacher education as incorporating two different conceptions: teaching about how to teach using a constructivist approach and working with teachers in a constructivist manner to examine their own understandings. Our intent is to expand the latter conception.

As we thought about definitions, we considered the advantages of definitions and labels as a means of simplifying complex thought and providing a starting place for understanding but struggled with the possibility that they could prove to be a substitute for thought about significance. Lave & Wenger (1991) state that "until recently, the notion of a concept was viewed as something for which clarity, precision, simplicity and maximum definition seemed commendable" (p. 121). They further suggest that one can better understand conceptualizations through relationships and interconnections than through concise definitions and boundaries. Congruent with our theoretical perspective, we tried to rethink the idea of a concise definition to include interconnected generative constructs linked to practice.

We chose to define constructivist teacher education (and organize this book) as the interaction of seven dimensions:

- Learning and development

- Authority and facilitation

- Action and reflection

- Autonomy and community

- Process and content

- Power and empowerment

- Critical thinking and multiple perspectives

Each dimension includes a pair of constructs that initially may seem to pull you in different directions. As you continue to read, you will see a more complex set of relationships. Constructivism often seems paradoxical, but then most important matters are of that nature. And constructivism is not one thing with a single determinant. For some it is an epistemology, a philosophy, or a learning theory. For others, it is spirit, a condition, a process, a decision, or a way of being. For us as a commission, it is the process and result of thinking, talking, arguing, reading, reflecting, and writing about a shared interest.

Vygotsky (1978) tackles the idea of paradoxical viewpoints in his discussion of learning and development. He suggests that the relationship between seemingly opposing viewpoints are not necessarily "opposing and mutually exclusive but have something essential in common . . . two process . . . are mutually dependent and interactive" (p. 81). In discussing each dimension, we delineate the relationships between the pairs of constructs.

While each dimension is discussed in the separate and linear fashion of a written work, in the practice or action of constructivist teacher education they all come into play. Think of constructivist teacher education like a child's pinwheel. With no wind, each blade (or dimension) is a clear and separate entity. As the wind picks up, the dimensions whirl, the edges blur and the pinwheel takes on a new look.

As you read each dimension, please enjoy and take note of the examples taken from life experiences in constructivist teacher education. Examples are included from pre-service, in-service and staff development programs, incorporating all levels from activities to supervision and courses to programs. We found that our distinction between teacher education and K–12 teaching became blurred; we couldn't talk about teaching teachers without reference to teaching children.

Our process of translating constructivist theory into teacher education practice was informative and invigorating. Our continual study, examining and extending our beliefs, knowledge and practice, through activity, reflection and discourse is an example of our social construction of constructivist teacher education. It led to each of us making our own meaningful connections between constructivist theory and practice in teacher education. With each chapter, authors include a brief biography of their experience with constructivist theory and practice to provide a context for their remarks.

Others (Bentley, 1998; Bettencourt, 1993; Gergen, 1995; Kessels and Korthagen, 1996) also have wrestled with the relationship between theory and practice. Bentley suggests that while constructivism can serve as a useful referent for education, practice is never a simple application of general rules to concrete situations. Citing Betttencourt (1993) he describes the relationship of theory and practice as a relationship of "mutual adaptation, of mutual questioning and of mutual illumination" (p. 47). Gergen (1995) suggests that in applying social construction and education practice, the social construction orientation itself is a "process in motion" (p. 29). He further suggests that rather than proposing definitive derivatives of theory, we seek to elaborate practices that are consistent with our current understandings of constructivist theories. This was our intention. Any prescription we make takes the status of a proposal or a working hypothesis; its utility is to be determined by those who re-construct it.

Researchers and practitioners will find *Reframing Teacher Education* as most helpful if used, not as a set definition or answers, but as a basis for conversation about constructivist teacher education. The commission generated this report from sincere conversations and we invite you into an extended dialogue.

Julie Rainer
Georgia State University

References

Bentley, M. (1998). Constructivism as a referent for reforming science education. In M. Laarochelle, N. Bednarz, & J. Garrison (Eds.), *Constructivism and Education* (pp. 233–252). Cambridge, UK: Cambridge University Press.

Bettencourt, A. (1993). The construction of knowledge: A radical constructivist view. In K. Tobin, (Ed.), *The Practice of Constructivism in Science Education* (pp. 39–50). Hillsdale, NJ: Erlbaum.

Kessels, J. & Korthagen, F. (1996). The relationship between theory and practice: Back to the classics. *Educational Researcher, 25* (1), 17–23.

Richardson, V. (1997). Constructivist teacher education: Building a world of new understandings. Washington, D.C.: Falmer Press.

Vygotsky, L. (1978). *Mind in Society: The Development of Higher Psychological Processes.* Cambridge, MA: Harvard University Press.

Foreword

FUNDAMENTAL QUESTIONS AND REVOLUTIONARY ANSWERS

What is the most effective way to educate and support our nation's future and current teachers? What types of experiences should preservice and in-service teacher education programs offer teacher learners? How do we develop and sustain a teaching corps that truly understands the nature of learning and uses these understandings to inform classroom practices? How do we prepare teachers to meet the many and varied challenges associated with schooling the students of the 21st Century? How do we help teachers meet increasingly higher expectations and be more accountable to their constituencies? How do we ensure that all teachers can teach so that all students will learn?

Teacher educators have grappled with these fundamental questions during recent years, and, as a result, both preservice and in-service teacher education programs are evolving in order to more successfully meet the field's needs. This book, *Reframing Teacher Education: Dimensions of a Constructivist Approach*, is, to some extent, a product of recent reforms in teacher education. However, its creators also intend for it to be an agent for further change. Commissioned by Edi Guyton during her tenure as President of the Association of

Teacher Educators and edited by Julie Rainer, this book represents a valid response to the questions posed above. Focusing exclusively on the principles and practices of constructivist teacher education, the authors present thought-provoking discussions that could inspire a revolution in how we teach teachers. Through careful explorations of the connections between constructivist learning theories and teacher-education practices, combined with detailed descriptions of the ways in which constructivist teacher educators "practice what they preach," the writers invite their colleagues to consider the power and possibilities of this approach.

Editor Rainer and her writing partners chose to structure their book around a set of seven apparent contradictions that emerge when we try to translate constructivist theories into educational practice. These seemingly contradictory dimensions actually represent predictable tensions that constructivist educators constantly strive to coordinate and balance. As we work to resolve these tensions and to provide the right experiences for our teacher learners, we stretch our own thinking and re-invent our own practice along and around each set of dimensional interactions—course after course, workshop after workshop, and cohort after cohort.

Linda Kroll and Paul Ammon introduce the seven dimensions with a discussion of constructivist theories and their implications for teacher education and then collaborate again to tackle the learning-development relationship. Additional contributors (Christie McIntyre, Teresa Harris, Sam Hausfather, Margaret Jones, Julie Rainer, Carrie Robinson, and Sandra Woolley) address, respectively, the other six dimensions: action and reflection, critical thinking and multiple perspectives, content and process, autonomy and community, authority and facilitator, and power and empowerment. These writers have studied and implemented constructivist education for many years, and their understandings of how theory informs practice and their wisdom about what complicates this work come through with clarity and conviction.

Each dimension has relevance for the entire spectrum of teacher education (in truth, for every teaching and learning situation!), regardless of whether the context is a preservice course sequence, a graduate program, or a professional development project. All of us who are engaged in the teacher education process can find a place for ourselves in this volume, no matter which facet we have responsibility for or where we are on our journey as constructivist educators.

The authors have written honestly about the pertinent and prickly issues surrounding constructivist education, and they have delved deeply into some messy and uncomfortable places. I know firsthand how challenging it is to consistently and appropriately apply what we know about learning to the art and science of teaching. It may seem extremely difficult (as Kroll and Ammon note in their Introduction) to implement a truly constructivist approach, given the intellectual rigor, meaningful reflection, and purposeful action that are required. However, the results are worth it.

As you read and reflect on these chapters, I hope that you will examine your beliefs and practices and critically appraise your teacher-education programs and projects. I hope, too, that you will tolerate some cognitive conflict as you ponder your work because it is through resolution of disequilibrium that we grow as professionals. And finally, I hope that you will reaffirm (or perhaps newly affirm) your commitment to the potential of constructivist teacher education. It does represent the paradigm shift in our teacher-education endeavors (Fosnot, 1996) that we so desperately need.

Sharon Ford Schattgen
Missouri Department of Elementary and Secondary Education

REFERENCE

Fosnot, C.T. (1996). Teachers Construct Constructivism: The Center for Constructivist Teaching/Teacher Preparation Project. In C. T. Fosnot (Ed.), *Constructivism: Theory, perspectives, and practice* (pp. 205–216). New York: Teachers College Press.

Professional Background:
Paul Ammon and Linda Kroll

Paul Ammon

Paul Ammon has directed the Developmental Teacher Education Program at Berkeley (DTE) since its inception in 1980, but his path into teacher education was rather atypical, as he has neither a degree in Education nor experience as a P–12 teacher himself. With a B.A. in Psychology and a Ph.D. in Child Development, and inspired during the sixties by Piaget's constructivist theory and by the new field of developmental psycholinguistics, he joined the Education faculty at Berkeley in 1966 with the goal of teaching doctoral students and carrying out educationally relevant research on the development of language and cognition. By the mid seventies it was apparent to him that developmental research would have little impact on education unless it informed the way teachers think about children as learners—which seemed most unlikely to happen those days in California, when the study of development was generally confined to a small portion of a ten-week educational psychology course in a one-year preservice program. At the same time, it also seemed important to gain a better understanding of how teachers do think about children and learning as they begin preparing to teach, and of how their thinking might change over time. These insights led to the founding, with several Berkeley colleagues, of DTE as a more extended preservice program in which the study of child development was treated as core knowledge, and to the beginning of research on the development of teachers' thinking about children and pedagogy. Both the program and the research have continued to evolve since then, with more and more attention to issues regarding diversity and educational equity. A past president of the Association for Constructivist Teaching, Paul remains active in that organization, as well as the American Educational Research Association, the Jean Piaget Society, the California Council on the Education of Teachers, and, now, ATE.

Linda Kroll

Linda Kroll is a Professor of Education at Mills College, in Oakland, California. She is the director of Developmental Perspectives in Teaching, the early childhood section of the Teachers for Tomorrow's Schools teacher education program. She has been at Mills since 1988. She has been a preschool teacher, a primary grade teacher and a teacher educator for thirty years. She has been concerned with children's development and a constructivist perspective on learning and development since she was a classroom teacher. Her research focuses on the development of children's thinking and understanding and teachers' learning about children's thinking and understanding. She has published work in children's literacy development and teacher learning and development. She is passionately committed to improving teacher education and children's learning, particularly in urban settings.

Constructivism and Teacher Education: A Vision, an Overview, and Seven Dimensions

Linda Kroll and Paul Ammon

The Association of Teacher Educators gave this commission a charge to write about constructivist teacher education. As we worked together, we saw that constructivist teacher education had the power to help all of us re-vision a world of learning and education where children, their families, their schools, and their communities could come together as life-long learners engaged in powerful learning, fulfilling the promise of democracy that universal public education leads us to hope for and anticipate (Oakes & Lipton, 1999). This introductory chapter describes our vision. It also provides an overview of constructivism, as we understand it, and of its implications for teaching and teacher education. Finally, it describes the organization of this book, and can be used as a road map for what will follow.

A VISION OF LEARNING AND TEACHER EDUCATION

As teacher educators we are especially concerned about the students who are not learning, who seem to be falling farther and farther behind. But even when students do seem to be learning by conventional standards, there are still concerns about the extent to which they are attaining the kinds of conceptual understandings and critical thinking skills they will need in order to put their knowledge to effective use, including the kinds of social understandings and skills needed to uphold democratic ideals. How can we best educate teachers so that they will have the knowledge and tools to address these concerns? How can teachers learn to provide learning opportunities for all their students? How can teachers inspire students to care about learning or about what they are learning? How can teachers engender an attitude of life-long learning in their students? How can teachers prepare their students to be contributing members of a democratic society? And how can we, as teacher educators, contribute to contexts that provide learning opportunities for all members of the educational community—students, parents, teachers, administrators, and other educational staff—to create an enthusiastic, inspired community of life-long learners?

What would an inspired community of learners be? Schools are already under fire for failing large numbers (and in some cases a majority) of our students according to some standards of assessment. In some ways, the extent of school failure may be overstated, where students are held to inappropriate or irrelevant standards, but, in other ways, schools are failing all students. They fail to provide an environment in which excitement about learning, in a community of collaboration and support, is the atmosphere. Schools today generally do not work well, either from a learning perspective or from a community perspective; rather they maintain a fairly mundane status quo. While educators and policy makers may regret the waste of human potential evident in the lack of conventional success for many students, they sometimes miss the point by failing to see that, in fact, we are short-changing all of our children and our communities. Moreover, they fail to see that the dominant model of instruction, a transmission model, contributes to the maintenance of this unsatisfactory status quo and offers no real solutions. The vision we hold here is one in which all members of the learning community—children, teachers, parents, administrators, staff, and even members of the wider community—find in the school a place of active learning where opportunities for discussion, collaboration, and intellectual stimulation are constant. We need a new vision in order to think "outside the box" (to use the current parlance) of traditional schooling and education.

Learning Theory and Educational Policy

Constructivism, as a theory of learning, provides us with a new lens with which to think about this vision. However, while constructivist views of the learning process are increasingly widespread among educational researchers and teacher educators, they are still relatively new, and the public and many policy makers still adhere to and believe in a transmission model of learning. Instead of that model being questioned, teachers and students are simply told to work harder. Thus, politicians and other policy makers have advocated longer school days and longer school years. Teachers and students are to be held accountable for more knowledge. Even President Clinton spoke about an end to "social promotion" as a panacea for school failure. While schools, and teachers in particular, have been under continuous criticism for failing the children in our schools, teacher educators have now begun to bear the brunt of the criticism. As the public (as represented by parent groups and elected officials) has come to believe that children are not doing well enough in school—are not learning what society needs them to know in order to be contributing members of a democracy—there has been a move to demand more accountability from the educational establishment at all levels.

A lack of confidence in teachers and schools has resulted in a demand for tests to insure that children are learning what they are supposed to know. Society has both the right and responsibility to know that schools are preparing children to be contributing members, but the solution of high-stakes testing to make sure that this is occurring results in teachers teaching to the test rather than students learning to be productive and responsible citizens. In addition, there is a growing national trend to require teachers to pass tests that indicate they have both subject matter knowledge and pedagogical knowledge. The PRAXIS II (a subject matter knowledge exam) is required for licensure in 36 states. In California, teacher credential programs must prove that they are preparing teachers to pass an examination in the teaching of reading, and prospective teachers must pass this exam that purports to assess their knowledge of the learning-to-read and teaching-to-read processes. On the one hand, there seems to be the belief that what is needed is more—that if teachers only knew more, our children would learn more in school. On the other hand, there is also the belief that teacher educators must be told what teachers need to be taught and what they, in turn, must teach.

Much of the criticism leveled at teacher educators may seem wrong-headed and unfair, but we cannot simply sit back and wait for the times to change again; we need to consider alternatives. We must be concerned about the students who are falling through the cracks, who are failing to thrive in our schools, and about the students who are doing "well" but still do not understand what they have learned as well as they could. Teachers must have methods and ways of thinking that enable them to provide opportunities that result in excellent outcomes for all students. In addition, schools must become places where not only students learn, but teachers, administrators, parents, and staff participate in an educational community that focuses on intellectually stimulating and fulfilling learning opportunities for all its members. Teachers and other adults will continue learning about teaching and children, while children will be learning what they need to succeed in the world. An even bolder view would have us create contexts in which adults, as well as children, could continue their personal as well as pedagogical learning.

What Should Be Learned?

The learning that occurs in school-based communities of learners is not just academic learning. Schools must prepare children to be contributing members of a strong and equitable society, which means social and moral learning must also occur. Teachers must understand and work with the communities in which they teach in order that all may contribute to this important work of preparing future productive citizens. The diversity of our student population must not be seen as a disadvantage, but rather as an opportunity for the social and moral growth of our communities as they make use of the funds of knowledge of all members (Moll & Greenberg, 1990). Social and academic learning are inextricably linked. In an atmosphere characterized by destructive criticism and by expectations that some members of society have less to contribute than others, no one feels safe to take risks, or to push him/herself to think about things in other than the most conventional ways. The social context affects what kind of learning can occur, and the quality of learning affects the kind of society we will have. Thus, both P-12 schools and schools of education need to think about a broader concept of learning than strictly academic learning.

While we are writing a monograph about teacher education, the context for the monograph is larger than that of the university or college or school district that prepares teachers. A common point of view often expressed in our society by educators, politicians, and the public alike is that education should be free of politics and that its focus should instead be to provide students with the academic and social skills necessary to succeed in life. Successful students are the measure of successful teaching. However, there are political consequences in carrying out this mission. Teacher education programs must guide their students to consider the political implications of their actions as teachers. It seems somewhat obvious that the official political rhetoric of economic competition would affect what teachers do in school. In several states (California, Texas, and Virginia to name a few) we can see the effects of politics on pedagogy, where one method of teaching literacy (a transmission method) is being supported by the legislature and the state board of education in response to what is seen as a failure on the part of the educational establishment (as represented by the schools and schools of education) to effectively teach children to read well enough to join the work force that the economy requires. Along the same lines, concern about how well American students measure up to the rest of the international community in mathematics and science education has been a significant political issue for some time (remember Sputnik?).

But politics and political effects occur on a much more essential and subtle level too. Every decision a teacher makes about curriculum has political ramifications. For example, choosing what to read in an elementary school classroom has consequences for all the students in that classroom. If a teacher chooses to teach a conventional list of readings that includes only children's books published before 1975, she will be disenfranchising not only children of color, who are not represented in the texts she has chosen, but also denying white children the opportunity to understand the richness and multiplicity of people within our society. A teacher education program must help teachers to consider the political and moral, as well as the pedagogical, consequences of curricular decisions. In a society that aspires to be a democracy, these programs must help their graduates remain committed to democratic principles of access and equity in education.

Education modeled on a transmission model of learning tends to reproduce the status quo. People who fit the conventional notions of knowing and being knowledgeable have more success. The conventional ways of knowing reproduce themselves. Thus, the same people and the same ideas continue to dominate education and educational communities. And the same people get left out or excluded from those same communities. In fact, the notion of a learning community within a transmission model seems contradictory. A transmission model assumes there are experts who have the real knowledge to pass on to novices. The social interaction is seen as unidirectional, where all the information goes one way (from teacher to student) and all the response goes the other (from student to teacher). The need for discussion or collaboration is minimal given the accepted "true" set of ideas. On the other hand, alternative ways of thinking about knowledge and the nature of knowing or learning give us a basis for creating different kinds of schools and genuine learning communities. Constructivist views of learning reconstruct our notions of what knowing and knowledge are and help us to see new ways of approaching education that allow all members of society to contribute in intellectually stimulating and socially important ways. While teacher education is not the only place to begin such a transformation, it is one place. We are a group of teacher educators and, as constructivists, we are beginning with what we know and looking at how we can construct more effective ways of creating learning communities within our own institutions and within the schools in which our students will eventually teach.

CONSTRUCTIVISM AND EDUCATION: AN OVERVIEW

This monograph is about constructivist theories of knowledge and their implications for teacher education. We say "theories" because there is not just one constructivist theory but a multiplicity of them (see, e.g., Fosnot, 1996; Phillips, 1995; Prawat, 1996). Steffe and Gale (1995) underscore this multiplicity by noting that a single colloquium series on alternative epistemologies in education included six different constructivist paradigms, which they identify as social constructivism, radical constructivism, social constructionism, information-processing constructivism, cybernetic systems, and sociocultural approaches to mediated action. While space does not permit us to go into detail about a large number of theories here, we nonetheless think it important to consider differences among constructivist perspectives, along with similarities, instead of focusing on just one perspective and putting the others aside. Thus we will use "constructivism" as an umbrella term (Larochelle, Bednarz, & Garrison, 1998) for a range of theories that offer various alternatives to the empiricist view that knowledge comes to us from the world "out there," and to the nativist view that knowledge is inborn. As background for the chapters that follow, we briefly discuss these three broad philosophical perspectives as they relate to each other and to education, and then consider some basic implications of constructivism for teaching and teacher education.

Empiricism, Nativism, and Constructivism

Empiricist perspectives provide the philosophical basis for transmission models of teaching—essentially the idea that showing and telling will generally suffice to bring about learning, especially when accompanied by guided practice and corrective feedback of the sort that is favored in behaviorist versions of empiricism. As we have already noted, transmission models continue to dominate our educational system, in spite of widespread dissatisfaction with current learning outcomes, and in spite of considerable interest in constructivism among educators over the past few decades, not to mention earlier interest in similar ideas under the banner of progressive education (Dewey, 1963). Constructivist approaches to education have gained acceptance in some places, but they are currently under attack in others. There are undoubtedly numerous reasons for the persistence of transmission models, and for hostility toward constructivism, including institutional inertia and the influence of political and economic forces that have a vested interest in the status quo. But there are also many hard working and well meaning educators who continue to believe in a transmission approach—in part, we suspect, because of its relative simplicity, and because it does seem to work in some respects (although we haven't asked often enough in what sense it "works," and why, and at what costs).

However, it is clear that the transmission approach doesn't always work, and when it doesn't—even with more engaging presentations, and with more practice, corrective feedback, remedial instruction, and so on—then proponents of transmission generally have two ways of explaining such failures. Either they pursue the empiricist perspective further, by blaming the out-of-school environment for not providing learners with the kinds of knowledge that would prepare them to learn in school (as in the concept of "cultural deprivation"). Or they turn to nativism for an explanation, by invoking the idea that the learners must lack some inborn ability or some biologically programmed readiness that is needed for the desired school learning to take place. Unfortunately this sort of nativist addendum to empiricist views of teaching leads all too readily to the conclusion that effective instruction is impossible in some cases, or is unnecessary in others. That is, because the ability to learn particular content is thought to be inborn, it is not seen as something we can cultivate. Either it is there or it is not—or perhaps it is not there yet, in the case of appeals to a kind of readiness that depends on sheer "maturation," in the form of organic growth, rather than past experience. Duckworth (1987, p. 31) put this last sentiment in the form of a complaint that might be uttered by educators who misinterpret Piaget's stage theory of cognitive development as a nativist/maturationist theory: "Either we're too early and they can't learn it, or we're too late and they know it already." In any case, the empiricist perspective, with or without the help of nativism, ultimately puts the onus for failed instruction squarely on learners and/or their families and communities, and therefore it leads to schools that maintain the status quo in our society, with all its inequalities.

The traditional alternative to the transmission model of teaching comes directly from nativist philosophy, particularly that of Rousseau, and it has generally been referred to as "romanticism" (Kohlberg &

Mayer, 1972). From a romantic perspective, children must be enabled to actualize their innate potential, with as little interference from others as possible. Thus the ideal learning environment is seen as one that most of us would consider highly permissive, and "teaching" is largely a matter of providing a rich environment and stepping aside to allow a natural process to unfold. However, while giving children a great deal of freedom can sometimes result in wonderful moments of discovery, it can also deprive them of the kind of guidance that would enable them to go much farther in their learning, and to become more effective participants in various communities around them. Not surprisingly, then, romanticism doesn't always work either. And when it doesn't, the main implication—for romantics—seems to be that those around the child should intrude even less and should simply wait for the natural process of development to occur. But most educators, already uncomfortable with a "wait and see" approach, find further waiting unacceptable. That probably explains why romanticism has never gained wide acceptance in our education system.

In contrast with both empiricism and nativism, a fundamental tenet of constructivism is that knowledge cannot be reduced to what comes from outside us, or to what comes from inside us, or to some simple combination of the two. Rather, knowledge emerges from human activity as people interact with each other and with the physical world, using their minds and bodies, and the material and symbolic tools made available to them by their cultures. Thus we actively construct our knowledge and do not passively receive it from experience or heredity. To be sure, experience and heredity make important contributions to our knowledge, but that is not to say that they constitute our knowledge in and of themselves. What is missing from such accounts is the crucial role of our *activity*, both as individuals and in concert with others. Our own activity transforms what comes from within and from without, and results in the construction of something that cannot be reduced to either. What we construct at any one time may later be reconstructed, and then reconstructed again, in the light of future experience and (sometimes) further maturation. Most importantly, though, it is what we have already constructed that gives us a basis for tapping the resources given to us by our nature and our experience, and for using them in the further construction of knowledge.

In contrast with both the transmission model and romanticism, constructivist teaching seeks to strike a balance between an overly curriculum-centered, teacher-controlled approach, and an overly learner-centered, laissez-faire approach. The key idea is to guide learners toward self-regulated activities that will lead to the construction of deeper, more powerful knowledge of curriculum content—activities that allow the learner to utilize whatever personal and social resources are available, including the knowledge they already have. Such activities can be physical or symbolic, individual or interpersonal, or—most likely—some combination of these, so long as they contribute to the construction of knowledge that is deemed worth having. When attempts to pursue this constructivist approach do not succeed, the appropriate response is not just to intensify what one has done before and then ultimately blame the learner if that doesn't work (as with a transmission model), nor is it to do less than one did before and hope for the best (as with a romantic model). Rather it is to reconsider the curriculum and the learners' resources for learning, in search of better matches between the two. Central to that search is the question of what knowledge learners already have.

An important implication of the foregoing discussion is that constructivism is not only about the *origins* of knowledge but about its very *nature* as well. In other words, knowledge is both constructed (process) and a construction (product). It is an interpretation or theory of what is "out there" (or "in there," in the case of knowledge about our psychological selves). If knowledge came entirely from outside the part of us that knows, or from an innate predisposition to know, then it would essentially be a copy of what is out there. From these empiricist and nativist points of view, to know something is to know it as it "really is." But even though we might often feel that we know things as they really are, it is not hard to find examples in our individual development and in our collective history where truths taken as self-evident have sooner or later proven to be wrong, at least in some respects. Both individually and historically, we have "known" our world to be essentially flat before knowing it to be spherical. The flat earth theory is not entirely wrong; it works quite well in guiding much of our everyday activity. But there are times when the flat earth theory doesn't work as well as the spherical earth theory, e.g., in navigating long voyages.

Moreover, there are other times when even the spherical earth theory doesn't work as well as one which holds that the earth is not perfectly spherical, but has a slightly larger girth at the equator than around the poles. Thus, from a constructivist perspective, the "same thing" can be known in different ways, and those different ways may be more or less useful for different purposes.

The link between knowledge and purpose is central to some rather diverse constructivist theories. For example, Lave and Wenger (1991), coming from a socio-cultural perspective, speak of knowledge being constructed through the activities of "communities of practice," while Piaget (1971), from a biological perspective, sees knowledge being constructed as a means of adaptation to the environment, which can include changing the environment as well as oneself. Thus, from an educational standpoint, it would appear that constructivism, in general, provides a theoretical basis for the venerable principle that instruction should be made practical. However, it would not be consistent with constructivism to interpret this principle in too narrow or literal a fashion. For one thing, some constructivists have shown great interest in the knowledge-generating power of such "impractical" activities as play and art. Moreover, practical activity, for many constructivists, includes not only doing but also reflecting—"minds-on" as well as "hands-on," to use some familiar terms in education. Reflection seems especially important when the goal of knowledge construction is understanding. In fact, the primary purpose of some human activities is simply to understand things better—to construct theories without having specific practical applications in mind (but then it's been said (Lewin, 1943) that there is nothing so practical as a good theory!).

When all is said and done, perhaps the most important questions for educators to ask about purposeful activities concern (a) what the learners' purposes are, and (b) how those purposes might lead them to engage in activities that produce knowledge consistent with the goals of instruction. But what are the goals of instruction? While it might be said that the general purpose of education, from a constructivist standpoint, is to facilitate the construction of knowledge, that seems to leave us with innumerable possibilities. Does constructivism have anything to say about the "large purposes" (Perrone, 1991) of education? We actually began to address that question in discussing our vision of learning and teacher education, and now we pursue it further.

Constructivist Perspectives on the Goals of Education: Implications, Questions, and Possible Answers

In general, the literature of constructivism suggests two overarching goals for education, goals that appear to be emphasized to somewhat different degrees by different constructivists. On the one hand, if we believe that knowledge is constructed in communities of practice, in order for those communities to pursue their practices effectively then we might say that a basic goal of education, broadly speaking, is to help individuals become full-fledged, central participants in the various communities of practice to which they belong or aspire to belong (Lave & Wenger, 1991). Such communities might include professional or vocational groups, families, and the citizens of local municipalities. As professionals, teachers participate in classroom and school communities of various sorts (e.g., the English Department, or the team of third grade teachers), and they might also be actively involved in the wider communities their schools serve, and in larger organizations of educators. On the other hand, if we believe that knowledge is constructed as people try to make sense of things in their own ways in order to adapt to their environments, then we might say that a basic goal of education is to help individuals achieve the kind of intellectual autonomy that enables them to think for themselves and reach their own conclusions, instead of relying entirely on authority or tradition to decide what they should do (Piaget, cited by Duckworth, 1964). Such autonomy might be expressed as differences of opinion among members of the same community, or as innovations in the community's practices. Examples of autonomy in teaching might include a teacher's ability to exercise her professional judgement in deciding how to go about teaching particular students, instead of relying on curricula and instructional practices specified by others, and in deciding how best to pursue her own professional development through a variety of experiences, on her own and with assistance from others.

Is constructivism giving us mixed messages about the goals of education? Do the goals of community and autonomy contradict each other, or are they actually compatible? Although we cannot develop the argument here, we believe that they are not only compatible but also mutually supportive, and both essential in a democratic society. We don't mean to deny the tensions that might arise between them, but to suggest that they can be seen as creative tensions. Chapter four of this volume addresses possible tensions between the goals of autonomy and community within teacher education, and offers constructive ways of addressing them.

Because we have described the goals of community and autonomy in very general terms, they may seem quite separate from the goals we generally think of with respect to the teaching of school subjects, or with respect to the teaching of teachers. Learning to collaborate and to think critically are all well and good, someone might say, but what about learning how to read and write and do mathematics, or how to teach reading, writing, and mathematics? It must be remembered, though, that communities of practice engage in practices with regard to *something*, and that autonomous thinkers think critically about *something*. Therefore the goals of community and autonomy entail all sorts of other goals as well. These are goals regarding the content and methods of thought and practice—the kinds of knowledge one needs to be a central participant in a community and an effective autonomous thinker.

It may seem, too, that the goals of community and autonomy are very long-term goals, having to do with the ways we want people to be eventually, once they have been educated. Constructivist educators do see them as long-term goals, but not just as long-term goals. If knowledge is constructed and reconstructed gradually, from collaborative interactions with others and from self-regulated sense making, then community and autonomy, in some form, are essential goals from the beginning of life—both for the long-term development of collaboration and critical thinking, and for the construction of all the other kinds of knowledge that make it possible for someone to participate in a particular community or to think autonomously in a given context. In other words, community and autonomy, in some form, are preconditions for the construction of knowledge at any level of education.

From a constructivist perspective, then, the goals of community and autonomy (and the other goals they entail) can and should be promoted by some form of instruction for any learner at any time, as was famously postulated by Bruner (1960). It is never too soon to start. To be sure, maturation and past experience create both potentials and limits vis à vis the knowledge that any learner can construct at a given time. But, as Vygotsky (1978, 1987) suggested so well with his concept of the zone of proximal development, a learner's current potential is generally realized through some form of assistance from others. Moreover, it seems both empirically and morally tenable for educators to assume that there is always some potential that has yet to be realized, even within the learner's current limitations, so that further assistance of some sort is always worthwhile.

The key to successful instruction is to make contact with the knowledge that learners have already constructed, and to help them build on it. In practice, this fundamental but deceptively simple-sounding principle of constructivist teaching immediately raises a host of questions. Exactly what are the various forms that current knowledge might take, and exactly how might teachers recognize them? Exactly what sorts of activities might lead to the further construction of knowledge, and exactly what sorts of constructions might result from those activities? Exactly how do people become increasingly autonomous constructors of knowledge, and exactly how do they become better able to function as constructive members of communities?

These are questions that teachers and teacher educators must address if they are to use constructivism as a guide for everyday practice. They are also questions addressed by constructivist theories, and answered by them in various ways, depending on the particular theory. What constructivist theory offers, then, is not a definitive answer to any of these questions, but a variety of answers—a variety of constructions regarding the construction of knowledge. It remains for educators to determine which of these constructions are particularly useful to them as they pursue the purposes of education in the particular contexts in which they work. Either deliberately or by default, educators do give specific answers to the above questions all the time, as they make choices regarding the particulars of educational practice. And the choices they make can have major consequences in the lives of their students. It seems morally imperative, therefore, that such choices be made as deliberately as possible, and that they be informed by powerful ideas regarding the nature of knowledge, learning, and development.

Our goal in this monograph is to consider some of the ideas available to us from constructivist theories, and to suggest how they might be useful in teaching and in the education of teachers. It is not our intention to summarize or evaluate the theories themselves, but to draw key ideas from them in order to explore the possible meanings of taking a constructivist approach to teacher education. However, we do encourage readers to look more deeply into the theories cited here, to gain a greater appreciation of the conceptual contexts from which the ideas have emerged. Much of the discussion in this monograph, and in the more general discourse on constructivism as it relates to education, can be traced back to Piaget (1970a, 1970b) and Vygotsky (1978, 1987), certainly two classic giants in the field. The recent revival of interest in Dewey reminds us, though, that earlier there was another giant, who spoke of his "belief in the office of intelligence as a continuously reconstructive agency" (Archambault, 1964, p. vii). Dewey's credentials as a constructivist are evident throughout his writings. However, Piaget and Vygotsky continue to be widely regarded today as the chief progenitors of major schools of constructivist thought in the social and behavioral sciences. Many of us who have been in education for a while first heard of constructivism during the sixties or seventies, when there was a great deal of excitement over the work of Piaget among some psychologists and educators. More recently, Piaget's influence in education has been eclipsed somewhat by the burgeoning interest in Vygotsky that began in the eighties and has continued through the nineties. Nevertheless, the current array of constructivist theories shows the enduring influence of both theorists, and it includes some that have been called "neo-Piagetian" and others that could be called "neo-Vygotskian."

All constructivist theories—including those proposed by Piaget and Vygotsky themselves—are best regarded as works in progress, because they have evolved over time and continue to evolve, as the originators or their followers investigate them further. We should not let the provisional nature of these theories discourage us from looking for useful ideas in them. In fact, from a constructivist perspective, all knowledge is provisional, so we have no choice but to "go with what we've got," keeping in mind that what we've got is subject to change, and that some ideas will prove more durable than others. Nor should we be discouraged by the apparent contradictions and tensions that we find between, and even within, particular constructivist theories. Such tensions, at least according to some constructivist perspectives, are inherent in the knowledge construction process itself, and are important motivators of further construction. Moreover, faced with a multiplicity of constructivist perspectives, we should remember the connection between knowledge and purpose, and consider the possibility that different constructivist ideas will be more or less useful for different educational purposes. For example, the Piagetian perspective may be especially useful for the purpose of exploring a student's current understanding of a concept through questioning, whereas the Vygotskian perspective may be more useful for attempts to support the mastery of new skills.

CONSTRUCTIVISM AND TEACHING: A SOMEWHAT CLOSER LOOK

It should be clear by now that just as there is no single constructivist theory, neither is there a single method of teaching that we can call constructivist teaching. There are, to be sure, certain teaching practices that tend to distinguish teachers who have a constructivist orientation from those whose work is based on a transmission model. For example, Kroll and Black (1993) found that elementary school teachers who had been prepared in a constructivist preservice program were more likely than highly regarded traditional teachers to make use of small group versus whole class activities, to allow students some choice in whom they worked with and how they went about completing an assignment, and to involve students in the process of evaluating their own work. However, each of these practices, as well as many others often associated with constructivist teaching, might be regarded as inconsistent with constructivism in some contexts, for both theoretical and practical reasons. Hands-on activities, for example, are widely seen as a hall-mark of constructivist teaching, but they can be counterproductive if they distract students from the kind of thinking that is required in order to construct the new knowledge that is the goal of instruction.

It should be clear, also, that constructivist teaching is not wholly unique and different from more traditional transmission or romantic approaches. There are times when constructivist teachers show and tell students things they need to know in order to proceed with a knowledge construction activity, and there are times when they allow them to engage in free exploration. From a constructivist perspective, it doesn't make sense to expect that children will construct, or "invent," arbitrary conventions like the correspondences between par-ticular letters and particular sounds in an alphabetic writing system. But it may make sense, at least sometimes, to have them experiment with such correspondences by inventing their own spellings, which they can then compare with conventional spellings as one means of coming to understand how the conventional spelling system works. So traditional transmission and romantic practices may be embedded in constructivist teaching as ways of assisting the knowledge construc-tion process, but constructivist teaching cannot be reduced to such practices, because learning cannot be reduced to receiving informa-tion or to "doing what comes naturally" in a presumably stimulating environment.

When we ask what else constructivist teaching might include beyond transmission and romantic practices, we should not be sur-prised to find that different constructivist theories sometimes lead us in rather different directions. Even a single theory, being a work in progress, may give us leads that seem ambiguous or downright con-tradictory. Indeed, before ending this introductory chapter, we will identify several basic tensions or apparent contradictions that can be found both between and within theories under the umbrella of con-structivism, and each of the following chapters will then focus on one of them. However, the challenges of applying constructivist theory to educational practice derive not only from these theoretical complexi-ties, but also from the complexities of practice itself, to which we turn now.

Challenges of Constructivist Teaching: Bringing the Learner and the Curriculum Together

At any level of education, from early childhood education to the preparation and continuing professional development of teachers, the challenges of constructivist teaching are many. They include both challenges that are intrinsic to any constructivist approach and challenges that are extrinsic and might therefore be present in some settings but not in others, such as severely limited resources or hostility toward constructivist practices. Without in any way minimizing the latter sorts of challenges, we focus here on those that are more intrinsic to constructivist teaching, paying particular attention to the need for ongoing assessments of learners and corresponding adjustments in the curriculum as keys to making a constructivist approach work well in practice.

If the activity of learners is central to the knowledge construction process, then there are a number of questions we must ask about learners before we can proceed with constructivist teaching. What do learners already know about the subject matter? What are their characteristic modes of thinking and of interacting with others? What do they believe about themselves as learners? What sorts of purposes or goals are most important to them? Again, these questions are answered in one way or another by all teachers, but often by default. That is, teaching is often based on implicit assumptions about learners—assumptions that have not actually been examined with respect to the particular learners at hand. Constructivist teachers try to address these questions in a more deliberate and informed fashion, and the answers they come up with may lead them to make a variety of different moves in teaching, depending on the subject and the context in which they are teaching it. Let us briefly consider each of the above questions further.

If knowledge is a construction that can undergo reconstruction, then the question of what learners already know is a question about the quality of their knowledge as well as the quantity. It is not simply a matter of asking "How much does a particular group of learners know?" Nor is it just a matter of asking whether or not their understandings are correct. To be sure, understanding is an important thing to ask about. However, the key question isn't "Do learners understand?" but *"How* do they understand?" From a constructivist perspective, learners are assumed always to have some understandings of the content being taught—some ways of thinking about it. Sometimes their understandings may be quite far from the kinds of understanding we want them eventually to have, but it is where we must start if we want to lead them toward better understandings. Moreover, students in the same class may have quite different understandings of the same content. Consequently, teachers must be prepared to offer students alternative learning activities, or activities that allow for multiple entry points, and they must also treat the diversity of perspectives among their students as a potentially rich resource for learning and development.

One of the great challenges a teacher faces is how to get in touch with learners' ways of thinking about the subject matter being taught. Counting right and wrong answers on tests of factual or procedural knowledge generally will not suffice. Alternative approaches to assessment include looking for patterns in students' errors, questioning students to determine how they have arrived at particular answers, listening to the kinds of questions students ask themselves, and seeing how they respond to various forms of assistance. While alternative methods such as these can be useful, each has its limitations and each may sometimes be impracticable in a given situation (e.g., asking students to give explanations when they have just begun to learn the language spoken by the teacher). Therefore it behooves teachers to have multiple means of assessing what students already know.

As we noted above, the need to have particular students in mind when asking "what works" applies not only to the process of assessment but also to instruction. However, to say that what makes for effective instruction depends on characteristics of the particular learners in question is not very satisfactory unless we can also say which characteristics are most likely to be relevant. Aside from the knowledge that learners have already constructed with regard to subject matter, there are other considerations as well. Since learning generally involves interaction with others, it matters what learners' typical ways of interacting are like. Researchers have found, for example, that various "participant structures" in classrooms (e.g., formal turn taking versus collaborative conversation) can be more or less comfortable for different students, depending in part on their cultural background (Au, 1980; Philips, 1972). Instruction that enables learners to participate by using familiar ways of interacting with others seems more likely to engage them in learning (although we should not neglect the possibility of fostering new styles of interaction as well).

It also matters what the learners' typical ways of thinking are like. The extent to which individuals actually have typical ways of thinking (general modes of thinking that cut across specific contexts and domains of content) is a matter of some controversy among constructivist theorists. However, many theories include the notion there are more general cognitive characteristics of some sort that vary from learner to learner. Sometimes they are seen as differences in thinking or learning styles that reflect different cultures and/or individual personalities, and sometimes they are seen as differences in ability that reflect major stages in the development of logical thinking or social perspective taking. The theory of multiple intelligences proposed by Gardner (1993) provides yet another way to look at differences in students' typical ways of approaching learning. Teaching in ways that are sensitive to such learner characteristics is made more challenging by the fact that an individual's "typical" ways of thinking may not be operative in some situations. Furthermore, they may also change over time. Indeed, constructivist teachers are generally interested in promoting changes—changes for the better—in the ways students use their minds, so that they will be able to construct better understandings for themselves. Nevertheless, it seems important for teachers to be aware that students may have particular ways of using their minds that are relatively stable over time, and that influence student behavior in a variety of situations.

Among the understandings that are consequential for learning are those that students have about themselves as learners and, more generally, as people. There is a large body of research, for example, on the development of metacognition, on what students know about their own learning processes and how they use that knowledge to guide their activities as learners (Flavell, Miller, & Miller, 1993). Another body of research is concerned with students' different "theories" about their own abilities (Dweck, 2000). Whether students believe their abilities are fixed or can be improved through learning, for example, affects their motivation in school.

With regard to motivation, the purposes students pursue while in school are many, extending well beyond, and often superseding, the goal of academic achievement per se. More often than not, students' purposes seem to be social in nature, having to do with their relations with others. Sometimes we are struck by the negative manifestations of students' social purposes, as when they tease other students or resist a teacher's attempts to establish trusting relationships with them. Drawing on the work of several theorists, Dalton and Watson (1997) have suggested that a great deal of what students do can be understood more positively in terms of the ABCs of motivation—that is, in terms of innate and normally adaptive desires for autonomy, belonging, and competence. Students generally value a certain degree of autonomy in choosing which activities to engage in. At the same time, they also value belonging to particular groups, and will engage in behaviors that gain and maintain group membership. In addition, they want to feel competent, which may include coming to better understandings of things, but may entail many other sorts of competencies as well, both academic and extracurricular. The purposes represented by the ABCs can work together, or they can conflict with one another. On the one hand, demonstrating a particular competency, for example, may gain one access to a group one aspires to join, and it may also earn one a certain degree of autonomy. On the other hand, other competencies may be negatively sanctioned by the same group and may therefore not be pursued in order to maintain affiliation with that group. Constructivist teachers, bearing in mind that knowledge is constructed through purposeful activity, try to create classroom communities— with extensions into the whole school and the larger community beyond—where students' positive purposes and school learning can support each other.

Given the way we have discussed constructivist teaching here, it may seem dauntingly difficult. Teachers who have begun to take a constructivist approach generally acknowledge that it is quite a challenging way to teach, and they may still feel that it is, even after they have had considerable experience with it. But they also tend to become strongly committed to it. In fact, we have found that, once teachers move beyond relying entirely on a transmission model, they usually say they would not go back. While constructivist teaching makes more demands on them, it also allows them to feel more in tune with their students and, therefore, more able to help them learn. There is often a genuine sense of excitement among educators when they see the "wonderful ideas" that students have (Duckworth, 1987), and "the power of their ideas" (Meier, 1995), in a constructivist learning environment. To feel that one has empowered students as thinkers, learners, and community participants can be extremely rewarding.

Of course the bottom-line question about constructivist teaching is whether it actually does enhance student learning and development. There are good reasons for thinking that it should—reasons grounded in basic theory and research of the sort that we have alluded to here. There is also enthusiastic testimony from teachers who have come to understand constructivism well enough to apply it effectively in their classrooms. And there is a growing body of evidence that supports constructivist teaching, from formal studies in which educational outcomes from learning environments that we would call "constructivist" are compared with those from other approaches (Darling-Hammond, 1997). It is not our purpose here to provide a systematic review of the various sources of support for constructivist approaches to teaching. Rather it is to regard the existing support as sufficient grounds for concluding that constructivism offers some highly promising perspectives on teaching, and to consider their implications for teacher education. The promise of constructivism can only be explored further to the extent that teachers understand its insights well and are able to use them in their teaching. The challenge for us as teacher educators, then, is how to help our own students become the kinds of teachers who will meet the challenges and enjoy the rewards of constructivist teaching.

Implications of Constructivism for Teacher Education

It follows from what we have said about constructivism and teaching that becoming a constructivist teacher is not just a matter of imitating what an exemplary model does. Nor is it a just matter of being instructed in the use of constructivist methods and having opportunities to practice them with feedback from experienced educators. While modeling, methods instruction, and coaching can all serve useful purposes in a constructivist teacher education program, they all have their limitations as well. Practices that are exemplary in one context may not be in another. There is no such thing as a standard and universally applicable set of constructivist methods for teachers to learn, and coaching in the use of particular methods per se doesn't address the crucial issue of the teacher's understanding. Constructivist teachers must not only have particular procedures at their disposal, but must also understand when and why those procedures are appropriate. Furthermore, they must be prepared to use their understandings as a basis for modifying familiar procedures, and even for inventing new ones, in order to fit their own particular needs and those of their students and the surrounding community.

Because teaching is a complex and demanding field of practice, and is always a political act, there are many knowledge domains in which teachers need to have well developed understandings. They include not only subject matter and pedagogy but also moral, social, and political knowledge as well. Moreover, while the teacher's knowledge in all of these domains can certainly be informed by experiences in contexts other than teaching, it must be reworked and integrated to fit the purposes of teaching. Constructivist perspectives on learning tell us that in order for all this to happen, teacher learners must do a great deal of conceptual work themselves, albeit in collaboration with others and with assistance from others. As teacher educators, our job is to help them do this conceptual work. As others have suggested (e.g., Ammon & Black, 1998; Ashton; 1992; Fosnot, 1989; Richardson, 1997), constructivism offers us guidance with respect to both the content and the process of teacher education, and therefore it has implications regarding the roles to be played by all the various participants—course instructors, master or mentor teachers, supervisors, school administrators, and of course the teacher learners themselves, their students, and their students' families.

With regard to the content of teacher education, we have already noted the variety of knowledge domains that are entailed in what teachers do and which, therefore, need attention in a teacher education program. One of these, the domain of pedagogy, is more or less unique to teaching, and may therefore be less well developed in the minds of prospective teachers than the domains that cut across other aspects of one's life. We have further noted that, from a constructivist perspective, pedagogy includes much more than a knowledge of teaching methods. It also includes understandings about the subjects taught, and about learners and how they learn what is being taught (understandings that are consistent with insights from constructivist theory and research). Thus, in a constructivist teacher education program, constructivism itself must be regarded as core content. Exactly how to help teacher learners understand the learning of school subjects from the perspectives offered by constructivists is a central challenge for teacher educators.

With regard to the process of teacher education, constructivism leads us to expect that teacher learners have much in common with other learners. That is, they construct knowledge through the purposeful activities they engage in, both individually and with others, using their previously constructed knowledge, and influenced by their typical modes of thinking and interacting with others. But teachers are also different from other learners. For one thing, they are not children or adolescents, but adults, and for another, they are preparing to engage in a range of activities that are more or less unique to teaching. Moreover, just as teaching differs from other kinds of activity, the various contexts for learning to teach differ from other contexts, and from each other as well. For example, practicum experiences in learning to teach typically take place in rooms full of young students for whom the teacher learner is at least partly responsible. For pre-service student teachers, these experiences usually occur during part-time work in another teacher's classroom—a teacher who has her own agenda, values, and practices, and to whom the student teacher is primarily accountable. On the other hand, inservice teacher learners generally have the greater autonomy that comes with working in one's own classroom, but they work full-time and are directly accountable to a wider community that includes other personnel at their schools and the families of their students. Both the similarities and the differences between the teaching environments of preservice and inservice teachers affect the kinds of purposeful activities they can engage in and, therefore, the ways in which they can learn and develop themselves.

In general, the circumstances surrounding pre-service and inservice teacher education open up unique opportunities for teacher-learners, but they also constrain teacher learning and development in many ways, as they entail important issues to be reckoned with aside from the teacher-learner's professional development—issues such as the well-being of the students in the room, the mandates of school, district, and state policies, and the interests of the students' families. Thus teacher educators are much like P–12 educators in having to adapt their practices to the complexities of the environments in which they work. And, like constructivist teachers, teacher educators must also adapt to the complexities of the learners whose development they seek to foster.

Contradictions, Dialectics, and Dimensions: Organization of the Monograph. How can we proceed to think further about constructivist teacher education? We have said that this monograph concerns the implications of constructivist theories for teacher education; we were charged with the responsibility of defining constructivist teacher education. As we have shown here, constructivism itself is a complex, multi-faceted theoretical perspective. These perspectives contain inherent contradictory ideas that must be addressed if we are to use constructivist theory to inform teacher education. For example, is knowledge individually or socially constructed (or both)? Are the goals of education to help individuals to become full-fledged community members or to achieve intellectual autonomy (or both)? Thus, constructivist teacher education is not so simply defined. If constructivism is essential to our vision of effective education, then we must address and reconcile these seeming contradictions. To begin our work in the commission, we discussed what sort of framework would be most effective to communicate our ideas and to help other teacher educators to understand our vision and to enable them to think about their own views on the issues we had identified. Our goal was to communicate a vision of teacher education that could contribute to changing the world for the better by educating prospective teachers to do more than simply replicate the status quo, to be more effective educators than their predecessors. Each member of the commission works in a program where learning with understanding, the achievement of social justice, and the education of citizens for a democratic society are articulated goals

(Oakes & Lipton, 1999). The mission of each teacher education program explains these goals somewhat differently, but all share a similar vision. We all see constructivist theory as helping us to achieve these goals.

Given this perspective, we constructed a framework for the monograph that would enable us to address the apparent contradictions in constructivism and to explicate our vision in constructivist terms. It seemed to us that this approach would be helpful to other teacher educators in thinking about their own practice from a constructivist point of view. In our discussion we identified seven pairs of seemingly contradictory ideas that could be drawn from applying constructivist theory to teacher education. Each of these contradictions came out of constructivist theory and seemed particularly relevant to teacher education. Each set of ideas is a dialectical pair in that within each set we have a contradiction of opposites that must be continually synthesized and resolved. Thus, for example, the contrasting notions of autonomy and community represent contradictory aspects of a teacher's persona. Simply put, we hope teachers will be both autonomous thinkers and collaborative community members. While these ideas appear to contain an inherent contradiction, both qualities are important aspects of a good teacher, particularly one who is committed to the ideals of social justice and equity in her classroom. We cannot have one idea without the other, since the very definition of one part of the pair depends on an understanding of the other. Rather than finding these apparent contradictions irresolvable, we find they provide a creative tension that allows us to reconstruct our notion of effective teacher education.

Each of these pairs represents an essential contradiction that teachers must continually consider. But no one pair represents the whole of a teacher's concern. Thus, we called each pair a dimension, implying that taken together, the set of seven dialectical pairs we have identified can help us better understand and manage the complexity of teacher education as a whole in order to be more effective in realizing our vision. The notion of a set of dimensions, the measurable extents, of applying constructivist theory to teacher education is a helpful one. By introducing a set of dimensions, we indicate that, while in contemplation we can consider one of the set, in action the others all come into play as well. We can better understand something by examining one aspect of it, but we must always remember that there are other aspects that impinge on our chosen aspect and thus, each dimension has implications for others. For example, consider a glass. We can know that the volume of the glass is 8 ounces, and have knowledge, therefore, of one dimension. But we don't really know that much about the glass unless we also have the height (another dimension) or the circumference (another dimension), the weight and so forth. We could also consider qualitative aspects of the glass, such as what it is made of, the color of the material. Each dimension is affected by others but can be considered separately in order to better understand that aspect of the glass. In the end, however, it is a whole glass that incorporates all the dimensions we have considered (and, quite possibly, others we have not). Considering the different dimensions of the glass will make its optimal use more explicit and understandable.

Each of the chapters that follow will consider aspects of teacher education within a constructivist framework from the perspective of a particular dimension. Each dimension gives us a lens on both theoretical and practical issues facing those of us who educate prospective teachers. By viewing teacher education through these different lenses, we hope to clarify different ways that one might think about designing teacher education programs that are constructivist in both theory and practice. This is not a book that will answer the question of how to create a constructivist teacher education program. Rather, the ideas we present here will hopefully help other teacher educators to think further and, perhaps, differently about their own practice. We hope these ideas will help other teacher educators to see how what they do can help to make teacher education a more effective contributor to change which will result in social justice and excellent educational outcomes for all children.

Here we briefly introduce each of the dimensions. Each dimension addresses particular aspects of teacher education. In reading each of the following chapters, it is important to keep in mind that ultimately one must be able to consider a teacher education program as a whole, with all of the perspectives working in concert. Each dimension is phrased as a balance between two dialectical concepts, a balance that is a coordination, rather than a contradiction, of conflicting ideas. In the ensuing disequilibrium, we are forced to consider both the contradictions and the coordinations of what we do. These dimensions help us to think about our goals for the teachers we educate, why these goals make sense and how we plan to achieve them.

Action-Reflection

This dimension is about the process of inquiry that accompanies good practice. The cycle of "knowledge-reflection-action-reflection-new knowledge" is one that underlies the practice of a constructivist teacher education program. Participating in such a cycle is an act of inquiry about one's teaching that provides for ongoing professional development for teacher educators and teacher candidates. Reflective examination allows one to act with intent. Teacher educators participate in this cycle themselves through conscious observation and constructed reflection for their students (e.g. freewrites). They continually examine what they are trying to teach and what their students seem to be learning. By sharing the results of this process with their students, they create a metacognitive reflective cycle on pedagogical learning and practice.

Teacher-learners are expected to apply the cycle of knowledge-reflection-action-reflection to their own practice, both as students in school and in the practice of teaching. Teacher education programs provide many contexts for this cycle to occur, both in a guided manner and independently. For example, in many teacher education programs, ongoing journals about student teaching are the norm. In some cases, these journals are dialogues between the student teacher and the cooperating teacher or supervisor, thus providing a guided action-reflection cycle. In other cases, these journals are private, but still provide an opportunity for the student teacher to practice action-reflection independently.

Content-Process

Inherent in the concept of constructivism is both content and process; content as what we learn, process as how we learn it. In the domain of teacher education pedagogical knowledge and subject matter knowledge are both important and both contain content and process aspects. Prospective teachers must reorganize their understanding of the content of their subject matter knowledge to what is referred to in the literature as pedagogical content knowledge. In addressing content, they must understand and coordinate both the structure of the discipline or content and analyze how it is one comes to know this content. In considering process, they must look at how they have come to know content and compare this to others' ways of knowing and learning, not assuming there is only one process.

Teaching prospective teachers, we must recognize the same challenge for ourselves. We must address the question "what is pedagogical content knowledge within a particular content area?" and simultaneously reconstruct our own understandings of the nature of the discipline. Embedded in this discussion is the recognition that disciplines are socially defined and constructed. We must continually reflect on the "what" of what we are teaching and the purpose such content serves. In addition, we must think about the construction processes that pedagogical and subject matter content understanding require on the part of beginning and experienced teachers, and conduct our own teaching in a manner that represents an awareness if the nature of learning to teach.

Autonomy-Community

Teacher-learners and teacher educators recognize the seeming contradiction of the autonomous learner who socially constructs his/her understanding. Teachers recognize that each student must construct his/her own understanding; what students need to learn cannot be "pasted" in. However, this learning process is a social one where individual understanding is constructed in the context of social interactions. The most commonly understood context is Vygotsky's notion of learning, which occurs under the auspices of an adult or more knowledgeable peer acting as a guide or facilitator. But learning can also occur in the context of teaching less knowledgeable peers or of collaboration with others whose partial understandings are complementary to one's own. Ultimately effective teachers are able to support individual learners in collaboration between the autonomous self and the social context in which they learn.

In addressing this dichotomy directly, teacher educators create contexts within their programs for teacher candidates to develop collegial relationships with one another, creating a community of learners. Within this community, teacher learners support one another's attempts to construct and reconstruct individual understandings about the subject matter, pedagogical content, children's learning and other relevant understandings. Learning within such a context will help teacher candidates learn to create similar supportive communities within their own classrooms. However, the connection between how teacher candidates are learning or being taught and how they might teach needs to be made explicit. Thus, an action-reflection cycle on collaboration and collegial relationships could be appropriate.

Authority-Facilitator

The dimension represented by this dichotomy refers to the role of the teacher in choosing the content and process of knowledge construction. An ongoing conundrum for the constructivist teacher is understanding that, while learners must construct their own understandings of content, there is content that is socially more or less useful; it is the responsibility of the teacher to make sure learners have the opportunity to construct understandings of this necessary content. On one hand, teachers who are constructivist in their orientation, recognize the role of teacher as coach or more knowledgeable learner, drawing on Vygotsky's notion of the zone of proximal development for teaching particular content. On the other hand, teachers are repeatedly confronted with decisions about which directions to encourage or support and which ones to ignore. Deciding what to teach and what content to present is the responsibility of the teacher, as is it her/his responsibility to create a context in which s/he can act to support students' construction of knowledge. For teacher-learners often this dichotomy is reflected more concretely in issues of classroom management and curriculum design. Teacher-learners struggle with the dual roles involved in creating a context of a community of learners that facilitates the learning of all members for which they have the ultimate responsibility. Thus, authority and facilitator must work in concert together.

Power-Empowerment

The notion of power is one rarely addressed directly in teacher education programs. Yet understanding who has which kinds of power and how all members of the learning community can be empowered is important in creating an environment in which democratic values are lived. While there are inherently inequitable power relations between students and their teachers, there is also the possibility for mutual respect between students and teachers in spite of this inequity. Teachers have more power for a number of reasons: they are generally older and more knowledgeable than their students about the content they are teaching; they have the responsibility for helping their students to learn that particular content. The combination of acknowledged expertise and responsibility creates a context for an inequitable power relationship. There are, in addition, secondary power attributes associated with social differences which, if unacknowledged, can interfere with the development of mutual respect; attributes such as middle-class status, gender, English language speaker status for example. If teachers are unconscious of the potential power inequities inherent in these different situations, then the inequities will manifest themselves in ways that interfere with the creation of an environment that encompasses democratic values. Students, on the other hand, have knowledge about their own communities, families and ways of learning that are useful knowledge for both learners and teachers. Mutual respect between teachers and students can be fostered by the acknowledgment on both sides of the "funds of knowledge" (Moll & Greenberg, 1990) which each can contribute. Such mutual respect is concretely reflected in responsive listening on the part of instructors to student questions and concerns, and constructive contributions on the part of students. Thus, in a program that recognizes the challenges of balancing this dilemma, students are willing to reveal their true thinking and instructors are willing to admit when they are unsure or unclear about their own ideas. Thus, students and teachers can continually learn from one another, in spite of the inequitable nature of their relationship.

Teacher education programs contain the same power inequities inherent in any classroom situation. Addressing the notion of power-empowerment directly and explicitly is often initially confusing to teacher learners, but ultimately the experience of mutual respect in teacher education can enable beginning teachers to create similarly respectful situations in their own classrooms.

Critical Thinking—Understanding Multiple Perspectives/Representations

Construction of knowledge is a process of coordinating multiple perspectives on many levels. As children mature, their ability to consider multiple perspectives grows. Thus, one can apply critical thinking to these multiple perspectives to construct new knowledge. However, all of us, in confronting unfamiliar content domains, tend to revert to simpler views of the subject matter, which often includes only one point of view. In addition, when considering subject matter we feel confident about, it is often difficult to address new possibilities, reflecting a certain rigidity in our thinking. As teacher educators, we must consciously consider what possible multiple perspectives to introduce regularly, to foster both flexibility and critical ability in our teacher learners. We must also continue to consider possible perspectives to foster continued flexibility in our own thinking and development.

Thinking critically allows one to evaluate multiple perspectives in social contexts as well. Knowledge acquisition is a socially mediated process that requires the consideration of multiple viewpoints of the different participants. Critical consideration, combined with flexible and sympathetic understanding of the perspectives of all participants, increases the likelihood of teachers and students acting with the good of everyone in mind. Thus, teacher-learners must think critically about possible multiple perspectives, as they choose the actions they will take. Clearly this dimension connects intimately with the action-reflection dimension by articulating particular aspects of reflection that are important for good teaching.

Learning-Development

The dilemma in this last dimension refers to how learning and development are sometimes differentiated in a way that implies conflicting approaches to education. That is, learning is often viewed from a transmission perspective, implying an active stance on the part of the educator (we can teach them what they need to learn), while development is often viewed from a romantic perspective, implying a "wait and see" approach (expose them to experiences and sooner of later they will develop the skills they need). In practice, this way of differentiating between learning and development usually results in an emphasis on learning, because that seems more proactive, while development is neglected. Conversely, learning and development are sometimes not differentiated at all, as development is thought by some to result entirely from learning. Here, there is no sense of a dilemma, but, once again, inadequate attention is paid to development.

From a constructivist perspective, learning and development are seen as different but mutually dependent processes. Learning can be thought of as particular changes in knowledge and skills while development can be thought of as broader systemic change. Development influences what is learned from specific experiences, and specific learnings can, in turn, influence the further development of whole knowledge systems. Thus, in order to foster lifelong learning, it is necessary to foster self-regulation with regard to both aspects of knowledge acquisition. However, teacher educators tend to be more concerned with the particular learning of teacher-learners than with their long-term development. But if teacher education programs are concerned only with particular learning, then once teachers are on their own, in their own classrooms, lifelong learning may be compromised. Teachers may be able to identify particular things they want to know, but be unable to make connections between specific learnings and their practice as a whole. On the other hand, if teacher education programs can provide support for ongoing development as well as ongoing learning, teachers are more likely to continue their lifelong learning process by continually pushing the envelope of their own individual zones of proximal development.

In differentiating learning and development, we see that teacher education programs have the potential to affect both. Self-regulation and lifelong learning require metacognitive knowledge about both one's own particular learning and one's own systemic change or development. It is evident that teacher education programs can affect particular learnings by providing teachers with appropriate instruction and learning opportunities. But teacher education programs can also support development, in two ways. First, they can help teachers understand the nature of development and reflect on their own development as teachers. Second, they can promote continued development by encouraging teachers to relate particular learnings to larger contexts—to make connections within and between the various knowledge systems that are relevant to teaching. Teachers with a constructivist perspective can identify how each particular learning will help them continue to achieve the goals they have set for themselves in contributing to the improvement of education for all children.

CONCLUSION

In addressing one of the dialectical dimensions described above, each of the chapters that follow provides a different lens on constructivist teacher education. The discussions in these chapters are based on ideas from various theories of constructivism, rather than from a single theory. However, each chapter subscribes to a basic tenet of all theories of constructivism regarding the central role of the learner's activity in knowledge acquisition. Because learners' activities are central, and because they vary from learner to learner, teachers must pay close attention to each learner's construction processes as well as to the curriculum or subject matter they are teaching. While it may seem self-evident that the learner, as well as the curriculum, must be the focus of the teacher's attention, it is how the learner's activity interacts with that of the teacher's, around the particular content to be learned, that differentiates a constructivist model of education from both transmission and romantic models.

Thus, the goal of this book is not to provide teacher educators with a set of constructivist practices for P–12 teachers. Nor is it to provide a set of practices that teacher educators can use "as is" in their own teaching. Rather, our goal is to help teacher educators think about how to actualize the promise of constructivism in their own particular contexts with their own teacher learners. Along with discussion of a dimension of constructivism as it applies to teacher education, each chapter also provides examples of how some teacher education programs have explored the contradictions within a given dimension in their own practices. Finally, each chapter addresses how its view of teacher education can contribute to realizing the vision we identified at the beginning of this introduction, the vision of creating a world of education where children, their families, their teachers, their schools, and their communities come together as lifelong learners engaged in powerful learning, contributing to a strong and equitable democratic society.

REFERENCES

Ammon, P., & Black, A. (1998). Developmental Psychology as a Guide for Teaching and Teacher Preparation. In N. M. Lambert & B. L. McCombs (Eds.), *How Students Learn: Reforming Schools Through Learner-Centered Education* (pp. 409–448). Washington, DC: American Psychological Association.

Archambault, R. D. (Ed.) (1964). *John Dewey on Education: Selected Writings.* New York: Modern Library.

Ashton, P. T. (Ed.). (1992). Constructivist Approaches to Teacher Education. *Journal of Teacher Education, 43*(5).

Au, K. H. (1980). Participation Structures in a Reading Lesson with Hawaiian Children: Analysis of a Culturally Appropriate Instructional Event. *Anthropology and Education Quarterly, 11*(2), 91–115.

Bruner, J. S. (1960). *The Process of Education.* New York: Vintage Books.

Dalton, J., & Watson, M. (1997). *Among Friends: Classrooms Where Caring and Learning Prevail.* Oakland, CA: Developmental Studies Center.

Darling-Hammond, L. (1997). *The Right to Learn: A Blueprint for Creating Schools That Work.* San Francisco: Jossey-Bass.

Dewey, J. (1963). *Experience and Education.* New York: Collier. (Original work published 1938).

Duckworth, E. (1964). Piaget Rediscovered. In R. E. Ripple & V. N. Rockcastle (Eds.), *Piaget Rediscovered* (pp. 1–5). Ithaca, NY: Cornell University School of Education.

Duckworth, E. (1987). *"The Having of Wonderful Ideas" and Other Essays on Teaching and Learning.* New York: Teachers College Press.

Dweck, C. S. (2000). *Self-Theories: Their Role in Motivation, Personality, and Development.* Philadelphia: Psychology Press.

Flavell, J. H., Miller, P. H., & Miller, S. A. (1993). *Cognitive Development* (3rd ed.). Englewood Cliffs, NJ: Prentice-Hall.

Fosnot, C. T. (1989). *Enquiring Teachers, Enquiring Learners: A Constructivist Approach for Teaching.* New York: Teachers College Press.

Fosnot, C. T. (Ed.). (1996). *Constructivism: Theory, Perspectives, and Practice.* New York: Teachers College Press.

Gardner, H. (1993). *Multiple Intelligences: The Theory in Practice.* New York: Basic Books.

Kohlberg, L., & Mayer, R. (1972). Development as the Aim of Education. *Harvard Educational Review, 42*(4), 449–496.

Kroll, L., & Black, A. (1993). Developmental Theory and Teaching Methods: A Pilot Study of a Teacher Education Program. *The Elementary School Journal, 93*(4), 417–441.

Larochelle, M., Bednarz, N., & Garrison, J. (Eds.). (1998). *Constructivism and Education.* New York: Cambridge University Press.

Lave, J., & Wenger, E. (1991). *Situated Learning: Legitimate Peripheral Participation.* Cambridge, MA: Cambridge University Press.

Lewin, K. (1943). Psychology and the Process of Group Living. *Journal of Social Psychology, 17*, 113–131.

Meier, D. (1995). *The Power of Their Ideas.* Boston: Beacon Press.

Moll, L. C. & Greenberg, J. B. (1990). Creating Zones of Possibilities: Combining Social Contexts for Instruction. In L Moll (Ed.), *Vygotsky and Education: Instructional Implications and Applications of Sociohistorical Psychology* (pp. 319–348). New York: Cambridge University Press.

Oakes, J., & Lipton, M. (1999). *Teaching to Change the World.* New York: McGraw-Hill.

Perrone, V. (1991). *A Letter to Teachers: Reflections on Schooling and the Art of Teaching.* San Francisco: Jossey-Bass.

Philips, S. U. (1972). Participant Structures and Communicative Competence: Warm Springs Children in Community and Classroom. In C. Cazden, V. John, & D. Hymes (Eds.), *Functions of Language in the Classroom* (pp. 370–394). New York: Teachers College Press.

Phillips, D. C. (1995). The Good, the Bad, and the Ugly: The Many Faces of Constructivism. *Educational Researcher, 24*(7), 5–12.

Piaget, J. (1970a). Piaget's theory. In P. H. Mussen (Ed.), *Carmichael's Manual of Child Psychology: Vol. 1* (3rd ed., pp. 703–732). New York: Wiley.

Piaget, J. (1970b). *Science of Education and the Psychology of the Child.* New York: Orion Press. (Original work published 1935, 1965.)

Piaget, J. (1971). *Biology and Knowledge: An Essay on the Relations Between Organic Regulations and Cognitive Processes* (B. Walsh, Trans.). Chicago: University of Chicago Press. (Original work published 1967.)

Prawat, R. S. (1996). Constructivisms, Modern and Postmodern. *Educational Psychologist, 31*(3/4), 215–225.

Richardson, V. (Ed.). (1997). *Constructivist Teacher Education: Building a World of New Understandings.* London: Falmer.

Steffe, L. P., & Gale, J. (Eds.). (1995). *Constructivism in Education.* Hillsdale, NJ: Erlbaum.

Vygotsky, L. S. (1978). *Mind in Society: The Development of Higher Psychological Processes* (M. Cole, V. John-Steiner, S. Scribner, & E. Souberman, Eds.). Cambridge, MA: Harvard University Press.

Vygotsky, L. S. (1987). Thinking and Speech. In R. W. Rieber & A. S. Carton (Eds.), *The Collected Works of L. S. Vygotsky: Vol. 1, Problems of General Psychology* (pp. 43–285) (N. Minnick, Trans.). New York: Plenum. (Original work published 1934.)

Professional Background:
Christie McIntyre

Christie McIntyre recently accepted the position of Clinical Instructor at Southern Illinois University in the Department of Curriculum and Instruction. She serves as a Center Coordinator for field experiences of preservice students. Prior to moving to Southern Illinois, Ms. McIntyre worked with the Early Childhood faculty at Georgia State University, where she continues to pursue her PhD in Early Childhood Education. At GSU, Ms. McIntyre served as co-facilitator in the Developmental Cohort program for preservice students and in the Education Specialist Cohort for inservice teachers. Both cohort programs are founded on principles of constructivism. While Ms. McIntyre has embraced constructivism as a teacher educator, her first experiences with constructivism were as a classroom teacher. She attended a Foxfire inservice while teaching in the primary grades, and the Foxfire Core Practices resonated with her own beliefs about teaching and learning. Soon to follow this inservice experience, she participated in the Collaborative Master's Program at GSU. Once again her beliefs were confirmed through the readings and experiences of the cohort. Practical knowledge of constructivist practices in the regular classroom and in the university classroom have provided Ms. McIntyre with an appreciation for the complex roles and responsibilities of being a constructivist teacher and teacher educator.

Action and Reflection in Constructivist Teacher Education

Christie McIntyre

> *"But others reflect, or give back in varied lights, all that strikes upon them. The dull make no response; the bright flash back that fact with an added quality . . . Moreover, slowness of response is not necessarily dullness; a thoughtful person waits to think things over"* (Dewey, 1933, p. 42).

Given the multiplicity of issues facing teachers today, it seems logical that reflecting on the outcomes of their practices would be a beneficial action for any teacher to engage in on a regular basis. The work of John Dewey and Donald Schon supports this practice of reflecting within teacher preparation programs. In *How We Think*, Dewey defines reflective action as the process of giving "active, persistent, and careful consideration of any belief or supposed form of knowledge in the light of the grounds that support it and the further conclusions to which it tends . . ." (Dewey, 1933, p. 9). Ultimately, theory and practice would merge in conscious thought and possible outcomes would be considered prior to actions. Teacher-learners should actively question their roles in the classroom; however, they often passively accept the established routines of a grade level, a school, or a school district without reflecting on the theoretical perspectives, social contexts, and personal experiences that influence their actions.

The relationship between reflection and action in constructivist teacher education is explored within this chapter.

Teacher educators want their students to develop a thirst for a deeper understanding of major issues and concepts in education, rather than to passively participate in the mastery of a set of skills. Encouraging them to discover why they do things a particular way in the classroom and the long/short-term effects of these decisions is paramount. This involves asking them to reflect on memorable experiences in their education. Identifying the impact of these experiences on current choices in the classroom can help one discover "why." For example, a negative experience with homogenous reading groups may motivate a teacher to look for alternative grouping strategies in her classroom. When major issues and their outcomes, like grouping strategies, are discussed in teacher education programs, the individuals begin to appreciate the multiple perspectives and approaches of their peers. Asking students to reflect on how they arrived at their conclusions can also provide us with insight into their understanding of the broader issues.

Reflecting on prior experiences and future actions is an integral component of the constructivist paradigm. A basic premise of constructivism is that students construct their new knowledge. Piaget's explanations of cognitive maps form the foundation for understanding how individuals construct knowledge, which leads to future actions. When confronted with an unfamiliar situation, we look for similarities to affirm our current knowledge; however, if similarities cannot be found, then we must deal with the contradiction in one of three ways:

> *(1) They might ignore the contradictions and persevere with their initial scheme or idea; (2) they might waiver, holding both theories simultaneously and dealing with the contradiction by making each theory hold for separate, specific cases; or (3) they might construct a new, more encompassing notion that explains and resolves the prior contradiction (Fosnot, 1996, p. 16).*

For example, during a reflective conference with a student teacher, the supervisor questioned the outcomes of a competitive spelling lesson and asked her to reflect on the impact of competition and cooperation in the classroom. The student teacher shared her reflection at the next conference, and it supported her initial decisions to provide competitive activities in the classroom. Although she is currently ignoring the 'contradiction' (as defined by Piaget), she had to reference the idea of cooperation, and in doing so, her transformed view of competition will now include its relationship to cooperation. While the contradiction may be provoked from an external source, it must be experienced internally to initiate development. According to Piaget, her disequilibrium has led to accommodation. This example also supports the dynamic nature of equilibration. Fosnot (1996) describes the process as a "dance of progressive equilibria, adaptation and organization, growth and change" (p. 14). The student teacher had to reorganize structures related to competition as she reflected.

Lev Vygotsky's zone of proximal development emphasizes the importance of a collaborative approach to making sense of our world. According to Fosnot (1996), he agrees with Piaget's belief that students construct knowledge as they reflect upon their experiences, however, he adds that an adult can enhance the construction by introducing "scientific" concepts (p. 18). Vygotsky describes scientific concepts as the more formal abstractions and the more logically defined concepts a student would encounter in the structured activity of a classroom. The "spontaneous" concepts acquired, according to Piaget, are essential to understanding scientific concepts. So, Vygotsky would support the presence of a more knowledgeable adult or peer, for example, during a reflective conference or discussion with students. When a teacher-learner debriefs a field experience in the presence of peers and a teacher educator, the scientific concepts can be explored in a meaningful context. The teacher educator uses knowledge of the teacher-learners' prior constructs to extend the discussion. This implies that teacher educators must redefine their role in the classroom.

Understanding the dimension of action and reflection is critical to developing a foundation for the other dimensions as they relate to constructivism. The first section of this chapter will explore the dimension of action and reflection as presented by John Dewey and Donald Schon. While Dewey addresses routine actions and reflective actions, Schon considers the roles of reflection-on-action and reflection-in-action. The second section will build on the work of

Zeichner and Liston (1996) who describe the differences in a technician and a reflective practitioner. As the dimension is clarified, examples of programs and courses are shared. The second section articulates the similarities and differences in these perspectives of action and reflection, as well as, proposes the implications for teacher educators.

MAJOR IDEAS ABOUT REFLECTION

Routine vs. Reflective Action

Dewey (1933) distinguishes reflective action from routine action, and he defines reflective action as a state of doubt that leads to the pursuit of a resolution. He refers to a 'stream of consciousness' (p. 3) when describing the random thoughts that run through our minds during the course of the day. The stream of consciousness usually has no purpose other than to allow ideas to flow without any consequence. The organization of a stream of thoughts towards a desired goal is a step in the direction of reflecting. Dewey describes the role of reflection as:

> *It emancipates us from merely impulsive and routine activity . . . enables us to direct our actions with foresight and to plan according to ends in view of purposes of which we are aware. It enables us to know what we are about when we act. It converts action that is merely appetitive, blind, and impulsive into intelligent action (Dewey, 1933, p. 17).*

Routine activities often dictate what a teacher does during the day. For classroom teachers, these activities range from taking the children to lunch at a set time to teaching multiplication facts in the third grade just because that is when the textbooks introduce it. Dewey (1933) cautions educators to consider the cost of "external monotony and internal routine" (p. 52). When we continue practices because they are familiar and produce predictable outcomes we may be robbing the children of an opportunity to explore their own interests in a thoughtful manner. He praises the role of curiosity and wonder and presents them as necessary factors for developing reflective thinking.

Within teacher education, action research projects are often used as a method to capitalize on the interest of teacher-learners and to foster reflectivity. The Collaborative Master's Program at Georgia State University encourages teachers to explore their wonderings through an action research project. Each teacher identifies a question related to his/her practice and chooses a method for data collection. Subgroups form based on common interests and provide support for the ongoing research. The subgroup establishes an agenda for periodic meetings where they may discuss literature, share ideas, or request experts to share their knowledge. As a part of the final paper and capstone, students report discoveries from action research projects. This exemplifies Dewey's (1933) notion that teachers should carefully examine their practice and the purpose of their actions with a summary of the outcome.

Another method for teacher-learners to discuss the issues pertinent to their classrooms and to critically examine their practice is discourse communities (Putnam and Borko, 2000). Again teacher-learners and teacher educators come together because they share a common interest in teaching or learning. Within the discourse community, participants engage in critical and reflective conversations challenging the arguments of peers in order to better understand the complexities of the topic. The collective knowledge of the group is greater than the sum of its individual parts (Putnam, p. 9). Action research projects and discourse communities enable teacher-learners to explore *states of doubt* through reflective action.

Dewey presents reflective action as a cyclical process similar to the scientific method (Dewey, 1933). When we encounter a situation where we are uncertain about the path or the outcome, we consider possible solutions, identify a potential course of action, modify our approach, and move in a direction consistent with our hypothesis. If the state of doubt persists, we will begin the process again. Reflective action seeks resolution.

Reflection and Experience

In Piaget's view, people "construct their knowledge through their actions on their environment" (Wadsworth, 1989, p. 186). This implies that experience interacts with knowledge. Following Dewey's premise (1933) that all experiences are not necessarily educative, educators should assume responsibility for guiding experiences toward an educative outcome. He suggests three conditions as criteria to be met in order for experiences to be considered educative. The first condition is that the students are interested in the topic/activity. Next, the project must have intrinsic worth to the student. Is this knowledge valuable information in the context they live in? Finally, the problem should "awaken new curiosity" and create desire for a deeper understanding of the critical issues (p. 216).

Engaging teacher-learners in meaningful experiences is only the beginning of a thoughtful inquiry of prior beliefs and behaviors (Kaufman, 1996). If the current structures of a teacher-learner's repertoire are not challenged, then they will teach the way they were taught. Most teacher educators agree that a field-based program that places the teacher-learner in a variety of teaching contexts will result in an expanded repertoire of experiences. However, few programs capture the essence of allowing students to explore the relationships between the "means and methods employed and results achieved" (Dewey, 1998, p. 104). This implies that through reflection a teacher-learner can consider the effects of the procedures employed and the outcomes on student learning. Insight cannot be imposed upon the teacher-learner, they construct it by reflecting on their experiences. So, the teacher educator is facilitating the attainment of knowledge through purposeful, educational experiences, rather than a profession of knowledge. A constructivist framework "emphasizes the growth of the prospective teacher through experiences, reflection, and self-examination" (McIntyre, Byrd, Foxx, 1996, p. 172).

Using a constructivist framework, Jadallah (1996) investigated the reflective insights of preservice teachers as they made curriculum and instructional decisions during their field experiences. He contends that their conceptual understandings of certain practices are dependent upon their prior experiences. Jadallah references Leinhardt and Greeno's work (1996) with schemata representations of knowledge as an explanation for the varying reflective insights of the preservice teachers. Schemata are cognitive maps/structures that have formed as a result of prior engagements in different environments. The depth of these prior engagements can also influence future insights in similar environments. Placing students in culturally diverse settings allows for the construction of new schemata; however, reflective conversations with peers, cooperating teachers, and teacher educators can strengthen the new schemata, thereby, creating a deeper understanding of the issues. Jadallah concludes his research with the following assumptions and interpretations: (a) teachers construct their understanding of teaching and learning by interpreting experiences; (b) reflective teaching is a process of analyzing and evaluating the relevance of curriculum and instructional practices for student and societal welfare; and (c) a dialogical process facilitates the development of reflective insights (p. 82–83).

Dewey's Three States of Mind

Dewey (1933) is often cited for the three states of mind that he attributes to reflective practitioners: open-mindedness, wholeheartedness, and responsibility. Open-mindedness is a willingness to consider multiple perspectives for a given situation. Wholeheartedness implies a commitment to seek out the most effective means for educating all students, even at the expense of an established routine. Finally, responsible teachers consider the intellectual and cultural consequences of their actions (Zeichner & Liston, 1996).

Teacher educators encourage these attitudes when they provide an environment that celebrates the new and respects the differences. At Southern Illinois University in Carbondale, teacher-learners analyze episodic events in their field placements from varying points of view. Through the eyes of the child, the teacher, a peer, and their own eyes, they consider the social, emotional, physical, and cognitive implications of an event. The different lenses facilitate an open-mind. Wholeheartedness is achieved by allowing teacher-learners to choose an episode of personal interest. The special education student may be more interested in shadowing a mainstreamed child, whereas, the physical education major may express an interest in the effects of a competitive group event. In their final reflection, teacher-learners are asked to broaden the lens and share how their beliefs about teaching and learning have changed. Reflective practitioners examine outcomes in light of their beliefs, hence a demonstration of taking responsibility for the outcome.

Reflection-on-Action and Reflection-in-Action

Donald Schon's work (1987) provides a different lens for viewing reflection. He differentiates between reflection-in-action and reflection-on-action and describes the nature of reflecting as a dialogical process. As a practitioner engages in conversations about a situation, s/he contemplates the issues to be resolved. If this conversation occurs simultaneously with the situation, then the practitioner is reflecting-in-action. As teacher educators, we often refer to this as "thinking on your feet" in the classroom. Reflection-on-action occurs either prior to or after a situation. For example, this process is facilitated by teacher-learner conferences that occur before and after observations.

Schon (1987) also demonstrates an appreciation for the process of discovery during reflection-in- and -on-action. In his description of a scene from Plato's Meno, he presents the paradox of searching for knowledge when you are not quite certain of what it is that you are searching for. Schon states, "the most important things—artistry, wisdom, virtue—can only be learned for oneself" (p. 83). Experiences followed by questioning lead to an understanding of the problems to be considered in a given situation. Following the observation of a lesson done by a teacher-learner, the observer and the teacher-learner can participate in a reflective conference where she "will recover for herself" the knowledge to be gained from that situation. This is in contrast to an approach to student teaching, where the student teacher is asked to show measurable gains in her performance of specified teaching techniques.

Naming and Framing Problems

Just as Dewey describes a state of doubt as an impetus for reflective action, Schon (1987) promotes the concept of "naming and framing problems" as an essential element of reflection (p. 4). He continues to say that "if (students) are to get a well-formed problem matched to their familiar theories and techniques, they must construct it from the materials of a situation that is, to use John Dewey's (1998) term, 'problematic'." When naming and framing a problem, the perspective of the teacher-learner and the context of the situation should be considered. For Schon, variations in context are called the "indeterminate zones of practice" (p. 6).

Scion's theories are consistent with the ideals suggested in Costa and Garmston's book, *Cognitive Coaching* (1994), which serves as a guide for constructivist mentoring experiences at Georgia State University. In a constructivist student teaching experience, the indeterminate zones of practice are defined by the student teacher during the planning conference. At this time, the student teacher describes the intended outcomes, the procedures, when the observation will take place, how long it will last, what data the observer could collect, and how it could be collected. Costa and Garmston encourage the teacher educator to be flexible. They define flexibility as respecting the teacher-learner's perceptions, cognitive style, belief system, gender, and ethnicity. These characteristics become the lens through which the teacher-learner will "name and frame" the problems relative to her situation. The shift in power places the teacher-learner in charge of her own learning experience. The following narrative describes a student teaching experience that demonstrates Schon's theories.

> A planning conference prior to an observation promotes reflection-on-action. As Nancy, a student teacher, rehearsed a lesson where she would be introducing centers about Native American heritage, she realized that she did not have enough time to introduce and implement the centers in her afternoon time slot. Nancy was "naming and framing" her problem. She began to reflect upon her observations of other teachers and brainstormed with the observer possible solutions to her problem. She decided to encourage her children to read the center signs, which described the objectives and activities, during the morning hours. She hoped that their familiarity with the centers would permit her to spend less time introducing the areas.

Nancy framed a second problem when she asked the observer to document whether or not the centers were meaningful activities. She also wanted her to interact with the children. Based on Nancy's definition of meaningful, the children were asked questions at different centers. Then, the activities were noted, as well as, how they related to her definition.

In the reflective conference, the observer, the cooperating teacher, and Nancy focused on Nancy's impressions of the lesson and the data collected. The cooperating teacher seemed most interested in the children's answers to the questions, and Nancy wanted to look at the data related to the center activities. As they compared the center activities to her definition of meaningful, Nancy realized that she had used the strategy of "fact finding" at several centers. She immediately began to think about alternative strategies for students to demonstrate their knowledge at some of these centers. Since Nancy had "named and framed" the problem, she readily took responsibility for the solution.

Providing the teacher-learner with a recipe for her problems would have been easier than facilitating her reflections through inquiry. The teacher-learner begins to construct an understanding of the classroom dynamics as she engages in conversations with her mentors. In the scenario above, the teacher-learner turns her attention to issues of time management and instructional strategies. As the cooperating teacher probes actual student responses relevant to Nancy's definition of what is meaningful, the team begins to reflect on how the students are interpreting their assigned tasks at the centers. The conversation has moved beyond the technicality of most observed lessons and has embraced the implications for the students' construction of knowledge. Schon (1987) favors a reflective practicum experience where the teacher-leaner acquires the kinds of artistry essential to competence in the indeterminate zones of practice (p. 18).

SUMMARY OF MAJOR IDEAS

Dewey sets up the dichotomy of routine actions and reflective actions. Noting that action is the common denominator, the presence or absence of reflection defines the dichotomy. Without reflection, teacher-learners become a product of past traditions. With reflection, teacher-learners can effect change in the context of their classroom, their school, and their community.

Schon and Dewey place experience as a central tenant for reflection. They also describe the process of reflection as a means for seeking resolution to a problem or inquiry. Schon's theories concentrate on the context of the inquiry and it is here that he differentiates reflection-in-action and reflection-on-action. The contributions of these two men are immeasurable in the area of teacher reflections.

IMPLICATIONS OF DEWEY AND SCHON'S WORK FOR CONSTRUCTIVIST PRACTICE

The Technician and the Reflective Practitioner

Zeichner and Liston (1996) set standards for reflective practitioners by contrasting them with technicians. The technician accepts reality as it is presented, does not question personal assumptions, and responds to situations without considering the context, as in Dewey's routine action. Whereas, the reflective practitioner exhibits the following qualities:

- examines, frames, and attempts to solve the dilemmas of classroom practice;

- is aware of and questions the assumptions and values he or she brings to teaching;

- is attentive to the institutional and cultural contexts in which he or she teaches;

- takes part in curriculum development and is involved in school change efforts;

- takes responsibility for his or her own professional development (p. IV).

These essential characteristics defined by Zeichner and Liston in their book, *Reflective Teaching* (1996), provide a framework for the following section to connect Dewey and Schon's theories regarding reflection to the practices of contructivist teacher educators.

A Reflective Practitioner Examines, Frames, and Attempts to Solve the Dilemmas of Classroom Practice. The ideas of Dewey, Piaget, and Schon support this first quality. Each of these men related knowledge acquisition to the resolution of a problem, which requires reflection. Zeichner and Liston (1996) contend that the reflective practitioner will view the problem within multiple frames to determine the best solution. These multiple frames are constructed from prior experiences with similar problems and from thoughtful consideration of future outcomes.

The earlier example of the teacher-learner defining her problem within the context of a cognitive coaching experience demonstrates the necessity of immersion in the field. The substance of the concerns was relevant only to her classroom; yet, she referenced observations in neighboring classrooms as she sought a solution to her dilemma. Another method dependent on field experiences is action research projects. While the cognitive coaching session focuses on an isolated moment in time, action research permits the teacher-learner to collect data over time, try out different frames, and suspend and revise her conclusions. Both cognitive coaching and action research support the process of defining a problem situated in the classroom experience of the teacher-learner.

A Reflective Practitioner Is Aware of and Questions the Assumptions and Values He or She Brings to Teaching. Descriptions of teacher education programs that espouse a reflective orientation often note the importance of identifying prior assumptions about education on the part of the teacher-learner (Laboskey, 1994; Noori, 1994; Zeichner & Liston, 1996). Within the constructivist paradigm, awareness of prior schemata is essential to understanding and interpreting routine and reflective actions in the classroom. Consider the teacher-learner who consistently praises children's work with generic statements like, "Good job" or "I like the work you are doing." Perhaps she does so because she believes positive affirmation motivates students to repeat the performance in the future. She may even recall her own attempts as a student to please teachers and to find favor. Unchallenged, her assumptions about student motivation may permeate yet another generation of learners. The routine action may appear harmless; however, it affects whose values are promoted in the classroom.

Many avenues are pursued within teacher education programs to address the prior assumptions of a teacher-learner. Upon entering a program, teacher-learners may be asked to reflect on memorable experiences they have had in education settings. Others use guiding questions that address the role of the teacher and beliefs about children, teaching, and learning (Kasten, 1996). Dialogue journals may also be used as an opportunity for the teacher educator to scaffold prior knowledge and apply the scientific concepts referred to by Vygotsky. While the methods differ, a constructivist teacher education program will address and challenge prior assumptions in light of new experiences and knowledge.

A Reflective Practitioner Is Attentive to the Institutional and Cultural Contexts in Which He or She Teaches. According to Dewey (1933), a reflective practitioner accepts responsibility for the implications of the institutional and cultural contexts by examining the environment, the prior experiences of the students, and the resources. Institutional contexts influence the resources available to teachers, including materials to support the curriculum, other personnel (music, P.E., art, ESOL teachers), monetary donations, and planning time. Even though these factors are predetermined, the reflective practitioner will reflect on how they affect the decisions she makes in the classroom every day. Will the teacher-learner ask her aid to work with a reading group, to translate classroom newsletters for ESOL parents, or to cut out apples for a bulletin board? Will the teacher educator provide time for students to debrief a multicultural field experience, to share journal insights during a *Dreamkeepers* (Ladson-Billings, 1994) book group, or to complete a quiz covering the multicultural chapter in the textbook? How we manage our resources is a reflection of our values.

To what degree does the classroom environment replicate the familiarity of the cultures of our children? Understanding the culture of someone else requires a self-analysis of our own culture. Again, asking teacher-learners to become familiar with their own assumptions may be a prerequisite to constructively considering the perspectives of others. To say that a teacher-learner is attentive to the cultural context implies that she is aware of how her actions in the classroom affect and are affected by the community within and beyond her classroom. She is accepting responsibility for the social and political consequences of her teaching as suggested by Zeichner and Liston (1996).

A constructivist teacher is seeking connections to the child's prior cultural experiences. Kathryn Au (1998) addresses the needs of students' of diverse backgrounds in literacy instruction. In her support of social constructivism, she emphasizes the role of the student's community in establishing values related to reading. She perceives the role of the teacher as one who mediates cultural understandings of print and its usefulness. At the forefront of her research, Au promotes the ideal that students must establish *ownership* of literacy. When students understand the purpose of their actions and how it will improve their present and future growth, they are motivated to invest in literacy activities. Motivation is also influenced by culturally relevant material and/or meaningful activities that build upon their personal experiences. For example, Au (1998) describes the positive outcomes of using "talk story" as a means for students to discuss previously read texts. Talk story is a form of communication indigenous to the Hawaiian culture. By including it as a communication vehicle for book discussions, students were beginning to accept personal responsibility for the comprehension of the texts, hence ownership of their learning. Discovering the critical role of practices like talk story is a result of reflecting on the cultural needs of a particular group.

A Reflective Practitioner Takes Part in Curriculum Development and Is Involved in School Change Efforts. Active involvement in curriculum development, rather than passive acceptance of the prescribed curriculum, requires a teacher-learner to give thoughtful consideration to the needs of her learners and its relationship to the learning goals. Teacher-learners can be empowered to create curriculum appropriate for their classroom and to critically examine the outcomes of particular learning goals within the school.

An example of merging student needs and learning goals for teacher educators can be found at Mills College in Oakland, California where faculty members have made a conscious effort to model the cycle of action and reflection. At an opening retreat in the fall semester, teacher-learners and faculty plan for the coming year. New program directions are discussed in relation to past experiences and the feedback received from candidates in past years. Many class sessions begin in the same way, with the professor reflecting on free-write data acquired at a prior class meeting or from teacher-leaner journals. As they reflect on their work, they report the results of their inquiries and demonstrate how the reflective process guides future actions.

A Reflective Practitioner Takes Responsibility for His or Her Own Professional Development. Zeichner's final characteristic of a reflective practitioner entails self-reflection. The cyclical nature of acting and reflecting on actions will lead the teacher-learner to an awareness of knowledge to be gained. However, this knowledge usually occurs as a result of sub-totaling prior reflections and analyzing strengths and needs. Dewey (1933) challenges educators to seek further professional development based on this prior analysis.

The Educational Specialist (EdS) program at Georgia State University encourages teacher-learners to pursue professional development through the National Board of Professional Teaching Standards (NBPTS) process. While participating in this process, teacher-learners are supported by their peers, prior NBPTS candidates, and faculty members. Teacher-learners create a portfolio that provides a window into their thoughts about teaching and learning. One of the core propositions for the NBPTS describes the National Board Certified Teachers as those who "critically examine their practice, seek to expand their repertoire, deepen their knowledge, sharpen their judgment, and adapt their teaching to new findings, ideas, and theories" (NBPTS, p. 2).

Final Implications

While state and national standards encourage a reflective strand within teacher education programs, viewing the role of reflection and action through the lens of a constructivist teacher educator has implications beyond its traditional roles. The ability to engage in the cycle of action and reflection is critical to the development of the teacher-learner. During the journey, s/he must wrestle with old constructs and accommodate new constructs. It is our responsibility, as teacher educators, to weave reflective action throughout our daily experiences with our students. Are we modeling an inquiry approach to education? How often do we pause during the course of a day with our students to share our own metacognitive processes regarding teaching and learning? Do we build on the prior knowledge and experiences of teacher-learners as a coach or do we carry out our course objectives without regards to our students' needs and prior constructs? Often times, we provide the "scientific concepts" prior to the student having an opportunity to explore the "spontaneous concepts." Are our practices consistent with the theories we espouse?

CONCLUSION

"Becoming conscious of actions and thoughts makes possible the revision and restructuring needed for cognitive improvement" (Silcock, p. 276, 1994). Reflectivity enables us to engage in conversations with our thoughts and therefore empowers us to be in control of future actions, rather than be bound to routine actions. The reflective discourse that occurs within our minds is built upon our prior understandings and projects into the future the implications of multiple courses of action. Careful consideration is given to values and assumptions, as well as, the cultural contexts of the students.

The quote by Dewey introducing this chapter challenges the teacher-learner and the teacher educator to take a second look in the mirror. What images are portrayed in the reflections of your students? Do you see lecture notes and a textbook? Perhaps, you see images of children in a classroom. Does the teacher-learner see her cooperating teacher in the mirror? The hope is that the reflection is one of an evolving practitioner actively pursuing educational changes that will ensure the success of all learners through personal reflections.

REFERENCES

Au, Kathryn H. (1998). Social Constructivism and the School Literacy Learning of Students of Diverse Backgrounds. *Journal of Literacy Research, 30*(2), 297–319.

Costa, Arthur L. & Garmston, Robert J. (1994). *Cognitive Coaching: A Foundation for Renaissance Schools.* Norwood, MA: Christopher-Gordon Publishers, Inc.

Dewey, John. (1933). *How We Think: A Restatement of the Relation of Reflective Thinking to the Educative Process.* Boston, New York: D.C. Heath and Co.

Dewey, John. (1998). *Experience and Education: The 60th Anniversary Edition.* West Lafayette, IN: Kappa Delta Pi.

Fosnot, Catherine Twomey, (Ed.). (1996). *Constructivism: Theory, Perspectives, and Practice.* Columbia University: Teachers College Press.

Jadallah, Edward. (1996). Reflective theory and practice: a constructivist process for curriculum and instructional decisions. Action in Teacher Education, 18, 2, 73-85.

Kasten, Barbara J. (1996). Helping Preservice Teachers Construct Their Own Philosophies of Teaching Through Reflection. (ERIC Document Reproduction Service No. ED 402 072).

Kaufman, Dorit. (1996). Constructivist-Based Experiential Learning in Teacher Education. *Action in Teacher Education, 18,* 2, 40–50.

Laboskey, Vivki Kubler. (1994). *Development of Reflective practice: A Study of Preservice Teachers.* New York: Teachers College Press.

Ladson-Billings, Gloria. (1994). *The Dreamkeepers: Successful Teachers of African American Children.* San Francisco, CA: Jossey-Bass.

McIntyre, D. John, Byrd, David M., & Foxx, Susan M. (1996). Field and Laboratory Experiences. In J. Sikula, T. Buttery, & E. Guyton (Eds.), *Handbook of Research on Teacher Education* (pp. 171–193). NY: Simon and Schuster Macmillan.

National Board for Professional Teaching Standards. (1994). *What Teachers Know and Should Be Able to Do.* Detroit, MI: Author.

Noori, Kathryn K. (1994). *A Constructivist Reflective Paradigm: A Model from the Early Childhood Program at Tuskegee University* (ERIC Document Reproduction Service No. ED 684-8718).

Putnam, Ralph T. & Borko, Hilda (Jan.–Feb., 2000). What Do New Views of Knowledge and Thinking Have to Say about Research on Teacher Learning? *Educational Researcher, 29,* 1, 4–15.

Schon, Donald, A. (1987). *Educating the Reflective Practitioner.* San Francisco, CA: Jossey Bass.

Silcock, Peter (1994). The Process of Reflective Teaching. *British Journal of Educational Studies, 42*(3), pp. 273–285.

Wadsworth, Barry J. (1989). *Piaget's Theory of Cognitive and Affective Development.* New York: Longman.

Zeichner, Kenneth M. & Liston, Daniel P. (1996). *Reflective Teaching: An Introduction.* Mahwah, NJ: L. Erlbaum Associates.

Professional Background:
Sam Hausfather

Sam Hausfather is currently the Dean of the School of Professional Studies at East Stroudsburg University of Pennsylvania. He came to college teaching after eighteen years teaching in elementary schools. Graduating college in 1972 with idealistic visions of changing the world through teaching, he spent several years teaching in small private schools in California experimenting with innovative alternative models of schooling. The approaches he used followed principles now associated with constructivism, such as integrated approaches, cross-age groupings, and curriculum designed with and by students. For ten years he taught in a small progressive public school district in rural California. Workshops in whole language led to deeper understandings and curriculum experimentation with constructivist approaches as well as the desire to learn more. After completing a master's degree in science education, he left California to attain a doctorate in Teacher Education. He taught in the teacher education program at Berry College (Georgia) while also serving as a laboratory school teacher, as director of field experiences, and then as Assistant Dean for Graduate Studies. His interests now include school partnerships, teacher education program redesign around constructivist principles, and conceptual change in students and teachers.

Content and Process in
Constructivist Teacher Education

Sam Hausfather

Teaching involves the process of leading learners to understand and use content. While content remains the goal of constructivist teachers, the process of learning becomes both method and goal as well. In the process of learning lies the roots of our understanding of content as well as our goal to create independent learners. The dichotomy between content and process disappears as we take a constructivist approach to knowledge and teaching. Content does not exist outside the process of acquiring that content (Tobin & Tippins, 1993). Controversies exist in taking this position. These controversies go to the very heart of our understanding of content and the ability to teach content to students. In this chapter I discuss implications of constructivism as a way of thinking about content, approaches to learning content that derive from cognitive research, and pedagogical content knowledge as an aspect of teacher education. Examples that illustrate these elements in the practice of teacher education are then given.

PERSPECTIVES OF CONSTRUCTIVISM
ON CONTENT KNOWLEDGE

Constructivism challenges the very core of our understanding of the nature of content (von Glasersfeld, 1993). The very nature of content is our beginning point, the philosophical basis of constructivism. Constructivism as an epistemology or way of knowing is based on a theory of knowing objective reality (Staver, 1998). Constructivism confronts the wishes of many disciplines to portray ultimate truths in a content area. Constructivism questions the separation between the observer and the observations, the knower and the known. "A constructivist perspective acknowledges the existence of an external reality but realizes that cognizing beings can never know what that reality is actually like" (Tobin & Tippins, 1993, p. 4). Traditional theories of truth postulate that knowledge corresponds to facts in reality. Constructivism views knowledge as being true in relation to other knowledge in an internally coherent network. This coherence view acknowledges that knowledge "works," without supposing that we can reveal an objective reality outside the individual and social interpretations of reality. Not denying an objective reality, human experience is seen as the only viable connection to the real world (Staver, 1998). Kuhn (1970) showed how understandings of the world progressed through revolutionary paradigm shifts that influenced how we as individuals experience the world. We know the world through our experiences, through the interface of our sensation and our constructed meanings of those sensations. While we would prefer to believe the world corresponds to our experience of it, constructivism posits that humans interpret the world in ways that cohere with reality (von Glasersfeld, 1989).

These views raise the most controversial aspects of constructivist perspectives. If content is a human construction, it can change over time. Although certain content areas are more clearly linked to human experience and interpretation as their source (the humanities, arts, and social sciences), the "hard" sciences including mathematics have the greatest difficulty with constructivist epistemology. A constructivist approach to the nature of content knowledge should effect how teacher educators look at content across many disciplines. English, history, and the social sciences are seen more as process and the result of personal viewpoints. Mathematics is seen as a social construction, and thus open to discourse as a method for understanding. The nature of science will continue to be debated given the various faces of constructivist thought (Good et al., 1993; Phillips, 1995). This raises questions about the approach teacher educators should take in developing teachers' approaches to knowledge. At the same time, the natural and mathematical sciences provide some of the greatest support for educational practices related to constructivism. In this dichotomy lies a source for continued exploration and discussion between teacher educators and content-area faculty.

CONSTRUCTIVIST APPROACHES TO LEARNING CONTENT

Constructivism brings important insights that speak to pedagogical approaches to learning content. Cognitive science has progressed to the point that clear implications are apparent in educational practice. Gaea Leinhardt (1992) has synthesized the research on learning that supports constructivism and summarized the implications around three fundamental aspects: multiple forms of knowledge, the role of prior knowledge, and the social nature of knowledge and its acquisition. While each of these aspects has clear implications for school practice, less has been written about how teacher education responds to these understandings about learning.

Research on learning has led to the understanding that there are both different types and amounts of knowledge. Declarative knowledge of content concepts and principles becomes powerful for students when it is connected with procedural knowledge of actions and skills (Best, 1995). Knowledge varies across content areas as we examine the different arrangements of facts, notations, and reasoning in different subjects. Knowledge varies within content areas as one looks at how documentation, arguments or explanations are structured in different disciplines. In addition, meta-knowledge, knowing what and how well you know, is seen as a powerful factor in developing understanding in students (Schoenfeld, 1987). The complexity of learning is highlighted by these multiple forms of knowledge. Knowledge is seen as not just the information, but an active process, retained when embedded in some organizing structure (Bereiter, 1985). The implications of the nature of knowledge on pedagogy point toward teaching that integrates content with using content, dissolving the line between content and process (Leinhardt, 1992). Active, problem-solving approaches should be apparent no matter what the content approach taken. Knowledge also does not exist in isolation. It must be connected to be incorporated into the deep understanding of students. Interdisciplinary approaches can strengthen the richness of separate disciplines while acknowledging their interrelationships and modes of inquiry (Martinello & Cook, 2000).

The separation of schools of education from schools of arts and sciences within the university often creates a situation where content courses are disconnected from courses on teaching methods and learning (NCTAF, 1996). While teacher education has sought to provide more integration of content with process within teacher education courses, the content prospective teachers learn in their arts and sciences courses is left separate and inactivated through the teacher education sequence. Teacher education faculty should work closely with arts and sciences faculty to plan and implement courses of study that provide strong disciplinary preparation linked closely with the methods and content of pedagogical studies. Teacher education programs should look closely at their own curriculum to determine the extent to which they model interdisciplinary integration of content areas and pedagogy.

Student prior knowledge has been shown to greatly impact their ability to understand content knowledge. Learning involves combining what you know with what was taught, continually connecting prior knowledge with new information (Leinhardt, 1992). This prior knowledge can facilitate, inhibit, or transform learning. In reading, comprehension has been shown to depend on what you already know or want to know (Smith, 1988). There has been much research into the nature of "children's science," the ideas and experiences students bring into class with them (Driver, Guesne, & Tiberghien, 1985; West & Pines, 1985). Research shows students hold tenaciously to their prior ideas. These alternative conceptions or misconceptions grow out of students' prior experiences with the world around them, and can interfere considerably with teachers' attempts to foster learning. Often the results of teaching produce unintended learning outcomes, as students combine existing ideas with the new ideas presented by teachers (Osborne &

Freyberg, 1985). Research in mathematics education shows students come to class with effective but alternative routes to mathematics processes that are often confounded by teaching (Carpenter et al., 1989). Research on the construction of history reveal students' tendency to see historical events in terms of individuals' personal intentions and interactions and to ignore the role of societal institutions (Barton, 1997).

The acknowledgment of alternative conceptions held by students has led to deeper understandings of the process necessary to deal with student constructions. Teachers need to surface students' prior knowledge, connect to it or challenge it, and allow students to build from and onto their prior knowledge. In order for students to accept the ideas taught by teachers, knowledge must present itself as intelligible, fruitful, and plausible. Beyond these qualities, students may also have to find dissatisfaction with their current knowledge and its use in understanding (Posner et al., 1982). This is a clear move away from a "discovery" approach to knowledge construction, where students construct knowledge solely based on their own experience. Instead, students must have the opportunity to test their knowledge within a social context, teachers may have to challenge some conceptions, and students must involve themselves in a process of constructing understanding (Watson & Konicek, 1990). Conceptual change instruction in science has emphasized a lesson format that includes an orientation phase, elicitation of ideas, restructuring of ideas, application of ideas, and reviewing change of ideas (Osborne & Freyberg, 1985). In mathematics, Cognitively Guided Instruction (Carpenter et al., 1989) emphasizes allowing students to surface their process ideas as the teacher leads students to see alternative routes to solving problems. Scardamalia and Bereiter (1985) have developed models for teaching writing that use a combination of modeling, coaching, scaffolding, and fading. The use of narrative has been shown to promote students' historical understanding and challenge students' prior conceptions (Levstik & Pappas, 1992).

Teacher education programs are caught in the bind of informing teacher candidates about the importance of prior experiences and misconceptions while also having to deal with these candidates' own prior experiences and misconceptions about both teaching and content. The "apprenticeship of observation" (Lortie, 1975), lengthy personal experience with schooling, prevents preservice teachers from searching beyond what they already know and questioning the practices they see (Feiman-Nemser & Buchmann, 1987). Teacher education programs must promote conceptual change in their students toward viewing schools as they could be, not merely as they are. In their content studies, preservice teachers' own misconceptions must also be challenged. Teacher education programs have the responsibility to work with faculty in arts and sciences to understand the preconceptions students bring to their classes and the approaches that will challenge these preconceptions. Through both having their own conceptions challenged and learning about the prior knowledge of their students, teacher candidates will be prepared to provide their students content linked with student prior knowledge.

Finally, the social aspect of knowledge provides clear implications in practice. As outlined above, learning is seen to be an active process of knowledge construction and sense-making. Beyond that, knowledge is understood as a cultural artifact of people. It is created and transformed by each individual and by groups of people (Vygotsky, 1978). Knowledge is distributed among members of a group, with the whole being greater than the sum of the parts (Brown, 1994). As a result, learning should involve talk, public reasoning, and shared problem solving. Too often the social environment of schools is counterproductive (Hausfather, 1996). Instead of a focus on individual achievement, learning should involve social interaction that supports thinking, surfaces prior knowledge, and allows skills to be used in the context of content knowledge. Students should be allowed to participate in communities of discourse that allow them to clarify, defend, elaborate, evaluate, and argue over the knowledge constructed (Brown, 1994). Cooperative learning has been shown to be a powerful vehicle to improve learning outcomes for students (Slavin, 1996).

Teacher education has a clear role in clarifying a vision of a social environment supportive to learning. Preservice methods courses must model collaboration between and among the teacher and students. College teaching has traditionally stressed individual processes over social processes in learning. Teacher education needs to provide opportunities where college students learn within social situations. College students should metacognitively experience zones of proximal development (Vygotsky, 1978) within college classrooms, working within cooperative or discourse groups while analyzing their own experience as a guide to their own teaching. Instructional conversations can occur within the classic Socratic seminar, where instructor and students together explore problems as a small community of learners. Pairing students for field experience placements in schools can provide peer collaboration which fosters deeper understandings of classroom situations.

These implications from cognitive science research lead us to understand the difficulty of separating content from process in learning. Research in teaching has identified the linking of content with the process of teaching that occurs as the teacher continually restructures subject matter knowledge for the purpose of teaching (Cochran, DeRuiter, & King, 1993). Termed pedagogical content knowledge (PCK), this concept links research on teaching with research on learning, helping determine constructivist approaches to learning content for teaching.

PEDAGOGICAL CONTENT KNOWLEDGE

Lee Shulman (1986) introduced the term pedagogical content knowledge as "the ways of representing and formulating the subject that make it comprehensible to others" (p. 9). This goes beyond knowledge of the content per se to include issues of teaching the content, including typical curricular choices, powerful ideas, common learning difficulties, and student conceptions in the specific subject. Shulman included PCK in the broader knowledge base for teaching, which included content knowledge, PCK, curriculum knowledge, general pedagogy, learners and their characteristics, educational contexts, and educational purposes (Shulman, 1987). PCK involves the transformation of content knowledge so that teachers can communicate it with learners during classroom practice. Teachers derive PCK from their understandings of content, their own teaching practice, and their schooling.

As such, it is impossible to distinguish PCK from either content knowledge or pedagogical process knowledge (Van Driel, Verloop, & De Vos, 1998).

Different scholars have included different aspects within their conceptualizations of PCK, although all agree PCK differs considerably from content knowledge and that it is developed through an integrative process during classroom practice (Van Driel, Verloop, & De Vos, 1998). Cochran, DeRuiter, and King (1993) renamed PCK as pedagogical content *knowing* (PCKg) based on a constructivist view of teaching and teacher education. Their model includes subject matter content and specific pedagogical knowledge but adds teachers' understanding of students and of the environmental context of learning. Understanding students includes student abilities and learning strategies, developmental levels, attitudes, motivations, and prior conceptions. Context includes teachers' understandings of the social, political, cultural and physical environment. Teachers should simultaneously experience these four components as they prepare for and progress through their career.

Research in pedagogical content knowledge reinforces the research in cognitive science (Cochran, DeRuiter, and King, 1993) and many of the implications listed above (Ashton, 1990). To enhance the development of PCK in our teacher candidates, teacher education programs should model and share teaching decisions and strategies with students by both education and content-area faculty. These faculty should have opportunities to demonstrate and reflect on how they use PCK in their own teaching (Cochran, DeRuiter, and King, 1993). Attention must be given to the context in which PCK develops, contexts that promote active simultaneous learning about the many components of teaching within the content area. These contexts must be similar to classroom environments, which suggest the incorporation of multiple field-based opportunities within the teacher education program. Early, continued, and authentic field experiences should include real teaching, much contact with experienced teachers, and reflection and feedback.

Although it is difficult to separate PCK from content knowledge, it appears as though a thorough and coherent understanding of content is essential to effective PCK (Van Driel, Verloop, & De Vos, 1998). Teacher education programs must assist preservice teachers in constructing a deep understanding of disciplinary content from a teaching perspective so it can be used to help specific students understand specific concepts (Cochran, DeRuiter, and King, 1993). This involves both working closely with arts and sciences faculty to understand pedagogical perspectives as well as integrating methods courses with or alongside content courses.

Balancing attention to the process of learning with the content of what is being learned will ultimately result in teachers better able to understand both their content and the learning of their students. Too often content is taught without any attention to process, or process is taught without a deep understanding of the nature of the content involved. Teacher education programs are struggling to find the balance. We now turn our attention to examples of program efforts that work to obliterate the lines between content and process.

ELEMENTS IN PRACTICE

Many teacher education programs throughout the country have identified constructivist principles as foundational to their teacher education mission and goals. As constructivism has taken hold, programs have worked to understand and create the links between content and process that are fundamental in constructivist approaches. We review here several programs at undergraduate and graduate levels that have given thought to these issues, with the assumption we can learn from the lessons of individual programs.

Berry College

There is much in teacher education that is process focused. This makes sense given the process nature of teaching. Generally, there is important content as well, such as the theoretical bases of constructivism in the work of Piaget, Vygotsky, etc. Berry College's undergraduate teacher education program tries to continually mix content with process, so as theoretical bases are discussed, applications can be discussed and modeled. The program is structured to involve a back and forth between college classroom and field experience, allowing students opportunities to continually test the content of teacher education against the process of teaching in real classrooms. There are aspects of the theoretical content where mastery is expected, both in demonstrations to faculty and on the national certification tests. Assessments are constructed which allow demonstration, both authentic and paper/pencil.

Subject-matter content (math, science, social studies, phonics, etc.) is a clear part of the responsibility of an undergraduate teacher education program. Faculty strive to model the way they want students to teach this content while at the same time teaching them the content. They realize that they can not teach all the content teachers should know. In today's world, can anyone know all the content they should? The emphasis goes more to big ideas, inquiries, and the attitudes necessary to help our students become life-long learners. This starts with an understanding of the nature of knowledge and how knowledge changes through time. It is important to give credence to students' preconceptions while at the same time understanding the currently accepted conceptions. Teacher education students must understand how to use the tools given to them to continue to learn. They must understand the content deeply in order to teach it. That involves delving into the content in a way not separate from content. As teacher educators, that also means the frustration of knowing you will not cover everything you hope to. Thus the importance of an attitude toward learning content. Teachers must not be afraid of exploring their own understandings and delving on their own to understand further. The tools at our disposition are powerful to do this, with the web, electronic encyclopedias, linked communications, etc. Faculty expect students to do the self-learning necessary to prepare well to teach others, both in college classrooms and in their field experiences. Faculty model for students their own attempts to keep up with the burgeoning knowledge in their fields and their continual revision and updating of courses. And faculty honor student expertise as they learn from student explorations into particular content. Content and process becomes as inseparable as teacher and learner.

What about the teaching of particular content? College faculty depend for much on their colleagues in the arts and sciences. Faculty are brought together to design the teacher education curriculum. Constructivist teacher education cannot occur in a vacuum. Too often students move from teacher education classes to arts and sciences classes where behavioristic techniques prevail. Teacher education faculty continue to struggle with the role of helping colleagues across campus understand changes in pedagogy. Teacher education faculty also deal with teacher education students as we expect them to deal with their own pupils. This involves surfacing students' alternative conceptions or misconceptions, and then bringing them to understand the alternative conceptions pupils will bring to the classroom. Content is thus revealed, making it approachable but hard. In the teacher education classroom, an approach to teaching content is modeled that begins with experiences orienting students to a content issue. Student ideas are then elicited, and a process of restructuring ideas is modeled which challenges student ideas and introduces accepted ideas. Students then have the chance to apply their ideas through experience, and review their change in thinking. This "constructivist teaching model" is taught not as a pattern to be reproduced but as a way of understanding constructivist teaching, allowing for variety based on context.

Although there is clear need for understanding of disciplinary content, that understanding must become a part of interdisciplinary thinking. Once one steps outside the classroom, there is little in life that narrowly follows disciplines. Berry College is in the process of breaking down course walls, moving all courses to become blocks team taught by professors bringing different perspectives together. A literacy block will bring together reading, language arts, and literature. An inquiry block will share math and science. An integrated arts block will allow social studies, art, music, and PE to create integrated units. A foundations block will bring together psychology and education. Curriculum brokers will ensure that technology, child development, special education, and second-language learners are integrated throughout all blocks. In this way, content areas will be given meaning within integrated blocks emphasizing active/inquisitory approaches to knowledge.

Georgia State University

The Collaborative Master's Program (CMP) at Georgia State University is a master's degree program based on constructivist principles and the work of Dewey. The ongoing nature of program allows for the following (Rainer & Guyton, 1999):

- living the process of a constructivist model is part of the content of the program;

- contextually bound part of work (classroom based) gives meaning to content and process;

- integrated content; and

- deep engagement of content.

Content is negotiated with students in the CMP. For example, work in math methods is begun by discussing current professional standards in mathematics education (NCTM) and the relationship of these standards to teachers' practice. As the teachers look at both of these in light of constructivist theory, they begin to ask questions of faculty and faculty of teachers. Together a very optimistic list of topics is generated that the group would like to explore together. Topics are sorted into relevant categories, for example, topics such as problem solving, critical thinking and technology are grouped together with the NCTM standards on communication and reasoning. After narrowing the list to a manageable set of integrated concepts, the ideas are discussed and assigned, including a time line and designation of individuals responsible for discussions and resources. Faculty members prepare a "proposed" agenda based on these decisions. As each class begins, the agenda is presented for additions and revisions. Faculty contributions include providing reflective questions, current research on the topics, and an activity involving children's literature and physical models. Teacher's contributions involve demonstrating effective practice, reflecting on changes in pedagogy, and sharing resources.

Teachers select one area about which they want to study in some depth, collaboratively in focus groups. Example topics have been teaching math, the teaching of reading, culturally relevant curriculum, assessment and evaluation. These groups design not only the content they will study, but also the process through which to study it. Each group has a faculty advisor for resources, coaching, and guiding. In addition to documenting the content knowledge teachers gain through this process, they are asked to document their own learning process. The goal is for them to be metacognitive and articulate about their own learning process. The learning frameworks help teachers design their current and future studies.

When teachers engage in designing the benchmark, rubric, capstone, and grading process, the understanding of assessment and evaluation becomes personal. These are probably the most challenging experiences of the year for teachers in the CMP. What teachers learn about assessment and evaluation of content becomes important to them personally. They learn much more than by reading. They are living the content.

Mansfield University of Pennsylvania

The teacher education program at Mansfield University of Pennsylvania works with inservice teachers in their classrooms to contextualize their content. The program encourages deep engagement with content.

In an emerging literacy course, students are held accountable for content by checking that they have completed a log based on chapters. Five or 10 entries are required depending on the length of the chapter. The entries include: one paragraph about an idea expressed in their own words and one paragraph about the reactions. The logs are used in small group discussions and in writing their final philosophy paper. The latter must demonstrate that they have grasped the critical content (the five major topics are specified that the paper must address).

Early Childhood Curriculum follows emerging literacy. The course included nine classes where students must work for two hours in second grade classrooms. They are observed on a rotating basis and create lesson plans and reflections after each class. During the rest of the course content is introduced using parts of several NAEYC texts.

Students develop a resource notebook organized around the seven topics and then make a concept map. This helps them link information they have from learned in many courses. However, it is difficult to separate the ones who are learning the content from others who may not be.

Mills College

Inherent in the concept of constructivism are the notions of content and process. The teacher education program at Mills College strives to help students think about this dichotomy as complementary. One program standard articulates this area as "Teaching for the acquisition and construction of subject matter knowledge." A primary focus of the Mills College credential programs is to help candidates think in different ways about the subject matter knowledge they already possess. Opportunities are provided for students to transform their content knowledge into working knowledge, often referred to in the literature as pedagogical content knowledge. That is, students analyze and reorganize their subject matter knowledge in ways that will make it possible for them to provide similar opportunities for their students to organize knowledge. In addition, candidates construct subject matter knowledge where necessary as a means to obtain and develop more pedagogical content knowledge in the future.

To emphasize the contrast and dichotomy of process and content, students engage with content at an adult level while thinking about the teaching of that content (or process) at the instructional level—whether it be for a child or an adult. For example, all elementary-education students participate in Writers' Workshop during the second semester. The semester ends with a publishing party and a collection of writing, and a contribution from each class member is published. In conducting the writers' workshop, the nature of learning to write (the content), aspects of writing (more content) and the pedagogical method (process or pedagogical content) is analyzed. In mathematics methods, students' own understanding of mathematics is often deepened as they see the math lessons modeled as a hands-on, how-it-really-works approach that they did not experience as first-time learners about algebraic thinking, rational number operations, or probabilistic reasoning.

In both the methodology classes and in child development classes, students examine children's learning of mathematics and literacy and apply that understanding to thinking about how best to teach the content. Thus, throughout the program there is a goal of coordinating the nature of the discipline, children's learning, instructional practice and an overall view of the curriculum.

CONCLUSIONS

Constructivist approaches to teacher education must deal with the issues of content and process, acknowledging the vital link between content and its acquisition. Constructivism challenges some basic understandings of content knowledge. At the same time, research supporting constructivist approaches brings insights to teacher education practice that makes for more powerful teaching and understanding of content. An understanding of the nature of pedagogical content knowledge leads teacher educators to work more closely with arts and sciences faculty to help students integrate their experiences in content courses with their experiences in teacher education courses. Examples of several teacher education programs reinforce these understandings.

These program examples share an understanding that content and process are inseparable. Programs consciously link methods courses with content, focusing teacher candidates on thinking in different ways about content. Modeling by teacher education faculty engages students with content while they learn strategies to teach that content. Content is negotiated with students, with an emphasis on concepts over facts. Courses are blocked across content areas to model interdisciplinary teaching and learning. Finally, efforts are underway to increase collaboration with arts and sciences faculty toward creating a seamless teacher education program.

Teacher education provides a multiplier effect. As we model approaches that lead our students to understand content deeply and to view content and process as inseparable aspects of knowledge construction, our students gain the perspectives and abilities to move their students to deeper understandings of content. Powerful teacher education should lead to students at all levels of schooling coming to better appreciations of the world around them. A constructivist approach shows us that content and process are not dichotomous. As more teachers come to that understanding, all students will benefit.

REFERENCES

Ashton, P. T. (1990). Editorial: Theme Issue on Pedagogical Content Knowledge. *Journal of Teacher Education, 41*(3), 2.

Barton, K.C. (1997). "Bossed around By the Queen:" Elementary Students' Understanding of Individuals and Institutions in History. *Journal of Curriculum and Supervision, 12*(4), 290–314.

Bereiter, C. (1985). Toward a Solution of the Learning Paradox. *Review of Educational Research, 55,* 201–226.

Best, J. B. (1995). *Cognitive Psychology* (4th Ed.). St. Paul, MN: West Publishing Co.

Brown, A. L. (1994). The Advancement of Learning. *Educational Researcher, 23*(8), 4–12.

Carpenter, T. P., Fennema, E., Peterson, P.L., Chiang, C.P., & Loef, M. (1989). Using Knowledge of Children's Mathematics Thinking in Classroom Teaching: An Experimental Study. *American Educational Research Journal, 26*(4), 499–531.

Cochran, K. F., DeRuiter, J. A., & King, R. A. (1993). Pedagogical Content Knowing: An Integrative Model for Teacher Preparation. *Journal of Teacher Education, 44*(4), 263–272.

Driver, R., Guesne, E., & Tiberghien, A. (Eds.) (1985). *Children's Ideas in Science.* Philadelphia, PA: Open University Press.

Feiman-Nemser, S., & Buchmann, M. (1987). When Is Student Teaching Teacher Education? *Teaching and Teacher Education, 3*(4), 255–273.

Good, R.G., Wandersee, J.H., & St. Julien, J. (1993). Cautionary Notes on the Appeal of the New "Ism" (Constructivism) in Science Education. In K. Tobin (Ed.) *The Practice of Constructivism in Science Education* (pp. 71–87). Hillsdale, NJ: Erlbaum.

Hausfather, S. J. (1996). Vygotsky and Schooling: Creating a Social Context for Learning. *Action in Teacher Education, 18*(2), 1–10.

Kuhn, T.S. (1970). *The Structure of Scientific Revolutions* (2nd ed.). Chicago: University of Chicago Press.

Leinhardt, G. (1992) What Research on Learning Tells Us about Teaching. *Educational Leadership, 49*(7), 20–25.

Levstik, L. S., & Pappas, C. C. (1992). New Directions for Studying Historical Understanding. *Theory and Research in Social Education, 20*(4), 369–385.

Lortie, D. (1975). *Schoolteacher: A Sociological Study.* Chicago: University of Chicago Press.

Martinello, M. L., & Cook, G. E. (2000). *Interdisciplinary Inquiry in Teaching and Learning* (2nd ed.). Upper Saddle River, NJ: Prentice-Hall, Inc.

NCTAF (1996). *What Matters Most: Teaching for America's Future.* New York: National Commission on Teaching & America's Future.

Osborne, R., & Freyberg, P. (1985). *Learning in Science: The Implications of Children's Science.* Portsmouth, NH: Heinemann Publishers.

Phillips, D.C. (1995). The Good, the Bad, and the Ugly: The Many Faces of Constructivism. *Educational Researcher, 24,* 5–12.

Posner, G.J., Strike, K.A., Hewson, P.W., & Gertzog, W.A. (1982). Accommodation of a Scientific Conception: Toward a Theory of Conceptual Change. *Science Education, 66,* 211–227.

Rainer, J., & Guyton, E. (1999, February). *A Constructivist Approach to Teacher Education.* A paper presented at the annual meeting of the Association of Teacher Educators, Chicago, IL.

Scardamalia, M., & Bereiter, C. (1985). Fostering the Development of Self-Regulation in Children's Knowledge Processing. In S. Chipman, J. Segal, & R. Glaser, (Eds.), *Thinking and Learning Skills: Research and Open Questions* (pp. 563–577). Hillsdale, NJ: Erlbaum.

Schoenfeld, A.H. (1987). What's All the Fuss about Metacognition? In A. H. Schoenfeld (Ed.), *Cognitive Science and Mathematics Education* (pp. 189–253). New York: W. H. Freeman.

Scott, P. (1987). *Children's Learning in Science Project: A Constructivist View of Learning and Teaching in Science.* Leeds, England: University of Leeds, Centre for Studies in Science and Mathematics Education.

Shulman, L.S. (1986). Those Who Understand: Knowledge Growth in Teaching. *Educational Researcher, 15,* 4–14.

Shulman, L.S. (1987). Knowledge and Teaching: Foundations of the New Reform. *Harvard Educational Review, 57,* 1–22.

Slavin, R. E. (1996). Research on Cooperative Learning and Achievement: What We Know, What We Need to Know. *Contemporary Educational Psychology, 21*(1), 43–69.

Smith, F. (1988). *Understanding Reading: A Psycholinguistic Analysis of Reading and Learning to Read.* Hillsdale, NJ: Erlbaum.

Staver, J. R. (1998). Constructivism: Sound Theory for Explicating the Practice of Science and Science Teaching. *Journal of Research in Science Teaching, 35*(5), 501–520.

Tobin, K., & Tippins, D. (1993). Constructivism as a Referent for Teaching and Learning. In K. Tobin (Ed.), *The Practice of Constructivism in Science Education.* Hillsdale, NJ: Erlbaum.

Van Driel, J. H., Verloop, N., & De Vos, W. (1998). Developing Science Teachers' Pedagogical Content Knowledge. *Journal of Research in Science Teaching, 35*(6), 673–695.

von Glaserfeld, E. (1989). Cognition, Construction of Knowledge, and Teaching. *Synthese, 80,* 121–140.

von Glaserfeld, E. (1993). Questions and Answers about Radical Constructivism. In K. Tobin (Ed.), *The Practice of Constructivism in Science Education* (pp. 23–38). Hillsdale, NJ: Erlbaum.

Vygotsky, L. S. (1978). *Mind in Society: The Development of Higher Psychological Processes.* Cambridge, MA: Harvard University Press.

Watson, B., & Konicek, R. (1990). Teaching for Conceptual Change: Confronting Children's Experience. *Phi Delta Kappan, 71*(9), 680–685.

West, L.H., & Pines, A. L. (Eds.) (1985). *Cognitive Structure and Conceptual Change.* Orlando, FL: Academic Press.

Professional Background:
Julie Rainer and Margaret Jones

Julie Rainer

I am currently an associate professor in Early Childhood Education at Georgia State University. My research focuses on the intersections among constructivist theories and teacher education. I came to higher education with a child development background after teaching multi-age pre-school and kindergarten for many years. I found many commonalities between the learning process of the adults and the children I taught. The principles of constructivism that supported my own learning and my teaching in kindergarten are also evident in the cohort of K–5 teachers that I work with in our Educational Specialist Program. In each setting, we were/are learners together, starting with many questions and struggling to become more knowledgeable and better at our practice. The application of my beliefs and knowledge to higher education brought dissonance and new questions. On reflection, I needed the same form of professional development that our teachers need. I needed (a) time to examine my context and practice in light of my beliefs, (b) support to take risks and reflect on them, and (c) colleagues with whom to share and develop new ideas. Opportunities, such as program development in my department and the work of this commission, provide this type of professional development. I thank ATE and the Commission members for the gift of time, support, and collegiality.

Margaret Jones

In 1981 when I was interviewing for my first classroom teaching position, I was asked by a large public school system to write about how I would teach my class about democratic citizenship. I promptly described how I would allow the children to create and implement their own democratic society within the classroom. I explained, in this 15-minute essay, that the only way for children to learn such a concept was by allowing them to "live" it. I didn't get that job, but I now realize that that essay was the beginning of my journey toward understanding and implementing constructivist theories in the classroom. After several years in elementary classrooms experimenting with this notion of allowing children to create their own learning experiences and actually living the curriculum, I formally studied constructivist theory at Indiana University before coming to Georgia State University's Early Childhood Education Department. Struggling to provide a meaningful master's program for practicing teachers, the Department took on a two-year study of John Dewey's work as it may relate to teacher development and learning. Through this study, the Collaborative Master's Program was born. As the co-director of this program, I find myself thinking about and trying to create the same sorts of learning environment for teachers as I did for my fourth graders 20 years ago. The learning never stops.

Autonomy and Community in Constructivist Teacher Education

Julie Rainer and Margaret Jones

This chapter addresses the constructs of autonomy and community as critical components in constructivist teacher education. Autonomy and community often hold political connotations; how and by whom governmental decisions are made. However, in light of constructivist learning theory, the two constructs become less about governing and more about personal and public knowledge and relationships. Autonomy encompasses the independent and personal arenas of understanding and being. It's about finding and using your own voice. It's about knowing yourself and articulating those beliefs and understandings. It's about "moral and intellectual self-regulation" (DeVries and Zan, 1994, p. 31). Community refers to the collaborative, shared, public arenas of understanding and relating. It's about sharing space—physically, emotionally, and intellectually. It's about belonging and responsibility. It's about finding a place for yourself within a group and preserving the group and its individuals. Within the traditional and political definitions of community and autonomy, the two constructs seem to be in competition with each other—individual needs versus group norms. However, constructivist interpretations imply not a competition but a dynamic dialectic: a process of change in which one concept transfers over and into and is preserved and fulfilled by it's opposite. Community is a group of autonomous individuals and autonomy is achieved in the context of a community. There is regular tension between the individual and the group, but this dialectic moves both of them forward toward continuous growth and strength from within (personal) and from without (public).

In the work of applying principles of constructivist theory to teacher education, the issues of autonomy and community are both theoretical and practical. In this chapter, we discuss autonomy and community, examining the dialectal connections and grounding them in constructivist theory. Based on this discussion, we then present examples to illustrate how to foster autonomy and community in the practice of teacher education.

AUTONOMY AND COMMUNITY
WITHIN CONSTRUCTIVISM

It is the essential and inseparable roles of individual development (personal) and social engagement (public) that provides the foundation for our discussion of autonomy and community. As suggested in the introduction, a fundamental tenet of constructivism is that knowledge emerges from individual activity in concert with interactions with the physical and social world. Piaget (1977) describes individual cognition not only in terms of global stages but also as equilibration, a dynamic process of progressive adaptation, organization, growth, and change. He also acknowledges the importance of contradictions, often arising from social interactions, in the cognitive structuring process. Vygotsky (1962) focuses on the effect of social interaction, language, and culture, suggesting that dialogue among peers and adults working in a zone of proximal development, and the inner speech that derives from it, facilitate the learning of scientific (or formal, culturally agreed upon) concepts.

Analyzing the work of both theorists, Cobb (1996), Fosnot (1996), and Rogoff (1990) suggest focusing on both the individual and sociocultural components of Piagetian and Vygotskyan theory. They find that a commonality among these perspectives is the inseparable relationship between the individual and the culture. Rogoff argues, "that individual effort and sociocultural activity are mutually embedded, as are the forest and the trees" (p. 25). She argues to keep both the individual and social environment in focus and to acknowledge that they build integrally on each other. Cobb suggests a complementary relationship between individual cognition and sociocultural perspectives and argues for coordinating the two perspectives rather than a forced choice. Fosnot synthesizes both perspectives and concludes that the focus should be on the interplay or dialectical interaction between the individual and the social world. She addresses the question of how individual representation interfaces with one' s social setting:

> *As ideas are shared within a community, new possibilities are suggested to the individual for consideration. These multiple perspectives may offer a new set of correspondences and at times even contradictions, to individual constructions. Of course, these perspectives shared by others are not "transmitted"; even the shared perspectives are interpreted and transformed by the cognizing individual. But as we seek to organize experience for generalization and communication, we strive to coordinate perspectives, to "get into the head" of others, thereby constructing further reflective abstractions and developing "taken-as-shared" meanings (p. 27).*

Application of these theories of individual and sociocultural development to education suggests the importance of an individuals' self-organization, equilibrium, and reflective abstraction, and the importance of dialogue within a "community of discourse engaged in activity, reflection, and conversation" (Fosnot, 1996, p. 29).

The dialectical relationship between the individual and community is also evident when examining the moral nature of teaching. In teacher education we not only teach specific skills but also shape attitudes and ways of looking at the world. This is particularly clear in the work of DeVries and Zan (1994) who remind us that constructivist theories have implications for sociomoral development as well as cognitive development. They provide a theoretical discussion of the parallels between Piagetian theory and a sociomoral atmosphere (an interpersonal atmosphere that fosters development). Similarly Noddings (1992) proposes a pedagogical ethic that supports individuals and groups caring for ideas, objects, and each other. Palmer (1998) further suggests that the heart of teaching is a complex and life-long process of self-discovery, particularly relating to identity and integrity. If education is moral in nature, then what does that mean for practice? Noddings suggests that moral education requires (a) showing how to care, (b) open-ended and genuine dialogue, (c) opportunities to practice caring relationships, and (d) affirming and encouraging the best in others.

AUTONOMY AND COMMUNITY: THE DIALECTIC

The implications of constructivist theory for education (Cobb, 1996; Fosnot, 1996; Rogoff, 1990) and the moral nature of teaching (DeVries & Zan, 1994; Noddings, 1992; Palmer, 1998) leads to our focus on the relationship between autonomy and community or coming to know yourself (individual) as one among others (society). Working in a constructivist paradigm, the dialectical tension between autonomy and community has been acknowledged and examined from many perspectives by current authors. Goodman (1992) discusses these social constructs from an ideological perspective; Fosnot and Rogoff from a psychological perspective, Palmer and Belenky, Clinchy, Goldberger and Tarule (1986) from an ontological and epistemological perspective; and Costa and Garmston (1994) and DeVries and Zan from educational perspectives. These perspectives provide a foundation for our work, particularly as related to autonomy and community.

Goodman (1992) argues that the dialectical tension between individuality and community must remain balanced for democracy to survive. He suggests that individuals must be "not only free but actually supported in their efforts to self-actualize . . . that each individual's self actualization can be fully realized only within a just and caring society" (p. 9). He further explains, "freedom within this context suggests non-exploitative psychological, social, and economic relations and the belief that our individual identities cannot be seen as separate from the organic interdependent system of humankind" (p. 9). Based on these arguments, Goodman suggests that teachers and children consider learning not only from the strong individualistic rationale provided by our heritage, economy, and popular culture but also from a connectionist perspective. He argues that the organization and practices of schools must be reformed to promote a critical democracy and "a *connection* to the lives of all human beings and other living things on our planet at the center of the educational process" (p. 28).

Fosnot (1996) looks at the dialectic from a psychological perspective of constructivism. In her synthesis of the cognitive psychology of Piaget and the sociohistorical psychology of Vygotsky, she concludes that "implied in all is the idea that we as human beings have no access to an objective reality since we are constructing our version of it, while at the same time transforming it and ourselves"(p. 23). She acknowledges the debate between those who advocate individual cognitive development or a sociocultural perspective but suggests we reframe our inquiry to look at the interplay between and complementary nature of the two constructs. Fosnot writes:

> The culture and the collective individuals within it create a dialectic such that the individual is disequilibrated; but reciprocally the whole is disequilibrated by individuals as they construct their environment. Thus individual thought progresses toward culturally accepted ideas but always in an open dynamic structure capable of creative innovation (p. 26).

Palmer (1998) discusses the nature of reality (an objective truth or a community of truth) and recommends the community of truth as an alternative to a mythical and dominant objectivism. He suggests that a community of truth represents knowing as a web of relationships including knower and subjects. In a community of truth there are no ultimate authorities and education is more than delivering propositions. Palmer further discusses objective and relational knowing and suggests that relational knowing takes our human capacity for connectedness and makes it a strength. In his representations of the two types of knowing, he does not advocate absolutism or relativism but a "transcendent dimension" (p. 105) that puts content at the center of the knowers and their knowing. In this model, the knower and the subject are both active agents. In his exploration of truth, he reminds us of the importance of knowers, knowledge, and the "conversations about things that matter, conducted with passion and discipline" (p. 104). For a more in depth discussion of the importance of content, see the chapter on Content and Process in Teacher Education.

DeVries and Zan (1994) in their work in kindergarten classrooms discuss autonomy as related to children's moral development and adult roles in this process. They discuss autonomy in terms of relationships and rules. Based on Piagetian theory, the authors describe autonomous adult-child relationships as "constructivist relationships"; one of "mutual respect in which the teacher minimizes the exercise of unnecessary authority in relation to the children" (p. 3). They contend that autonomous relationships operate through cooperation that "means striving to attain a common goal while coordinating one's own feelings and perspective with a consciousness of another's feelings and perspectives" (p. 49). This conception parallels Costa and Garmston's (1994) definition of holonomy discussed next.

Within an educational context, Costa and Garmston (1994) introduce the concept of holonomy, which has potential for balancing the tension between autonomy and community. Holonomy is defined as "individuals acting autonomously while simultaneously acting interdependently within the group" (p. 3). More specifically,

> *Autonomous individuals set personal goals and are self-directing, self-monitoring, and self-modifying. They are constantly experimenting and experiencing, they fail frequently but they fail forward, learning from the situation. However, they are not isolated or mechanical in their work, they also participate significantly in their organization. They operate in the best interests of the whole while simultaneously attending to their own goals and needs. In other words they are at once independent and interdependent—they are holonomous (pp. 131–132).*

In their work on teacher development, Costa and Garmston (1994) further describe holonomous persons as possessing five states of mind: efficacy, flexibility, craftmanship, consciousness, and interdependence. Efficacious people are optimistic, self-actualizing and self-modifying.

They think their efforts make a difference. Flexible people are able to step beyond themselves and look at situations from differing perspectives. They tolerate ambiguity and doubt, trust their intuition, and can deal with a variety of simultaneous activities. Craftsman-like people generate and hold clear visions and goals, monitor their progress toward goals and continuously strive to improve performance. People who enjoy a state of consciousness are metacognitive. They articulate well-defined value systems and apply internal criteria for decisions they make. Interdependent people seek collegiality and grow through reciprocity. They hold their values as they lend their energies to the achievement of group goals. These states of mind describe the characteristics we hope to nurture in constructivist teacher education programs.

AUTONOMY AND COMMUNITY WITHIN CONSTRUCTIVIST TEACHER EDUCATION

From constructivist theory, we have a view of knowledge as emerging from a complementary relationship between individual constructions and social interactions. Looking specifically at autonomy and community in the context of constructivist theory and teacher education, we find a rationale for relational knowing, the strength of connectedness, and the importance of knowers and content that matters. Each of these has implications for teaching and teacher education. If autonomy and community both have merit in constructivist practice, then we want individuals who are thoughtful, reflective, and meta-cognitive about themselves, content, and pedagogy. They also should be able to interact with, dialogue about, and share in each of these areas, all in the context of relationships. We are striving for autonomous individuals in a community, or an autonomous community.

This section is organized using key concepts in constructivist theory (knowledge creation and social interaction) and seven areas of practice to illustrate constructivist teacher education in a variety of contexts. In knowledge construction, we examine: (a) making content the center of learning; (b) knowing yourself as a teacher and learner; and

(c) balancing the self and the group. In social interaction, examples illustrate (d) creating a respectful and trusting community; (e) collaborating to learn; (f) empowering individuals to contribute to the community; and (g) balancing power in relationships. Examples range from course activities to programmatic structures. While presented separately and sequentially, there is continuous overlap among these constructs and examples. We share descriptions of how teacher educators have fostered autonomy and community within their own teaching experiences.

Knowledge Construction in Teacher Education

A key point in organizing our discussion of autonomy and community and areas of practice in constructivist teacher education relates to knowledge. Knowing is viewed as relational and connected (Fosnot, 1996; Goodman, 1994, and Palmer, 1998). We learn socially; coming to know by interacting with people, content, and context. The dialogue of interaction builds, clarifies, and extends our knowledge. Sharing, listening, and struggling with ideas and processes create meaning for the individual as well as the group.

From an autonomy perspective, individuals must read, discuss, reflect, and articulate their beliefs in order to create a collaborative or connected reality. Individuals analyze what they think, believe, and know (being metacognitive) in light of others' thinking, in order to clarify and extend their own thinking. From a community perspective, a group also creates its own knowledge; a reality built on the experiences of the individual and the group. Bringing what you know and combining it with what others are saying brings a group to a shared or common understanding that is more meaningful to everyone. The context for the interaction between individuals and groups also includes the content or subject matter as a component of a constructed reality. Since knowledge takes its meaning through context, the individual, the content and the group must be considered, acknowledged, and valued. (See also the chapter on Content and Process in Constructivist Teacher Education.)

Content as Central in Teaching and Learning. Richardson (1997) addresses the topic of subject matter in constructivist classrooms and concludes that since teacher education has its own specific content, that content should be considered in planning and implementing constructivist practice. In constructivist practice, teacher-learners participate in individual and collaborative learning experiences designed to facilitate the construction of content, and process as content (Costa & Garmston, (1994). These experiences allow learners to actively engage knowledge (content and pedagogical) with others at personal and public levels of understanding. They also provide structure for processes such as examining personal beliefs and understandings, reflection, collaboration and group development of conceptual ideas.

In the public domain, teacher-learners in Mills College's Teachers for Tomorrow's Schools program participate in several group projects. One such project entails a group of students from different specialization areas exploring some overarching concept (e.g., scientific literacy, change, and point of view) and demonstrating how this concept could be taught at four different grade levels. Students must coordinate their different autonomous perspectives on the subject matter to create a common and agreed upon understanding. Group presentations include how these lessons are developmentally, conceptually and pedagogically related to one another, illustrating a spiraling curriculum. This presentation of content requires dialogue, collaboration, making connections, and individual and group development of conceptual ideas.

The Foxfire approach (Teets and Starnes, 1996) provides many opportunities for teacher-learners to construct knowledge in a professional development course. In small groups, teacher-learners engage the Foxfire core practices (see Teets and Starnes), and analyze them in light of their successful teaching experiences. They reflect on memorable learning experiences and generate criteria for teacher and student roles and meaningful learning. Teacher-learners also examine curricular goals and objectives for relevance to their practice and then plan projects to meet these goals and objectives. Teacher-learners are continually asked "What do we need to do to ensure that you will be ready to implement the approach when you return to your classroom?" (Teets and Starnes, p. 37). This experience of engaging content encourages reflection, balancing teacher and student relationships, and developing learning based on curricular and content goals.

In Georgia State University's Collaborative Master's Program (CMP) in Early Childhood Education, the entire group of teacher-learners (the cohort) participates with the faculty to define the guiding framework for the 15 month program of study. This process begins with groups of teacher-learners selecting a book illustrating constructivist practice (selected from a list provided by the faculty; see resource list). Groups are given guiding questions that help distill the pedagogical assumptions embedded within the chosen book. Groups then share the knowledge gained from each book through a jigsaw process, with the task of articulating commonalties among the pedagogical assumptions. From this set of assumptions, the cohort derives the knowledge, skills and attitudes (KSA) that one must possess in order to teach according to the assumptions. The cohort constructs not only an understanding of constructivism, but they also participate in the definition of their program. It is in the quest of gaining these knowledge, skills and attitudes that the curricular and assessment experiences for the program are negotiated. These experiences encourage knowledge construction through guided questioning, examining and developing content, and facilitating collaboration.

Knowing Yourself as a Teacher and Learner. The previous examples primarily illustrate knowledge in the public domain. Knowledge must also be addressed in the personal domain. In order for individuals to be able to participate in the public articulation of conceptual understandings, they must first possess self-understanding. For example in the jigsaw process above, individuals must know what they know and be able to articulate it at whatever level of understanding they possess. They must be able to balance their own learning with group needs. This personal domain of knowledge construction clearly links to the reflective nature of constructivism. Teacher-learners must be reflective and metacognitive about their understandings and their practices; about who they are as teachers, how they teach, and why they teach the way they do.

At Mills College, elementary pre-service teachers write a Self as Teacher paper as one program instance of a guided reflection and examination and understanding of practice. Teacher-learners are guided through a systematic reflection of a self-selected aspect of their teaching in order to clearly articulate who they are as teachers, encouraging the development of autonomous behavior in teaching. At Georgia State University, teacher-learners spend an entire year reflecting on who they are as teachers with the goal of being able to articulate their own personal pedagogy. This process begins with an analysis of personal learning autobiographies, searching for values and beliefs about teaching and learning imbedded in personal experiences. Next teacher-learners analyze specific classroom practices (lesson plans or routines) to uncover their underlying values and beliefs. Teachers are then encouraged to synthesize their discovered beliefs about teaching and learning, seeking congruence with what they say they believe and what they do in their classrooms. It is through these personal understandings that learners are able to bring their understandings to the public construction of knowledge. Without this personal element of understanding, no communal understanding could occur.

Another way that teacher-learners are encouraged to get in touch with and rework their own understandings is through free-writes. In the CMP, teacher-learners are asked to free-write (write whatever comes to the pencil) prior to whole group discussions. This allows an opportunity for the teacher-learner to articulate his/her own ideas and understandings prior to the group discussion. It helps develop a personal voice, a thoughtful contribution to the public domain. It is through this personal made public that the construction of the group knowledge moves forward.

Balancing Self and the Group. A key point of our discussion of autonomy and community has been to examine the dialectical relationship of the individual and the group, emphasizing the need for a balanced interplay between independence and interdependence (Costa & Garmston, 1994; Goodman, 1992). The development of holonomous persons requires structures and processes that encourage knowledge construction through both individual and collaborative development.

Focus groups are one way that knowledge construction is encouraged in the CMP. These groups represent a balance between the public and the personal domain. Focus groups are small groups of faculty and teacher-learners who come together to study a topic of personal interest in depth. The groups develop their learning agendas for exploring and creating knowledge relevant to their personal and program goals. They meet once a week for several months providing time for the development of content and process. For example, one focus group investigated the nature of constructivist assessment and the implications it had for their practice; another group explored the role of problem solving in children's development of mathematics. Focus groups provide a structure that encourages individuals to read, talk to experts, and observe children, and then come together to discuss ideas and share examples of the implementation of these ideas in their classrooms and schools. These processes encourage individuals to articulate their ideas in the safety of a small group with similar interests. In addition to engaging content, the process requires collegiality, participation, dialogue, negotiation, and decision making. Focus groups exemplify the importance of both knowledge construction and social interaction.

Social Interaction in Teacher Education

The social nature of knowledge creation moves us to look closely at relationships. Relationships, both personal and professional, are embedded in autonomy and community in constructivist teacher education. At the beginning and at the end of the twentieth century, authors advocated participation in relationships as one role of schools and teachers. Dewey (1916) presented a view of schools as miniature communities and emphasized the potential of relationships for both students and teachers' growth. Noddings (1992) suggested a form of schooling that emphasized relational development. She concluded that school organization, curriculum, assessment, and teacher preparation are keys to moving toward caring relationships. In order to move toward meaningful relationships, constructivist teacher education must include structures and processes for creating a respectful and trusting community, collaboration, empowering individuals' ownership in and contributions to the community, and balancing power in relationships.

Creating a Respectful and Trusting Community. An essential element for relationship development is a caring, respectful, and trusting community. In order to reach this ideal community in teacher education, it is important to encourage commitment and get to know people on many different levels, both personally and professionally. Examples to encourage personal and professional relationships are described as ways to facilitate a respectful and trusting community.

An activity that promotes personal relationships occurs in an undergraduate emergent literacy class at Mansfield University of Pennsylvania. Teacher-learners write and then read publicly a picture book based on a childhood memory. These picture books share aspects of people's personal lives that endear the group toward one another. Students laugh and cry together, creating a climate of intimacy and inclusiveness.

As part of the CMP, all participants (both faculty and teacher-learners) attend a two-day retreat in the north Georgia mountains. An outside facilitator leads the cohort through a series of team building activities with the goal of relationship building and establishing a shared experience upon which all future experiences can build. As one of the team building activities, participants are asked to bring to the retreat three artifacts that represent some aspect of their lives. (Examples of artifacts include photographs, books, a quilt, and a seashell) At the retreat, 15–20 minute segments are set aside throughout the retreat for people to share their artifacts and thus some aspect of their personal life. This activity opens up people's hearts and minds as the group begins to form.

Another activity, less focused on the individual, is called "Fears in a Hat." At the start of the retreat, all participants anonymously write on an index card a fear they have about the next three days. After placing these cards in a hat, each participant selects one of the "fears" to read aloud to the group. The person reading acknowledges the fear, shows empathy and understanding toward the writer, and then offers words of support that may help the individual cope or overcome her fear. This activity has touched on fears such as sharing living space with strangers, lack of physical prowess, bugs, meeting the expectations of the group, and doubts about being liked. Even though no one knows who holds the specific fears, the fears become public. It's a powerful experience to know that others share your fears. These team building activities allow people to get to know each other, and it establishes an expectation that everyone work together to create a caring and risk-free environment within which to work. As faculty and students get to know each other, the boundaries between people and their roles become blurred, especially related to issues of power.

Another activity designed to promote personal relationships and a risk-free environment is the establishment of agreements or group norms. On the first day of the CMP, the agreement process begins with a singing activity taken from Mara Sapon-Shevin (1995). One of the cohort faculty begins the first class meeting of the program by teaching a song to the cohort. After singing she asks, "Why do you think I started with singing?" Eventually someone asserts that it builds a sense of community. From there, we discuss communities we have been a part of, sharing stories from our past. Once several stories are shared, the faculty member asks who would be willing to lead the group in the next song. Amidst lowered eyes and looks of terror, the faculty member then asks who would rather die first than lead a song. Most hands are then raised. The discussion moves to the circumstances needed in order for someone to be comfortable leading a song. The issue that emerges is safety. People want to feel safe before they take risks.

At the retreat, the outside facilitator follows up on initial conversations about safe-spaces by leading a conversation about successful groups. When have you been in a successful group? What are the qualities that make it good? This list of qualities is then turned into group norms that the community will agree to live by. Examples of norms include "I am open-minded and flexible with other people's thoughts, ideas, concerns, comments in my work; I will seek out and honor individual voices, ideas, concerns, comments in my work; I take my concerns to the appropriate people (instead of complaining to a third party and expecting them to intercede)." The agreements hold each person accountable for supporting the relationships established. They make public the behavior norms needed to continue the caring, respectful, and trusting community established at the retreat. The agreements are re-negotiated periodically throughout the year. Are these agreements still working? Has anything been missed? Are any changes needed? Is there any agreement that gets less than adequate attention by the community? What agreements have been mastered? Through this public attention to personal relationships, a risk-free environment is maintained.

These experiences illustrate structures and activities that encourage individuals to create relationships different than those of traditional university classrooms. Relationships are more inclusive, open, trusting, collegial, supportive, and caring. By creating a safe environment for opening hearts and minds, participants find connections, build a foundation for continued work as individuals and as a group, and begin a dialogue about learning together.

Collaboration and Professional Relationships. Even though forming personal relationships in the community is essential to constructivist teacher education, relationships that center on professional growth and development provide a forum for such personal relationships to flourish. Teachers struggle together with common professional questions, contexts of teaching, and/or pedagogical style, with the common goal of becoming better teachers. These issues of teaching and learning become the content of discussions in the learning community. Professional relationships provide the juncture for knowledge and the human elements of teacher education to coincide. They provide an opportunity for teachers to collaborate on issues by sharing work, addressing diverse perspectives, and supporting each other in their growth.

One strategy that promotes professional relationships and provides an opportunity for collaboration occurs at Mills College. Within their credentialing program, there are four specializations: Early Childhood Education, Elementary, English and Social Studies, Math and Science. Students are primarily involved with those from their own specialty; however, there are monthly meetings with groups that consist of cross-specialty groupings. Teacher-learners are reminded that everyone is a teacher first, a specialist second, and that teachers have more in common across grade levels and content areas than they have differences. Groups are challenged to find these commonalties and to learn to work collaboratively with one another as they develop as teachers and learners. These groups provide a sense of professional community and encourage sharing multiple perspectives. The curriculum project described previously in this chapter (Content as Central to Teaching and Learning section) is carried out in these groups.

At Berry College in Rome, Georgia, after team building initiatives like the ropes course and class meetings, teacher-learners are placed in pairs for an intensive junior-year field experience. These pairs observe and coach each other as well as team teach within their P–12 placements. The professional relationships formed are extremely powerful as these beginning teachers develop.

As part of the CMP at Georgia State University, teacher-learners form benchmark groups for periodic assessments. These groups are self-selected groups of 3–4 teacher-learners and two faculty members that remain constant throughout the 15-month program, meeting once every 6–8 weeks. The purpose of these benchmark groups is to provide teacher-learners with the ongoing opportunity to share their work and receive feedback from peers and faculty. Teacher-learners select some aspect of their work, either classroom or graduate work, to reflect upon and share with their group. Written reflections are distributed prior to the actual meeting so that group members come prepared to interact with peers and their work. These sessions consist mostly of coaching, suggesting, questioning, and sharing expertise and experience. At these benchmark meetings, the work made public is often taken to a more thoughtful and meaningful level through the collaborative process.

We find experiences and time dedicated to collaboration and developing professional relationships as integral to constructivist teacher education. Teachers interacting and sharing strengthens their knowledge and their practice, both individually and collectively.

Empowering Individuals to Contribute to the Community. A third element that contributes to social interaction and the establishment of meaningful relationships within an autonomous community is the invitation for and support of empowered individuals. This element also relates to knowledge construction in that for individuals to be able to contribute to the knowledge creation of the community, they must first be encouraged to self actualize (Goodman, 1992, Richert, 1994). That is, they must be able to articulate what they know, and then they must feel comfortable sharing their knowledge (or themselves) within the total community. To accomplish this, individuals are invited to participate in decision making and encouraged to take ownership for their learning.

One structure utilized in the CMP at Georgia State University to encourage empowerment of teacher-learners is Book Groups. On a monthly basis, self-selected groups of students choose a book to read together. These groups meet at least twice. Each book group then shares with the cohort their interpretations of the book and how it has influenced their classrooms or thinking. These groups not only allow teacher-learners to collaboratively make meaning of their readings, but they also provide a forum through which they can contribute to the whole community's shared understandings. In self-selecting books to read, teacher-learners are trusted to make meaningful choices and generate knowledge as they pursue program and personal goals. It is one way they are empowered to direct their own learning.

A decision-making strategy called Fist-to-Five provides an opportunity for empowered individuals to express their ideas. When making group decisions, all participants are asked to show their level of support for the idea being discussed by raising anywhere from zero (fist) to five fingers. Hands showing five fingers are in complete support of the idea. Hands showing three fingers minimally support the idea, but are willing to agree to it without reproach. Hands showing a fist are in no way in support of the idea and will oppose any effort toward the idea. It is agreed that anyone showing zero to two fingers must share with the group their dissatisfaction and then the discussion continues. In reaching consensus, all participants' ideas are heard and the group works together to reach an agreement that all can support. It provides one way for an individual to remain autonomous within a community, for personal thoughts and relationships to exist in concert with professional needs.

At Berry College, teacher-learners are empowered as they take an active role in curricular design, logistics, and assessment. This is accomplished at the course level through formal and informal mechanisms used to surface student knowledge, interest, and ideas. At Berry College, they begin courses by asking teacher-learners to list their goals and the specific knowledge, skills, and dispositions they hope to learn. Class sessions include opportunities to respond to class activities and suggest future directions. Curriculum is built to include teacher-learners prior knowledge and interests, which means letting go of the predetermined syllabi.

A structure of the CMP at Georgia State University, called faculty liaisons, invites teacher-learners to contribute to the curriculum. Faculty liaisons are self-identified cohort members with a specific interest in a content area, who take on the role of liaison between the community and the faculty member responsible for that content. For example, a math liaison would talk with the cohort to determine their needs and interests in teaching mathematics then communicate these ideas, negotiating with the faculty member in planning university classes and workshops. This process continues with liaisons providing feedback to faculty members as classes continue throughout the semester. This role requires university faculty to listen and consider teacher-learners needs and interests, while requiring teacher-learners to interact with cohort members and take responsibility for the direction of their learning in the community.

These opportunities and experiences give voice and ownership to teacher-learners and contribute to autonomous thinking as well as community development. Together faculty and teacher-learners share understandings, pursue goals, and take an active role in their learning, bringing individual perspectives together with the support of a group. Empowerment is strengthened through democratic and cooperative processes that promote the coordination of individual feelings and perspectives with a consciousness of other's feelings and perspectives: balancing the personal with the public.

Balancing Power in Teacher Education. Empowering teacher-learners is connected to balancing the power in teacher education. When establishing relationships within a constructivist teacher education program or course, attention must be given to power in relationships, as well as in curriculum and assessment. A meaningful distribution of responsibility and power manifested in an atmosphere of caring are both important elements of constructivist teacher education. These require not only different experiences but also new roles for participants.

Activities designed to create respectful environments and meaningful relationships (discussed in previous sections) also work toward leveling power among teacher-learners and university faculty. However, balancing power also requires new roles for teacher educators and teacher-learners. Constructivist roles require all participants to consider themselves learners. Kaufman (1996) describes constructivist roles and practices in a teacher preparation program at the State University of New York at Stony Brook. These include: creating interdisciplinary experiences, providing opportunities for reflection and collaborative discourse, posing problems that connect university and fieldwork experiences, creating curriculum in response to emerging needs, and assessing teachers authentically. These roles provide opportunities for all participants to build relationships and construct knowledge. Dillon (1995), writing with five teachers, describes his experiences to foster ownership of learning in his class at McGill University. He begins with a general framework of four key principles and readings that describe teachers' efforts to live those principles. Since this framework is his construction of knowledge, he also provides teacher-learners with the space to create their own, more specific construction of knowledge. He describes his role as providing collaborative experiences that embody the key principles and supporting teacher-learners as they direct and maintain their own learning efforts.

Teacher-learners are also changing roles in the learning process. In learner-centered work, they become curriculum planners and builders, leading and participating in spirited conversations and negotiations, and inquiring deeply into content as it relates to their practice. Teacher learners initiate and solve problems, develop and nurture supportive relationships, reflect on and refine their learning process, and design and participate in authentic types of assessment.

Inviting teacher-learners to engage in designing the assessment processes and products for a course or program, makes explicit the issues of power and relationships. In a respectful environment, the evaluative processes cannot follow the "gotcha" approach. True autonomy within a community of meaningful relationships implies an emphasis on self-evaluation and formative assessment. In this process, the understanding of assessment and evaluation becomes personal and professional, individual and collaborative. Assessment is probably the most challenging of experiences.

In the CMP at Georgia State University, teacher-learners are involved in the design of their assessment and evaluation. The assessment experience occurs during the benchmark meetings as described in an earlier section of this chapter. The evaluative experiences center on a cohort-designed rubric. Teachers create a rubric with specific behavioral descriptions that evaluate each of the program goals. This rubric is designed at the start of the second semester of the program, after teachers have had an opportunity to become familiar with program goals and ideals. After the rubric is designed, teachers plot themselves on each dimension and collect artifacts that document their evaluation. Teachers then share this self-evaluation with cohort faculty during a one-on-one conference. During this conference teachers and faculty distill future goals for the teacher and brainstorm strategies through which to obtain these goals. Also during this conference, notes are made about the effectiveness of the rubric, questions about its criteria, etc. After all teachers have participated in the self-evaluation conference, the rubric is re-examined, clarifying criteria and discussing appropriate documentation.

What teachers learn about assessment and evaluation of content is that assessment is a respectful process, with moral consequences (Wiggins, 1993). They experience assessment based on relationships and an atmosphere of trust; one that encourages knowledge construction. They are living the content. Teacher-learners are also sharing in a powerful process traditionally open only to faculty members, a key element to balancing power in relationships.

CONCLUDING THOUGHTS

We have discussed the relationship between autonomy and community as mutually embedded (Rogoff, 1990), as complementary (Cobb, 1996). and as a dialectical interaction (Fosnot, 1996). Building on these conceptions and our experiences in teacher education, we propose the concept of synergy, from the Greek word *synergos*, meaning working together, to help us understand the dialectical relationship between community and autonomy. While autonomy and community may be viewed as discrete and dichotomous concepts, often in tension, they need not be in opposition. Their interaction, with the "I and the we" supporting each other, produces a total that is greater than the individual effects. This interaction is a collective and concurrent effort of individuals within a group. It requires strong individual voices and combined effort or cooperation. It suggests a collaborative nature for educating teachers, where individuals, personally and professionally, are empowered to construct knowledge in a supportive community. In a study of community in the Collaborative Master's Program (Rainer and Guyton, 1999), one teacher's description provides a glimpse of the complexity of this phenomenon.

> *A learning community is one in which each member has a voice and actively contributes to the group as a whole. The community values each member's ideas and works together to find shared meaning. Individual differences and strengths are accepted and encouraged. The community offers a safe place where ideas can be shared and learners can grow and change (Sp98, Resp. 101).*

In this same study, an interview with a university faculty member echoes and extends this description:

> *There's work you do to build and maintain community, the safe place where there's equitable exchange of mine and ours; but there is also everybody's individual work, and the work we do together—my work, our work, community work. Everybody brings something and takes something away (Sp98, Int.CF).*

These perspectives converge in agreement with Goodman (1992) and Smith (1994) that a dialectic relationship exists between autonomy and community, that an emphasis on individualism (heteronomy) has occurred in society and schools, and that a balance or interplay between the values of autonomy and community must be encouraged to maintain a critical democracy. Westheimer's (1998) findings in case studies of two schools indicate that autonomy and community may indeed seem to be strange bedfellows, but that teachers in a faculty community "gain (rather than lose) a sense of identity and individuality through their participation in the community" (p. 146).

Specific to teacher education, Tom (1999) suggests that teaching as collegial work is an integral component of a conceptual framework for professional development. Smylie and Conyers (1991) review conceptions of teaching in relation to teacher development and conclude that if teaching is a "complex, dynamic, interactive, intellectual activity" then "teachers will require substantial autonomy to make appropriate instructional decision... and at the same time teaching can no longer be viewed as an individual activity. It must be considered a collective enterprise. Teachers will have to work and learn together to be successful in their classrooms" (p. 13). A continued, in-depth look at the nature of knowledge construction and relationships, as related to autonomy and community, becomes paramount for teacher education.

REFERENCES

Belenky, M., Clinchy, B., Goldberger, N. & Tarule, J. (1986). *Women's Ways of Knowing.* NY: Basic Books.

Cobb, P. (1996). Where Is the Mind? A Coordination of Sociocultural and Cognitive Constructivist Perspectives. In Fosnot (Ed.), *Constructivism: Theory, Perspectives and Practice* (pp. 34–54). NY: Teachers College Press.

Costa, A. & Garmston, R. (1994). *Cognitive Coaching: A Foundation for Renaissance Schools.* Norwood, MA: Christopher Gordon Publishers.

Devries, R. & Zan, B. (1994). *Moral Classrooms, Moral Children: Creating a Constructivist Atmosphere in Early Education.* NY: Teachers College Press.

Dewey, J. (1916). *Democracy in Education.* NY: Macmillan.

Dillon, D. (1995). Teaching and Learning Together in Teacher Education: "Making Easter." In Dudley-Marling and Searle (Eds.), *Who Owns Learning?: Questions of Autonomy, Choice and Control* (pp. 190–212). Portsmouth, NH: Heinemann.

Fosnot, C. T. (1996). *Constructivism: Theory, Perspectives and Practice.* NY: Teachers College Press.

Goodman, J. (1992). *Elementary Schooling for Critical Democracy.* NY: SUNY Press.

Kaufman, D. (1996). Constructivist-Based Experiential Learning in Teacher Education. *Action in Teacher Education, 18*(2), 40–50.

Lambert, L., Walker, D., Cooper, J.E., Lambert, M.D., Gardner, M.E., & Slack, P.J. Ford (1995). *The Constructivist Leader.* New York: Teachers College Press.

Noddings, N. (1992). *The Challenge to Care in Schools.* NY: Teachers College Press.

Palmer, P. (1998). *The Courage to Teach.* San Francisco, CA: Jossey-Bass.

Piaget, J. (1977). *Equilibration of Cognitive Structures.* NY: Viking.

Rainer, J., & Guyton, E. (April, 1999). *Coming Together—Respectfully: Learning Communities in Teacher Education.* Paper presented at the Annual Meeting of the American Educational Research Association, Montreal, Canada.

Richert, A. (1992). Voice and Power in Teaching and Learning to Teach. In L. Vali, (Ed.), *Reflective Teacher Education.* Albany, NY: SUNY Press.

Richardson, V. (1997). *Constructivist Teacher Education: Building a World of New Understandings.* Briston, PA: Falmer Press.

Rogoff, B. (1990). *Apprenticeship in Thinking: Cognitive Development in Social Context.* NY: Oxford University Press.

Smith, H. (1994). Foxfire Teachers' Networks (Viewed through Maxine Green's *The Dialectic of Freedom*). In J. Novak, (Ed). *Democratic Teacher Education* (pp. 21–46). Albany, NY: SUNY Press.

Sapon-Shevin, M. (1995). Building a Safe Community for Learning. In Ayers (Ed.), *To Become a Teacher* (pp. 99–102). NY: Teachers College Press.

Smylie, M. & Conyers, J. (1991). Changing Conceptions of Teaching Influence the Future of Staff Development. *Journal of Staff Development, 12*(1), p. 2–16.

Teets, S. & Starnes, B. (1996). Foxfire: Constructivism for Teachers and Learners. *Action in Teacher Education, 18*(2), 31–39.

Tom, A. (1999). Reinventing Master's Degree Study for Experienced Teachers. *Journal of Teacher Education, 50*(4), 245–254.

Vygotsky, L. (1962). *Thought and Language.* Cambridge, MA: MIT Press.

Westheimer, J. (1998). *Among Schoolteachers: Community, Autonomy and Ideology in Teachers' Work.* NY: Teachers College Press.

Wiggins, G. (1993). *Assessing Student Performance.* San Francisco, CA: Jossey-Bass.

Professional Background:
Carrie Robinson

I am currently an Associate Professor in the Department of Literacy Education at New Jersey City University. As a professional student and lifelong learner, I have spent most of my career in higher education administration and teaching after a very short but enjoyable time as an early childhood educator. Prior to my decade of experience in teacher education as a field experience director and a faculty member in educational leadership, educational technology, and literacy education, I spent a decade providing technical assistance and professional development activities for educators who were providing a second chance or first opportunity for adult learners to become literate or acquire a formal education. My work as an adult educator provides the foundation for my role as a constructivist teacher educator. Building on the tenets of andragogy, I approach the teacher education classroom with an understanding of how adult learners acquire, modify, reframe, and utilize their experiences and expertise to build, scaffold, and construct knowledge in meaningful and authentic ways.

I have been an active member of ATE since 1989. I have served on two national planning committees and chaired the Fiscal Affairs Committee for one three-year term. I was Chair and Vice Chair of ATE's Multicultural Education Special Interest Group. Prior to my involvement in the Commission on Constructivist Teacher Education, I was also a member of the Commission on Gender Equity in Education.

I am one of ATE's representatives to NCATE's Board of Examiners. I completed a term on ATE's Board of Directors at the end of the 2000 Annual Meeting. I am privileged to currently serve as president-elect (2001–002) and will proudly become president of ATE at the conclusion of the 2002 Annual Meeting in Denver, Colorado.

Authority and Facilitation in Teacher Education

Carrie Robinson

> *Sometimes looking into a classroom is a bit like looking into a beehive: the uninformed visitor might see lots of bees moving in many directions with no apparent logic, but the beekeeper knows what each bee is doing and how many an activity fits within the overall pattern. (Source unknown)*

Two people viewing an accident may recount that accident focusing on different aspects of the event that was observed. Some people looking at a glass may see it as half full. Others looking at the same glass may, however, describe it as half empty. Two people observing a classroom or an academic event and/or experience may see two very different things. One person may concentrate on what the teacher is doing. Another person may focus their observation on what the children are doing. Another person may focus on the interaction between students and teacher while yet another person may focus on the interactions between and among students.

The metaphors of teacher educator or teacher as authority and teacher educator or teacher as facilitator can both be documented in the literature and observed in constructivist teacher education in the P–12 school setting as well as on the university campus. The purpose of this chapter is to explore and discuss these two metaphors as they are manifested in the context of the constructivist teacher education setting.

This chapter builds upon Marlow & Page's (1998) definition of constructivism as "constructing knowledge, not receiving it; thinking about and analyzing (crap detecting), not accumulating and memorizing information; understanding and applying information, not repeating back; and being active, not passive learners" (pp. 9–13). Additionally, Driscoll's (2000) conditions for constructivist instruction including "complex and relevant learning environments, social negotiation, multiple perspectives and multiple modes of learning, ownership in learning, and self-awareness of knowledge construction" (p. 373) are the theoretical basis for the exploration of the dimensions of teacher educator as authority and teacher educator as facilitator in the constructivist teacher education setting. In conclusion, this chapter examines the characteristics of the two metaphors in practice, provides examples of the two metaphors in teacher education settings, and demonstrates, using portfolios as one of multiples assessment measures, how these metaphors may be concretely observed in higher education as well as P–12 school environments.

METAPHORS OF SCHOOLING

Morgan (1985) describes people as having different lenses through which they view events, organizations, and people. Bolman and Deal (1997) use the term reframing to analyze individual and organizational behavior through one of four frames, which may also be described as lenses or metaphors: the structural frame, the human resource frame, the political frame, and the symbolic frame. Each of these frames contains a different image of the essence of schools as organizations. Each of the frames captures a different but significant slice of reality of the school as an organization. Each frame offers a different conception of the organizational dynamics of schools and provides a different formula for interaction within the university or school setting.

Each frame has its own strengths and its own limits. None is a frame for all seasons and situations, but each frame has much to offer to anyone who hopes to understand the school as an organization and identify the strategies that foster effective participation in the educational process.

According to the tenets of the structural frame, schools and universities as organizations are bureaucracies wherein the roles of all constituent groups are clearly defined. This frame assumes that schools work best when goals and roles are clear and when the efforts of individuals and groups are well coordinated through both vertical and lateral strategies. The human resource frame, on the other hand, views the school or university as an organizational entity that functions like an extended family that is primarily concerned with the welfare, personal, and social needs of all constituents. It presumes that schools work best when individual needs are met and the school fosters a caring, trusting work and learning environment. The political frame advances the idea of the school or university as an organizational setting like a jungle with multiple conflicts and competing interests on both individual and group levels. This frame identifies the limits of authority and the inevitability that resources are too scarce to fulfill all demands. Schools and universities are viewed as political arenas where groups jockey for power. The symbolic frame centers attention on symbols, meaning, and faith. Every human organization creates symbols to cultivate commitment, hope, and loyalty. Symbols govern behavior through informal, implicit, and shared rules, agreements, and understandings. Thus, the symbolic frame views the school and the university in the context of its culture and relies more on the meaning of events than on what happens within the organizational setting of the school or university.

Advancing the reframing concept in the academic arena, one's metaphor for teaching and/or schooling (Morrison, 2000) frames one's educational epistemology. According to Morrison, "people use metaphors—positive, negative, or a mixture of both—to describe their beliefs about schools and schooling. The metaphors teachers (and teacher educators) use shape their teaching and professionalism" (p. 93). Therefore, the metaphor of schooling that educators, teacher educators, teachers, school personnel, P–12 students and candidates use as their lens influences their teaching practices and learning expectations of P–12 students and candidates and frames their views about professionalism. Morrison identified six metaphors for teaching: teacher as student, teacher as facilitator, teacher as sage, teacher as coach, teacher as leader, and teacher as researcher (p. 16). As the focus of this chapter is on the dimensions of authority and facilitation in constructivist teacher education, this chapter will only discuss the metaphors of teacher educator as facilitator, teacher educator as sage, and teacher educator as coach as manifested in the constructivist teacher education setting.

ANDRAGOGY VS. PEDAGOGY IN CONSTRUCTIVIST TEACHER EDUCATION

"A child centered constructivist curriculum focus on children's thinking and learning" (Oakes and Lipton, 1999, p. 111). Teacher education faculty like their P–12 colleagues often use pedagogy, the art and science of teaching children, as the theoretical foundation for instruction. This perspective may be the result of the fact that higher education institutions are by and large set up as they were when the typical college student or teacher education candidate was a person just having graduated from high school. Today's college student or teacher education candidate, however, is often a person who has been out of school and in the workforce for a number of years prior to entering college. Thus, the tenets of adult education or andragogy, the art and science of facilitating the learning process for adults, would be a more appropriate paradigm for the teacher education sequence. Applying the aforementioned Oakes and Lipton quote to teacher education, this chapter advocates the paradigm that a candidate-centered constructivist curriculum should more appropriately focus on how adults, not children, think and learn.

Malcolm Knowles (1969, 1973), the father of adult education, established a set of very useful guidelines that could be used by higher education faculty in general and constructivist teacher educators specifically to facilitate the development of adult learners in the university classroom. According to Knowles (1969), adult motivation is based on experiences and/or perceived needs and interests; adult learning is life-centered; experience is the richest resource for adult learning;

adults have a deep need to be self-directing; and individual differences among people increase with age.

Knowles (1973) also identified five major differences between adults and children/youth that are important considerations for the constructivist teacher educator:

- Self-concept: adults are not dependent personalities but tend to be more self-directed learners.

- Experience: adult use experience to build, scaffold, and construct meaning.

- Readiness to learn: adults learn to prepare for a role not to learn for the sake of learning. Thus, adults want to see the utility of what they are learning and are not willing to learn information to be stored merely for usage later.

- Orientation to learning: adults wish and expect to have immediate application of information, skills, and concepts learned. They favor learning activities that foster the problem-centered frame of mind.

- Adults experience a tension between teaching and learning.

Applying Knowles' principles of andragogy in the constructivist teacher education setting, teacher education candidates are adults that could clearly more appropriately benefit from enrollment in constructivist teacher education sequences that incorporate an understanding of how adults learn and how adults differ from children instead of the traditional professional education sequence that is often built on a model of pedagogy.

TEACHER EDUCATOR AND TEACHER AS AUTHORITY

Universities, colleges of education, and departments of education as well as school districts operate in the broader context of society and thus must simultaneously address and respond to national/federal issues, state issues, institutional issues, accreditation issues, school issues, classroom issues, candidate and P–12 student issues, personnel issues, and resource (human and non-human) issues. Doyle and Hartle (1985) view education as a national concern, a state responsibility, and a local function. Their belief manifests itself in the current educational reform agenda which espouses a series of national education goals that have particular impact on the roles of teacher and teacher educator as the authority or more knowledgeable learner.

AMERICA 2000 was the educational reform agenda established by former President George Bush and the state governors in 1990 (National Education Goals Panel, 1994). AMERICA 2000 placed a high priority on the basic subjects of English, science, mathematics, history, and geography and enumerated six national goals that were to be accomplished by the American educational system by the year 2000. In 1994, former President William Clinton modified AMERICA 2000 and signed GOALS 2000: Educate America Act that espoused creating learning communities all across America and codified the six goals established in 1990 and added two new goals that included teacher education and professional development, as well as parental involvement and participation. Again, those eight goals were to be accomplished by the American educational system by the year 2000 (National Education Goals Panel, 1994).

GOALS 2000 clearly outlined the federal educational agenda that states were responsible for implementing through local municipalities and school districts under the former Bush and Clinton Presidential administrations. Current President George W. Bush's federal education initiatives espouse the belief of *leaving no child behind*. This focus as well as the foci of the two aforementioned federal administrations also clearly support the metaphor of teacher and teacher educator as authority.

Many states, municipalities, and P–12 school districts are still involved in GOALS 2000 activities and initiatives. Table 1 summarizes GOALS 2000 (National Education Goals Panel, 1994, pp. 8–11). These GOALS are germane to this chapter's exploration of teacher educator and teacher as authority.

Table 1 GOALS 2000: Educate America Act

Goal 1	Ready to Learn	By the year 2000, all children will start school ready to learn.
Goal 2	School Completion	By the year 2000, graduate rates will increase to at least 90 percent.
Goal 3	Student Achievement and Citizenship	By the year 2000, students in grades 4, 8, and 12 will demonstrate (through testing) competency over challenging subject matter including English, mathematics, science, foreign languages, civics and governments, economics, art, history, and geography. Every school in America will ensure that students use their minds well, so they may be prepared for responsible citizenship, further learning, and productive employment.
Goal 4	Teacher Education and Professional Development	By the year 2000, the teaching force will have access to programs for the continued improvement of their professional skills and the opportunity to acquire the knowledge and skills needed to instruct and prepare all American students for the next century.
Goal 5	Mathematics and Science	By the year 2000, United States students will be first in the world in mathematics and science achievement.
Goal 6	Adult Literacy and Lifelong Learning	By the year 2000, every adult American will be literate and will possess the knowledge and skills necessary to compete in a global economy and exercise the rights and responsibilities of citizenship.
Goal 7	Safe, Disciplined, and Alcohol-and Drug-free Schools	By the year 2000, every school in the United States will be free of drugs, violence, and the unauthorized presence of firearms and alcohol and will offer a disciplined environment conducive to learning.
Goal 8	Parental Participation	By the year 2000, every school will promote partnerships that will increase parental involvement and participation in promoting the social, emotional, and academic growth of children.

According to Oakes and Lipton (1999), "schools tried to match the organizational efficiencies of factories that were producing such abundant manufactured goods. These efficiencies required smooth-running classrooms where many students would all do the same academic work at the same time" (p. 240). These bureaucratic/structural and political realities of schools are visible manifestations of Bolman and Deal's (1997) structural and political frames.

The teacher educator and the teacher are both expected to know the content and process of knowledge construction. Ways of knowing (Morrison, 2000) include knowing through experience, knowing through authority, knowing through reason, knowing through intuition, and knowing through active construction. Attending specifically to the concept of knowing through authority, briefly let us examine the behaviors and expectations of candidates and teachers. Teacher educators and teachers have historically been perceived as authority figures. Teacher educators and teachers are perceived as authoritative sources of knowledge. They are expected to know what to teach. They are also expected to know when it should be taught, in what sequence, and under what conditions. Under some circumstances, teacher educators and teachers are viewed as the sole source of academic knowledge and the candidate or P–12 student is viewed as a tabla rasa, a blank slate, or an empty bank waiting to be filled. Constructivist teacher education, however, rejects that belief.

The metaphor of teacher educator and teacher as authority provides the raison d'etre for the expert to function in the role of curriculum mapper. The content of knowledge construction, often referred to as curriculum design (Boyer and Baptiste, 1996; Shrenko, 1994), requires teacher educators and teachers to organize and lead the teaching and learning process in ways that ensure that learners have numerous high quality opportunities to construct their own understandings of the content being presented. In order to accomplish this goal, the teacher and the teacher educator must have a solid knowledge base that can be utilized to determine what to teach and what content to present, when and in what sequence (Morrison, 2000; Stipek, 1998).

Using the metaphor of teacher educator or teacher as more knowledgeable learner, in the context of this chapter—constructivist teacher educator or teacher as authority—the tenets of pedagogy encourage teachers and teacher educators to utilize Vygotsky's Zone of Proximal Development (Slavin, 1994; Soderman, Gregory, & O'Neill, 1999) to determine what students can accomplish independently or with assistance. The craft of adult education (Draper in Barer-Stein and Draper, 1994), on the other hand, identifies three major points that constructivist teacher education faculty should take into consideration when outlining and planning courses in the professional education sequence: adults can and do learn; adults can and do take responsibility for all aspects of learning (planning, participating, and evaluating); and adults are teachers as well as learners.

While the context of the P–12 curriculum can be directly traced to federal (GOALS 2000) and state (e.g., New Jersey State Department of Education Core Curriculum Content Standards, 1996) initiatives, the content of courses taught in the teacher education sequence is often predetermined based on the approved course syllabus (Grunert, 1997) which is placed on file in the education department and/or the college of education. As the more knowledgeable content area learner, the teacher educator prepares and distributes a course syllabus that serves as a learning contract wherein the following are identified: a course description including the purpose of the course, the course objectives, course content (the topics to be covered), the required textbook(s) and reading assignments, course requirements, instructional procedures, outcomes assessment, resources (print and non-print). It is imperative that adult learners (candidates) understand and subscribe to the purpose of the course (Knowles, 1973). The course syllabus is an excellent vehicle for assisting adult learners to accept ownership for their learning in a particular course and determining ways that they can utilize their prior knowledge and experiences to build, scaffold, and construct meaning. This outcome is best achieved in the constructivist teacher education setting when the teacher educator employs the metaphor of teacher educator as facilitator or coach (see discussion of teacher education as facilitator in the next section for further discussion of this point).

According to Slavin (1994):

> *Constructivist approaches to teaching emphasize top-down rather than bottom-up instruction. "Top-down" means that students begin with complex problems to solve and work out*

or discover (with the teacher's guidance) the basic skills required. . . . This top-down processing approach is contrasted with the traditional bottom-up strategy in which basic skills are gradually built into more complex skills. In top-down teaching, the tasks students begin with are more complex, complete, and "authentic," meaning that they are not parts or simplifications of the tasks students are ultimately expected to perform, but they are the actual tasks (p. 225–226).

The constructivist teacher educator must determine what those tasks are, when those tasks should be assigned, and how to organize those tasks to best facilitate P–12 student and candidate achievement. The teacher as authority must utilize Vygotsky's Zone of Proximal Development to assess what tasks are appropriate for which P–12 students and candidates. The concept of the zone of proximal development reminds the teacher as authority to determine what tasks candidates and P–12 student are capable of doing alone or in collaboration with others.

From the lens of teacher and teacher educator as authority, the teacher has more experience, expertise, and the professional preparation to meet this professional challenge. Thus, "the teacher's role is to guide, focus, suggest, lead, and continually evaluate the progress of the students" (Marlowe and Page, 1998). Evaluating the progress of students includes providing direct instruction when and where appropriate.

Marlowe and Page (1998) affirm that "a constructivist student/ teacher communication system does not mean that the teacher gives up responsibility. Although a major role for students in the constructivist classroom is to direct their own learning, they do not have license to do whatever they want" (p. 57). While allowing candidates and P–12 students to make choices is a goal in the constructivist classroom, sometimes the candidate or P–12 student has no choice. Curriculum requirements may be specified by the state, the teacher education unit and/or the school district. Standardized testing and test preparation may also be mandated. The curriculum may also dictate certain books to be read at certain grade levels or in specific courses. See Chapter 3 for a discussion of content and process in constructivist teacher education.

In conclusion, Morrison (2000) describes "the teacher as a 'sage on the stage,' a repository of knowledge, wisdom, and expertise. The sage, like a guru or Zen master, challenges learners and models the importance of learning how to think" (p. 16). This view of the teacher and teacher educator as authority provides the foundation for the teacher and teacher educator's role as facilitator of the learning environment.

Examples of Teacher Educator as Authority

Georgia State University's Collaborative Masters Program (CMP) provides one of many examples of the role of constructivist teacher educator as authority. In the CMP Program, this dimension is seen in two newly created roles—that of "cohort faculty" and "faculty on retainer." Two cohort faculty members coordinate the program and provide consistent guidance for the cohort group over the 15 month period. They are responsible for program and community development. Cohort faculty manage the logistics of scheduling as well as other administrative tasks; facilitate democratic decision making within the community; coach teachers in their classrooms; and are responsible for the assessment process (representing more facilitative roles). Faculty on retainer, provide faculty expertise, technical support, resources, and coaching as needed by participants rather than as prescribed by a course schedule (representing more authoritative roles). These six faculty are assigned a course load and are retained for approximately 33 hours of "access" during the four semester program, providing opportunities for content integration and flexible schedules for faculty to meet with large and small groups or individuals. It is balancing the expert knowledge that faculty bring to the table with the discovery and construction of knowledge for individual teachers. It's about what Dewey names the "mature guide." See Chapter 4 on autonomy and community in constructivist teacher education.

In other programs, candidates and P–12 students defer to the teacher educator or teacher as the voice of authority and more knowledgeable learner. Teachers and teacher educators affirm that respect for authority as they set course expectations and standards, organize the content and topics to be covered within the course, provide direct instruction when and where appropriate, and identify resources and instructional strategies. Constructivist teachers and teacher educators also utilize their role of authority to design cooperative learning experiences and clinical experiences.

The issue of grades and grading presents a special challenge for the constructivist teacher educator but is another example of the role of teacher educator as authority. The traditional university grading system assigns to all teaching faculty the responsibility for the submission of grades, to the appropriate department on campus, that reflect how the student has successfully or unsuccessfully satisfied the course requirements as outlined in the course syllabus. A common tension in the constructivist teacher education setting is sometimes the discrepancy between the grade posted by the faculty and the grade that candidates feel that they have earned based on the effort expended in a particular course rather than their demonstration of completion of course goals and objectives. See Chapter 6 for a discussion of power and empowerment in constructivist teacher education.

TEACHER EDUCATOR AND TEACHER AS FACILITATOR

Morrison's (2000) definition of teacher as facilitator states "Teachers are professionals who set the stage, organize the environment, and make it possible for students to learn. They are 'guides on the side.' Constructivist teacher educators as facilitators view students as active learners who are responsible for their own learning and capable of learning on their own" (p. 16). This view respects the fact that many learners are self-directed and need to be provided with a supportive academic environment in which they are encouraged to think outside the box or take academic risks without fear of failure or retribution.

The metaphor of teacher as coach views "exhorts and encourages students to perform to the limit of their individual capabilities, to train for future performance, and to contribute to the team. They also show and demonstrate skills and behaviors" (Morrison, 2000, p. 16). Herein the constructivist teacher educator demonstrates that she or he is the more knowledgeable learner by capitalizing on teachable moments to facilitate meaningful connections between school and society without expecting that P–12 students and/or candidates will learn or memorize information merely for the sake of adding it to the "bank" to be utilized at some unknown time and place in the future.

According to Lenz, 1998, it is important for constructivist teacher educators to recognize that

> *adult learners are people whose lives are overflowing with commitments, obligations, burdens of one sort or another. They have jobs or professions that occupy a substantial portion of their time, or domestic responsibilities, or in many cases, both. The time and energy they invest in learning must compete with all the personal, social, family, community, and other tasks, responsibilities and diversions that press upon the lives of most adult (p. 2).*

Understanding this view and recognizing that adults live and function in an increasing complex world, the needs of adult learners are more appropriately met in the constructivist teacher education setting when one subscribes to the metaphor of teacher educator and teacher as facilitator. "The teacher who creates optimal conditions for learning, becomes a facilitator of learning rather than a dumper of information" (Schrenko, 1994, p. 7). This metaphor advances the view of students as active learners who are responsible for their own learning. In addition, students are viewed as being capable of directing their own learning. Teacher educators and teachers facilitate the learning process by setting the stage, organizing learning environments, and creating environment conducive to learning. In the context of this metaphor, teacher educators, teachers and school personnel, candidates, and learners are intimately involved in the learning process, help determine the content of instruction, help establish how learning is organized, and influence the terms and conditions of the evaluation of learning.

Adults are motivated to learn as they experience needs and interests that learning will satisfy. Therefore their needs and interests are appropriate starting points for organizing and facilitating learning activities in the constructivist teacher education classroom. Since the adult's orientation to learning is life-centered, the appropriate units for organizing candidate learning in teacher education settings are life situations not subjects. It is imperative, therefore, that teacher educators find ways to connect educational theory to real classrooms and P–12 learners in concrete and meaningful ways.

Experience is the richest resource for adult learning. The core methodology of adult learning is the analysis of meaningful learner-centered experiences. Adults bring a wealth of life experiences to the teacher education classroom which should be utilized and incorporated into courses on a regular basis.

Adults have a deep need to be self-directing. The role of the teacher educator as facilitator is to foster engagement in a process of mutual inquiry as opposed to the role of teacher educator as authority with the responsibility for transmitting knowledge to the candidate and then evaluating the candidate's conformity to the transmission model of instruction.

Individual differences among people increase with age. Teacher educators must make optimal provision for differences in style, time, place, and pace of learning. Reflective of the tenets of andragogy, teacher educators as facilitators of constructivist teacher education must encourage candidates to reflect upon the knowledge base that they are constructing and relate it in meaningful ways to school settings using actual classrooms or case studies as field or clinical experiences.

The course syllabus may more appropriately be used in constructivist teacher education settings to frame the professional education course and also as a springboard to collaborate with candidates and P–12 colleagues about the course assignments to be completed, the weight to be allocated to each assignment, the learning activities that will be undertaken to meet course objectives, and how candidates and P–12 students will document growth regarding the course's objectives. In addition, candidates, faculty, P–12 students, and P–12 personnel may jointly develop the rubrics that may be utilized to assess candidate and P–12 student growth and performance.

According to Oakes and Lipton (1999),

> *Constructivists suggest that, like most of real life, thinking is complex and disorderly. Sometimes we take years to make sense of ideas and experiences; sometimes making sense happens*

overnight. That's what we really hope for when we tell someone to "sleep on it." And sometimes understanding happens in a flash. "Aha!" is a sure sign that someone has suddenly made sense out of confusion. These ideas wreak havoc with teaching strategies that rely on tight schedules and precise five- or seven-step lesson plans with a tidy progression from presenting new information to practice to reinforcement of learning (p. 74).

Slavin (1994) affirms this view by reminding the teacher educator and teacher as facilitator that they must create the environment in which candidates and P–12 students can construct meaningful, authentic, and useful knowledge. The teacher educator or teacher facilitates the process of education by creating the contextual setting in which candidates and P–12 students construct knowledge "by teaching in ways that make information meaningful and relevant to students, by giving students opportunities to discover themselves, and by teaching students to be aware of and consciously use their own strategies for learning" (p. 225).

Examples of Teacher Educator as Facilitator

During the internship component of Georgia State University's CMP program, cohort faculty make monthly visits for coaching. The agenda of these visits is determined by the teachers. Faculty try to arrange the schedule so that at least part of the time they are at schools the teachers are free to talk (planning periods). This is best illustrated by the following CMP anecdote. A fourth grade teacher was working on class meetings as part of her goal to incorporate student voices into her classroom. The first field visit was spent exploring the teacher's goal and the purposes behind that goal. Through this conversation, the faculty member suggested readings, strategies, and resources to help the teacher reach this goal. At the second visit, the teacher and her students were still struggling with the class meetings. The teacher asked the Georgia State faculty member to sit in on the class meeting. In the midst of the meeting, the teacher stopped the discussion with the students and asked the faculty member, what do you think about what is going on here? She invited the faculty member along with the students to reflect on the process. The role of the faculty member was more like a team player/facilitator with the teacher and her students. The faculty member was able to bring some expertise and an outsider's perspective to the process these fourth graders were experiencing. Field visits thereafter continued the reflection and discussion around that goal in addition to covering other classroom and/or teacher development goals.

Employing the role of constructivist teacher educator as facilitator may be more of a challenge at the undergraduate or preservice candidate level. Depending of the age and experience of those learners, they may be more inclined to expect teacher educators to conduct classes in more traditional ways. However, graduate candidates and inservice teachers often eagerly recognize that they have a lot to contribute and are sometimes more willing to facilitate their own learning process in order to expand, scaffold, and construct a more extensive knowledge base and repertoire of instructional strategies.

Rubrics developed collaboratively by candidates and P–12 students and the constructivist teacher educator provides an opportunity for the teacher educator to function in the role of facilitator and meet the demands of the assessment process. Students may be asked to design a rubric for the evaluation and assessment of course assignments. Another strategy includes encouraging candidates to conduct research to identify rubrics that have been used for assignments and recommend how they might be modified to fit the current assignment. Utilizing a rubric also encourages the candidate to engage in Knowles' (1973) process of taking responsibility for all aspects of learning: planning, participating, and evaluating.

Use of Portfolio in Authority and Facilitator Constructivist Teacher Education

In response to a plethora of calls to raise standards and promote and produce academic excellence (Doyle & Pimentel, 1997) and utilize multiple measures to assess student learning outcomes (Gardner, 1985), many universities and districts have identified the portfolio (Campbell, Melenzyer, Nettles, & Wyman, 2000; Cole, Ryan, Kick, & Mathies, 2000; Fogarty, 1998; Mabry, 1999; McLaughlin & Vogt, 1996; Schurr, 1992; and Soderman, Gregory, & O'Neill, 1999) as one vehicle that may be utilized to provide a more authentic measure of student performance. According to Cole et al. "portfolios provide authentic and meaningful documentation of students' abilities. Curriculum, instruction, and assessment intersect via portfolios, tying the three together effectively for students" (p. 9).

"A portfolio will have multiple, but not conflicting, purposes" however, "portfolio usage reflects the curriculum and instruction that students receive (Cole et al., 2000, p. 13). The portfolio is a vehicle that may be utilized by constructivist teacher educators and teachers whether one employs the metaphor of teacher educator or teacher as authority or teacher educator or teacher as facilitator. See Table 2 illustrating Portfolio in Authority and Facilitator Constructivist Teacher Education (Cole et al, 2000, p. 13).

Most candidates are required to take six credits in literacy education as part of their thirty-credit professional education sequence. *Teacher as reflective urban practitioner* is the conceptual framework for the professional education sequence in the College of Education at New Jersey City University (NJCU). This conceptual framework includes four frames: (1) Reflective Practitioner Framework, (2) Professional Education Framework, (3) Process Framework, and (4) Urban Education Framework. The four frames are described below.

The Reflective Practitioner Framework is built on a professional knowledge base, action taken as a result of acquiring that knowledge base, the candidate's construction of knowledge, and reflective thinking about how best to use that knowledge base in an urban setting. This framework encourages the education professional to be thoughtful, responsive and responsible, and to utilize personal experiences, feedback from the education process, the context of school and society, and personal values to make sound educational decisions. As candidates explore the Reflective Practitioner Framework, they are encouraged to examine the following: How do my decisions affect my students and

Table 2   Portfolio in Authority and Facilitator Constructivist Teacher Education

	Teacher as Authority Teacher Educator Centered	Teacher as Facilitator Candidate Centered
Process	**Top Down Process** The portfolio process is predetermined by department, teacher educator, district, principal, and/or teacher with or without student input.	**Bottom Up Process** The portfolio process is determined by the candidate or P–12 student based on the mutually identified goals and objectives.
Contents	The artifacts included in the portfolio reflect the requirements established by the department, the district, the principal, the teacher educator, and/or the teacher.	The artifacts included in the portfolio reflect the interests of candidates, P–12 students, faculty, parents, the college of education and/or the school district.
Organization	Departments, faculty, and or districts specify how portfolios should be organized to document how knowledge has been constructed.	The teacher educator, department or district may propose organizational structures or portfolio processes as a springboards for negotiation of the portfolio process and product. Candidates and/or P–12 students determine how to organize the portfolio in order to demonstrate personal growth and development.
Evaluation	The criteria for portfolio evaluation are predetermined by the department, faculty, and/or district. Portfolio grades may be utilized to determine placement, promotion, and/or the award of course credit.	Teacher educators, teachers, candidates, and P-12 students mutually determine the criteria that will be utilized for portfolio evaluation. The portfolio is one of multiple assessment measures utilized to determine placement, promotion, and/or course credit.

others with whom I work? How could I have done things differently? What information do I need to improve?

The Professional Education Framework provides solid support for the development and process of the other three frameworks. It contains the understanding of the content to be taught: subject matter, curriculum, and instructional strategies. It also includes knowledge of the student, the student's community, and a functional repertoire of instructional approaches appropriate for urban school settings. As candidates explore the Professional Education Framework, they are encouraged to examine the following: What do I know about my students that will help me teach them? What do I know about the family and community of my students? What do I know about the subject matter, curriculum, and instructional strategies?

The Process Framework describes the steps that enable the education professional to acquire, modify and reframe, and utilize knowledge leading toward reflective practice. As candidates explore the Process Framework, they are encouraged to examine the following: How will I learn more to improve my teaching? How will I practice using what I have learned? How will I change, grow, and reflect on what I know?

The Urban Education Framework acknowledges the links between and among cultural diversity and learning, abilities and potential, motivation and effort, and resiliency. The Urban Education Framework presents a proactive perspective that empowers the education professional to view learners in the urban environment as capable, motivated, and resilient. As candidates explore this framework, they are encouraged to examine the following: How does the urban environment affect learners? In what ways are my students capable, motivated, and resilient? How can I support cultural diversity and learning?

The Department of Literacy Education at NJCU adopted a policy requiring that portfolios be used as one of multiple assessment measures in the required courses in the professional education sequence. The faculty utilize the portfolio assessment process to assess and evaluate the growth and performance of candidate's work in the literacy courses. The portfolio assessment process was adopted because it allows candidates to assemble multiple measures of their work over time. In addition, candidates as well as faculty direct the process and shape the evaluation. The collection of candidate work gives the faculty a clear picture of how candidates have acquired literacy strategies over the course of the professional education sequence. In addition, the portfolio assessment process is utilized because it may be used to inform the candidate of their strengths and weaknesses and helps them to develop a plan for personal and professional improvement.

The literacy component of the professional education sequence at NJCU includes six credits spread across three undergraduate courses: LTED 330 FOCUS: Reading, Language and Literacy—3 credits, LTED 350/360/370 Early Childhood/Elementary/Secondary Literacy Workshop—2 credits, and LTED 470 Concurrent Language Arts Seminar. The Literacy Education Department portfolios serve as maps of candidates at different stages of development. However, each portfolio should contain a reflective statement that addresses the following questions:

1. What is my philosophy of teaching?

2. What is my approach to the teaching of literacy?

3. What theoretical viewpoints best represent my philosophy of teaching and my approach to literacy instruction?

4. What have I learned in this course?

5. What would I like other professionals to know about my performance as a student, as an educator, and as an individual interested in lifelong learning?

6. What materials and/or artifacts have I collected from my classmates colleagues that might be useful to me in my present/future placement/classroom?

7. What materials and/or artifacts have I created that might be useful to me in my present/future placement/classroom?

The reflective statement is an essential component of the literacy portfolio and should clarify, evaluate, and summarize the meaning and significance of various experiences that impacted on the candidate's growth toward being a reflective urban practitioner while enrolled in the professional education sequence.

The literacy portfolios must also demonstrate an understanding of the New Jersey Core Curriculum Language Arts Literacy Standards (New Jersey Department of Education, 1999). The Language Arts Literacy Standards are:

- All students will **speak** for a variety of real purposes and audiences.

- All students will **listen** actively in a variety of real purposes and audiences.

- All students will **write** in clear, concise, organized language that varies in content and form for different audiences and purposes.

- All students will **read** various materials and texts with comprehension and critical analysis.

- All students will **view,** understand, and use nontextual visual information.

The *FOCUS* course is the first literacy education course taken by candidates at NJCU. Students enrolled in that course are learning about the foundations that foster and support literacy growth. Portfolios in that course are developmental in nature. Their intent is to encourage students to connect with their own literacy history and to begin to develop a philosophy or theoretical outlook on how language is developed and literacy acquired. The Early Childhood, Elementary, and Secondary Language Arts Workshops focus on strategies, techniques, and materials candidates can use to foster and support literacy development in their P–12 classrooms. Portfolios from these courses should demonstrate and showcase the candidate's understanding and application of concepts and theories studied in these courses. The Concurrent Language Arts Seminar offers candidates the opportunity to rethink their student teaching experiences and to further build their repertoire of instructional strategies to foster the development of literacy in P–12 classrooms. The candidate's portfolio for this course should reflect the student teaching experience and also showcase their talents as future literacy educators.

A health education candidate enrolled in one of this author's LTED 330 FOCUS: Reading, Language, and Literacy courses struggled with the concept of developing a literacy portfolio as one of the multiple assessment measures that were required for satisfactory completion of the course. During the term, the candidate repeatedly questioned her department's requirement that she as a future educator complete a literacy course as part of her professional education sequence. She completed all of the mandatory assignments but always raised an objection to having to learn anything about literacy when she was planning to teach at the secondary level. The entire class was speechless when she entered the class the day portfolios were due carrying five shoe boxes. Most of the class was under the mistaken impression that she was probably completing her holiday shopping until the class began to share their experiences with the portfolio process. E.C. (pseudonym) was anxious to share her experience as she was proud of her ability to finally see the relevance of literacy to everything that is done in the classroom—whether it is an elementary, middle, secondary, or higher education setting. Comparing *feet* and *literacy*, E.C. introduced her portfolio as follows:

Feet . . .	Literacy . . .
• are the base of our body.	• is the base/foundation of education.
• help us maintain our balance.	• balanced literacy is what I will strive for.
• take us where we want to go. They carry us from place to place.	• travels with us through all aspects of life.
• change and grow as we develop.	• grows and changes with a person as they develop.

E.C. created her table of contents by cutting oak tag into the shape of socks. According to her portfolio's introductory statement, "This portfolio contains five shoeboxes. Each one represents a particular stage of literacy development. Inside every shoebox will be information and/or demonstrations of my acquired knowledge from the course, FOCUS, Reading, Language, and Literacy, according to the stage of literacy development it refers to." E.C. had purchased the five pairs of shoes exclusively for her portfolio. Each shoe box represented a stage of literacy development ranging from the infant to the professional and was matched with one of the course objectives. Prior to sharing her portfolio process and the contents of her portfolio with the class, E.C. taped one of the shoes in each box to the top of the box.

The first shoe box, the infant shoe box, explored the psychological and cognitive factors of literacy development. The second shoe box, the emergent literacy shoe, ranged from the pre-kindergarten to second grade child and focused on learning about language and emergent literacy and their role in the development of literacy outcomes. The third shoe box, her middle school shoe, focused on learning about the theory and practice associated with creating a literate environment. Shoe box number four, the high school shoe, focused on learning about the impact of socioeconomic, sociological, social, personal, familial, cultural, intellectual, physiological, and neurological factors on the development of literacy. The fifth shoe box, the professional shoe, explored how to use reflection to guide instructional practice. E.C. used index cards that increased in size to represent that stage of literacy development, to demonstrate what she had learned about literacy development in the context of that particular stage. Clearly, she was able to demonstrate, in meaningful and tangible ways, her awareness and/or mastery of all content areas covered within the course in a comprehensive but simple manner.

Revisiting Marlow and Page's definition (1998), E.C.'s portfolio provided concrete and tangible evidence that she did not just receive knowledge but was able to build, scaffold, and construct meaning based on the knowledge that she acquired. Additionally, it was clear that she did not just memorize or accumulate knowledge but was also able to analyze the information in meaningful ways. E.C. did not just repeat back the information covered in class but demonstrated that she clearly understood the literacy concepts that were explored. Last but by no means least, it was also evident that E.C. became an active learner as well as a teacher as she demonstrated how she took responsibility for directing how own learning experience.

E.C. also demonstrated the tenets of andragogy as espoused by Knowles (1973). It was evident that she could and did learn a content that she in the beginning questioned the value of adding to her professional repertoire. She took responsibility for all aspects of her learning: she planned, participated, and evaluated her learning experience and her literacy portfolio. To accomplish the task of constructing a literacy portfolio, E. C. functioned as both a teacher and a learner.

It is this author's firm belief that E.C. was able to complete the task of developing her first literacy portfolio so successfully after her initial resistance because she was enrolled in a literacy courses wherein the principles of andragogy and constructivist teacher education were affirmed and the dimensions of teacher educator as authority and teacher educator as facilitator were balanced.

CONCLUSION

What do we teach? When do we teach it (knowledge, skills, domains)? How do we teach? Why do we teach what we teach? The preparation that teacher educators provide for candidates can "ensure conformity and preserve the status quo or it can create new metaphors and paradigms for thinking and teaching that lead to significant social change. . . . We can prepare teachers who are clones or robots who do as they are told or we can foster a love of learning, produce critical thinkers, and develop creative, socially responsible citizens" (Curtis and Curtis, 1994, p. 1). Also, see Chapter 7 on critical thinking and multiple perspectives in constructivist teacher education.

In conclusion, this chapter has explored and discussed the dimensions of teacher educator as authority and teacher educator as facilitator in constructivist teacher education. It also examined the characteristics of the two metaphors in constructivist practice, provided examples of the two metaphors in constructivist teacher education, and demonstrated, using portfolios as one of multiples assessment measures, how these two metaphors are manifested in constructivist teacher education as well as P–12 school environments. Thus, this chapter provides a snapshot of the discussion of the sometimes competing dimensions of teacher educator as authority in constructivist teacher education and teacher educator as facilitator in constructivist teacher education. To continue this discussion, some of the questions that constructivist teacher educators might further ponder regarding the dimensions of teacher educator as authority in constructivist teacher education and teacher educator as facilitator in constructivist teacher education, include but are not limited to: Do we individualize instruction the way we ask our candidates to in order to foster P–12 student achievement? Do we take into account diversity and individual differences? Do we participate in setting our own agenda—in our classrooms? on campus? in P–12 settings? in the arena of the politics of education? Do we let people have authority that they should not? Do we respect teachers' knowledge? Do we give teachers and candidates the authority to meet the task we have assigned? Are we engaged in mutual inquiry and reflective practice?

Jones (1986) very aptly describes the competing tensions between the metaphors of teacher educator as authority (sage on the stage) and teacher educator as facilitator (guide on the side) in the following statement

> *To be a respectable teacher, I need to know a lot but not teach it. Teaching it all may overwhelm students and is a form of showing off. I keep reading for my own knowledge, not simply to tell students what I read. My preparation is largely indirect; if I have a lot in my head, I can pull it out whenever a question comes up, discussing ideas with students whose experiences are making them think (about the topic) (p. 24).*

The foundations of andragogy and pedagogy as well as the practice of constructivist teacher education support the teacher educator in the roles of teacher educator as authority and teacher educator as facilitator in university as well as P–12 settings. Reframing these roles, when and where appropriate, provides one vehicle that faculty at universities and schools as well as other educational settings might successfully utilize to provide opportunities for teacher educators, teachers, other school personnel, candidates, and P–12 students to successfully create and sustain constructivist education settings that will ultimately lead to improved academic achievement for *all* teachers and *all* learners.

REFERENCES

Barer-Stein, T. & Draper, J. A., editors (1994). *The Craft of Teaching Adults, Revised Edition.* Malabar, FL: Krieger Publishing Company.

Bolman, L. & Deal, T. (1997). *Reframing Organizations: Artistry, Choice, and Leadership, Second Edition.* San Francisco, CA: Jossey-Bass.

Boyer, J. & Baptiste, P. (1997). *Transforming the Curriculum for Multicultural Understandings.* San Francisco, CA: Caddo Gap Press.

Campbell, D. M., Melenyzer, B. J., Nettles, D. H., & Wyman, Jr., R. M. (2000). *Portfolio and Performance Assessment in Teacher Education.* Boston, MA: Allyn and Bacon.

Cole, D. J., Ryan, C. W., Kick, F., & Mathies, B. K. (2000). *Portfolios Across the Curriculum and Beyond.* Thousand Oaks, CA: Corwin Press, Inc.

Curtis, M.& Curtis, D. (1994). *Training Teachers: A Harvest of Theory and Practice.* St. Paul, MN: Redleaf Press.

Doyle, D. P. & Hartle, T. W. (1985). *Excellence in Education: The States Take Charge.* Washington, DC: American Enterprise Institute.

Doyle, D. P. & Pimentel, S. (1997). *Raising the Standard: An Eight-Step Action Guide for Schools and Communities.* Thousand Oaks, CA: Corwin Press, Inc.

Driscoll, M. P. (2000). *Psychology of Learning for Instruction, Second Edition.* Needham Heights, MA: Allyn and Bacon.

Fogarty, R. (1998). *Balanced Assessment.* Arlington Heights, IL: Skylight Training and Publishing Inc.

Gardner, H. (1985). *Frames of Mind: The Theory of Multiple Intelligences.* New York, NY: Basic Books.

Grunert, J. (1997). *The Course Syllabus: A Learner-Centered Approach.* Boston, MA: Anker Publishing Company, Inc.

Jones, E. (1986). *Teaching Adults: An Active Learning Approach.* Washington, DC: National Association for the Education of Young Children.

Knowles, M. S. (1969). *Higher Adult Education in the United States: The Current Picture, Trends, and Issues.* Washington, DC: American Council on Education.

Knowles, M. S. (1973). *The Adult Learner: A Neglected Species.* Houston, TX: Gulf Publishing Company.

Lenz, E. (1982). *The Art of Teaching Adults.* New York, NY: Holt, Rinehart & Winston.

Mabry, L. (1999). *Portfolios Plus: A Critical Guide to Alternative Assessment.* Thousand Oaks, CA: Corwin Press, Inc.

Marlowe, B. A. & Page, M. L. (1998). *Creating and Sustaining the Constructivist Classroom.* Thousand Oaks, CA: Corwin Press, Inc.

McLaughlin, M. & Vogt, M.E. (1996). *Portfolios in Teacher Education.* Newark, DE: International Reading Association.

Morgan, G. (1985). *Images of Organizations.* Beverly Hills, CA: Sage.

Morrison, G. S. (2000). *Teaching in America, Second Edition.* Boston, MA: Allyn and Bacon.

National Education Goals Panel. (1994). *The National Education GOALS Report: Building a Nation of lLearners.* Washington, DC: National Education Goals Panel.

Oakes, J. & Lipton, M. (1999). *Teaching to Change the World.* Boston, MA: McGraw-Hill College.

Schrenko, L. (1994). *Structuring a Learner-Centered School.* Palatine, IL: IRI/Skylight Publishing, Inc.

Schurr, S. L. (1992). *The ABCs of Evaluation: 26 Alternative Ways to Assess Student Progress.* Columbus, OH: National Middle School Association.

Slavin, R. E.(1994). *Educational Psychology: Theory and Practice, Fourth Edition.* Needham Heights, MA: Allyn and Bacon.

Stipek, D. (1998). *Motivation to Learn: From Theory to Practice, Third Edition.* Boston, MA: Allyn and Bacon.

Soderman, A. K., Gregory, K. M., & O'Neill, L. T. (1999). *Scaffolding Emergent Literacy: A Child-Centered Approach for Preschool through Grade 5.* Needham Heights, MA: Allyn and Bacon.

Professional Background:
Sandra Woolley

Twelve years ago when I became a teacher educator I was uncomfortable in the role of "teacher as expert" because I was accustomed to working with experienced inservice teachers in my recent roles as principal and curriculum director. In those capacities I had developed a collaborative leadership style. I believed in empowering adults as learners. As I began teaching early childhood methods courses at Mansfield University of Pennsylvania I formed partnerships with classroom teachers who were using active learning methods and I modeled similar methods in my methods courses. These classroom teachers did not call themselves constructivists but they were experimenting with teaching, assessment, and behavior management strategies consistent with constructivist learning theories. As preservice teachers progressed through a series of early childhood courses I taught, I gathered anecdotal evidence that students' beliefs about teaching and learning were changing. However, I had a nagging concern that these changes might be temporary, especially if students found themselves teaching in schools using more traditional methods.

In 1998 I joined the ATE Commission on Constructivism to learn more by collaborating with other teacher educators who were experimenting with constructivist approaches. I have not been disappointed. As we have worked together I have forged productive professional friendships while deepening my theoretical and practical understandings of constructivism. The experience has been both exhilarating and intellectually stimulating.

Power and Empowerment in Constructivist Teacher Education

Sandra Woolley

The dimension of power and empowerment addresses the balance of power between teachers and their students. Who decides what will be learned? Who controls classroom activities? Who talks and whose voice is valued? And who evaluates students' learning? Traditionally, teachers have assumed all of these responsibilities. However, teachers who believe in constructivist theories of learning attempt to reduce their dominance, thereby empowering students to assume a more active role in their own learning.

This dimension is also influenced by the balance of power among others—parents, community members, and politicians—interested in the education of today's youth. What are the goals of schooling? How and to whom are schools accountable? What curricula should children study? Are all children served equally well by schools? Answers to these questions shape teaching and learning in today's schools. However, issues of power are rarely discussed in teacher education programs, except in the context of administrators' leadership of schools or teachers' management of students' behavior. Teachers, focused primarily on students, curricula, and pedagogy, frequently do not pay attention to the political and organizational forces that impact their teaching and students' learning.

Like the constructs autonomy and community, power and empower have political overtones. Negative connotations are associated with using power to control others, especially if for personal gain. Wasserman (1990) calls this use of power, "power over," versus "power-to," (p. 7) which refers to the positive feelings generated in children or adults when they are empowered to accomplish a difficult task. Dictionary definitions of power include the ideas that persons with power have authority or influence over others, and that they have the ability or capacity to act. To empower someone means to enable them by giving them sufficient power or authority. Power can be viewed as a limited resource (if you have more power then I will have less) or a shared resource that holds potential for both personal and institutional change. As with autonomy and community, synergy can exist between giving up power and empowering others; that is, a leader with an inclusive concept of power can actually generate more total power by empowering others (Richert, 1992).

This chapter begins with a brief history of how the constructs of power and empowerment have been used in education and a discussion of why teacher educators interested in constructivist approaches want to shift the balance of power from themselves toward their students. Then, three issues critical to empowering students are explored: (a) involving students in the design of curriculum, (b) helping all students find their voices, and (c) assessment and grading of students' learning. Examples from teacher education courses and programs illustrate practical solutions to the difficult and persistent problems each of these issues presents. The chapter concludes with a few cautionary remarks.

POWER AND EMPOWERMENT IN EDUCATION

Most teachers have considerable control over how they organize their classrooms, manage student behavior, and plan and teach daily lessons. Jarvis (1997) suggests that teachers have power by virtue of their role, and that it is difficult for them to abdicate this power even if they want to. He argues that teacher power is not bad, as long as teachers intend to use it in the best interests of their students. French and Raven (cited in Payne & Cangemi, 1998) outline five types of power: coercive, reward, legitimate, expert, and referent. Teachers frequently possess all five types. They have coercive power based on their ability to administer negative consequences, for example, asking embarrassing questions or giving low grades. Reward power rests on the teacher's ability to deliver something of value, such as information, high grades or recommendations. Legitimate power is accorded to anyone who occupies the role of teacher. Teachers must earn expert power by demonstrating knowledge of their subject area. Referent power refers to the influence teachers have over students, if students admire and respect them.

Traditionally, teachers' power has not extended beyond their classrooms. Many teachers feel that their teaching is more and more controlled by standardized tests and required texts and curricula (McNeil, 2000). During the decades of the sixties, seventies, and eighties research based on a behaviorist model of learning focused on identifying effective teaching strategies that all teachers could learn and on developing "teacher-proof" curricula. Researchers, not teachers, were considered to be the experts on teaching. In the eighties and nineties recognition increased that many contextual factors influence teaching and learning. Effective methods of teaching could not guarantee success in all situations. Respect grew for qualitative and action research studies focused on understanding the context of teaching and learning and the perspectives of the participants. The focus of teacher education also shifted from a technical rational model to a professionalization of teaching model, which stimulated interest in reflective teacher education (Valli, 1992). In the latter model, empowered professionals are autonomous, self-renewing, and self-directed. They are capable of more than executing curricula designed by others. They make decisions while teaching and reflect on those decisions to continually improve their own teaching and their students' learning.

In the last fifteen years there has been a trend toward empowering teachers to participate in the operation of their schools. In a ten-year study of principal leadership Hall & Hord (1984) discover that behind successful principals were other change facilitators, usually teachers, who were critical to the successful implementation of school improvement efforts. More recently, Lambert, Walker, Zimmerman, Cooper, Lambert, Gardner & Slack (1995) proposed a theoretical model of leadership based on constructivist principles of learning that broadens the definition of leader and leadership. In this model leadership is defined as "the reciprocal processes that enable participants in an educational community to construct meanings that lead toward a common purpose about schooling" (p. 29). Leadership resides in the function, not the role or the person. Anyone in the school organization—administrators, teachers, parents, or students—can function as a leader by leading processes that work toward greater common understandings and the accomplishment of common goals. "Constructivist leadership can be distinguished from current notions of leadership that are influencing education and business in a number of ways, particularly in reference to who leads, the role of constructivist learning, and the need for community" (p. 29). Goodman (1992) suggests that if teachers work in hierarchical, bureaucratic schools in which they have limited power to participate in making the school what it is, they will probably not "think of or act in ways that will increase the power and participation of their students when it comes to organizing their classrooms" (p. 63). Richert (1992) cautions that the voice of empowered teachers, who are able to act in accordance with what they know and believe, may not always be welcomed in schools as they are currently organized until a more inclusive concept of power is accepted. Lambert et al. (1995) recommend that teacher educators must look at the bureaucratic forms of our educational organizations and question how they can be made more constructivist. Teacher educators must also ask how they can prepare their students to be future change agents when working in traditional settings.

WHY TEACHER EDUCATORS EMPOWER THEIR STUDENTS

Why do teachers who believe in constructivist theories of learning want to shift some of their power to their students? A primary reason is to improve their students' learning by encouraging them to assume a more active role. Teacher educators try to help teacher-learners construct understandings related to course topics by having them articulate their own ideas and confront the ideas of others. To facilitate this process they provide choices and ask students to assume responsibility for their own and others' learning. Research on adult learning (Knowles, 1990) has established adults' preference for active learning methods, including a desire to relate new learning to prior experiences and to apply new insights to current problems. Even adults with little formal schooling are self-directed, independent learners when they are motivated by a need to know something. Knowles created the term "andragogy" to describe teaching methods that support adult learning. He contrasted andragogy with pedagogy or traditional methods for teaching children who are expected to receive knowledge more passively. Like adult educators, teacher educators who use constructivist practices want to empower teacher-learners to be self-directed, life-long learners.

Another reason teacher educators want to empower their students is to find a more effective way of influencing teacher-learners' beliefs and practices related to teaching and learning. Guyton (2000) defines "powerful" programs as ones that have the power to change teachers and ultimately to change their students. "Powerful teacher education is that which produces good teachers who are able to teach all the children who come to their classrooms" (p. x). In contrast to other fields such as law or engineering, students enter teacher education programs with knowledge about teaching and learning. Lortie (1975) described students' years of K–12 schooling as a long apprenticeship during which they form opinions about teaching. The difficulty in changing preservice teachers' beliefs—for example, from a traditional transmission model to a more active constructivist model—has been blamed on the short duration of course and program interventions, the critical timing of field and university-based experiences, conflicting pedagogical perspectives of universities and schools, disciplinary backgrounds of preservice teachers, and the powerful socializing influence of the school culture (Mayer-Smith & Mitchell, 1997). A difference is observed between the pedagogical content knowledge and classroom actions of teachers who have completed a teacher education program and ones who have not (Richardson, 1996), but it appears that teacher educators need more powerful approaches.

Since teachers tend to teach as they were taught and since many preservice and inservice teachers have learned in classrooms based on a transmission model of teaching, many teacher educators believe that they must model constructivist approaches. Then, they try to help teacher-learners become aware of what is happening in the teacher education classroom by stepping back and asking, "What do you think of the changed teacher and student roles and the shifting balance of power? If this works for you as a learner, do you think a constructivist approach would work for your students?" It is not enough to lecture about constructivist learning theories. Teacher-learners need the opportunity to participate in a community of teacher-learners to make their beliefs about teaching and learning more explicit and to empower them to act on their beliefs as leaders or change agents in their respective schools.

SHIFTING THE BALANCE OF POWER FROM TEACHERS TO STUDENTS

Empowering students sounds deceptively easy. In fact it is difficult, requiring changes in the roles of both teachers and students. This section with a practical focus introduces three issues that appear critical if teacher educators wish to shift power from themselves to their students. Although these issues overlap, each issue will be discussed separately, followed by course and program examples that illustrate practical solutions to the dilemmas introduced.

Issue One: Involving Students in the Design of Curriculum

Teachers who believe in constructivist theories of learning face the dilemma of how to balance their desire to empower their students by involving them in the design of curriculum with teachers' responsibilities to ensure that students learn the required formal knowledge in each subject area. Formal knowledge refers to "concepts, premises and understandings that have been debated and pretty well agreed upon within discourse communities that are larger than the classroom. . . . This formal knowledge is represented in textbooks, standards, testing programs, the teacher's understandings, etc." (Richardson, 1997, p. 4). The basic question teacher educators must answer is who or what is the authority in the classroom? Will certain answers be judged correct (i.e. the formal knowledge presented by the textbook or the teacher) or will a variety of student understandings be accepted and valued? Constructivist theories of learning suggest that curricula and teaching need to take into account students' prior knowledge, interests, and ways of knowing. However, with increased demands for accountability, neither teachers nor teacher educators can ignore the standardized tests their students must pass.

Different theories of knowledge, teaching, and learning are at the heart of this issue. Traditionalists view "knowledge as truth discovered by experts, and teaching as the transmission of that knowledge to students" (Oakes & Lipton, 1999, p. 108). Constructivists agree that there is a growing body of formal knowledge in each discourse community or subject area, but believe that understandings of that knowledge must be constructed by each individual. Content and the process of learning content are equally important and inseparable (see chapter on Content and Process by Hausfather). Psychological constructivists, focused more on the cognitive development of individuals, seldom address issues of power, authority, or the place of formal knowledge in their writings (Richardson, 1997). For social constructivists, however, the social context is instrumental in learning. Cultural meanings are shared through social interactions and formal knowledge enters into school learning as tools within the social situation. "There is no representation of reality that is privileged or 'correct.' There are, instead, a variety of interpretations that are useful for different purposes in differing contexts" (p. 8). All students bring funds of knowledge (Moll & Greenberg, 1990) with them into the classroom. "All students possess multiple frames of reference with which to construct knowledge by virtue of their ethnic background, race, class, gender, language usage, religious, cultural, and political identities, as well as such characteristics as their sexual orientation and physical appearance" (Ellsworth, as cited in O'Loughlin, 1992, p. 337). Social constructivists believe that teaching must promote interactions between learners' prior and new knowledge and involve them in conversations for internalization and deep understanding of ideas.

Social constructivist theories provide a theoretical basis for reformers' calls for involving students in the design of curricula. Reformers ask questions about "the influence of politics and power relations and their effect on the production of knowledge and the types of knowledge which are legitimized" (Oakes & Lipton, 1999, p. 27). There is an enormous conflict now between traditionalists who want schools to standardize the curriculum around a canon of history and literature that embodies traditional ideas, values, and universal truths, and reformists who argue that the modern approaches to curriculum do not provide suitable conditions for social justice in schools and society (Oakes & Lipton, 1999). The traditionalist perspective is represented by E. D. Hirsch, author of a 1988 best-seller, *Cultural Literacy*. "Hirsch argues that progressive reformers' emphasis on projects, 'discovery learning,' and other 'anti-subject matter' methods have brought curricular anarchy to U.S. schools. Teachers working from a constructivist and social justice perspective are the primary targets of Hirsch's outrage" (Oakes & Lipton, 1999, p. 129). Reformers call for a culturally democratic or multicultural curriculum that acknowledges many cultures, helps the less powerful acquire the cultural tools of the dominant Anglo-American culture, and creates a democratic forum for exploring conflict and oppression.

Examples of Involving Students in Curricular Design. The Foxfire Project (Wigginton, 1975, 1989) is perhaps one of the oldest and best known examples of involving students in the design of curricula. For over thirty years Foxfire has encouraged English teachers to engage students in the study of local customs and traditions and has published students' work. Core Foxfire principles illustrate a conscious balance in the curriculum between incorporating students' interests and motivations and ensuring that students learn the required content. Although one principle emphasizes the need to plan the work teachers and students do together around the desires and concerns of students, another principle emphasizes that the work must have academic integrity. This means that an academic community larger than the classroom would judge the content worthy of students' investigation.

For years the Foxfire project has been disseminated to teachers around the country through workshops. Teets and Starnes (1996) explain that these workshops have been more successful since they have focused on the constructivist principles necessary "to do" Foxfire, rather than on the production of a successful magazine. In a level one Foxfire workshop for teachers, trainers model the Foxfire process. The workshop begins with some activities that help teachers identify their needs and interests. Then, teachers are asked to reflect on their own learning experiences and make a list of qualities of good teachers and of memorable learning experiences. Teachers also describe a particularly successful lesson or series of lessons that they have planned and carried out with children. Then, the Foxfire core practices are introduced. The parallels between the core practices and teachers' memorable learning experiences are usually clear. Teachers also consider which of the core practices they already use by analyzing the lesson they described. The rest of the course is focused on helping each teacher develop individual plans for adding one or more Foxfire practices to their teaching.

Several features of the Georgia State Collaborative Master's Program (CMP) program illustrate ways of involving students in the design of curriculum. Students are given many curricular choices throughout the program, but within a framework of goals and processes established by the program faculty. Program goals and assigned readings are "givens." Initially, teacher-learners select a reading group and participate in a cooperative learning activity to report on the required books to all of the cohort members. Book groups are also formed around areas of interest to support students' action research projects.

In addition, throughout the program students are given many choices about how to accomplish program goals, including what topics and subtopics to emphasize and what resources to consult in the process of learning. An illustration is provided by one instructor's use of a curriculum planning document recommended by Wiggins and McTighe (1998) at the first of several class sessions on the teaching of mathematics. Teacher-learners were first asked to categorize course content as "worth being familiar with," "important to know and do," and "enduring understandings." Then, in small groups students combined individual ideas on charts, eliminating redundancies and representing their group's thinking in the three categories. The next step was to reach consensus as an entire class around what they thought to be "enduring understandings" and "important to know and do." These ideas became the content covered in the next several classes. This planning process gave teacher-learners a voice in the development of their curriculum and resolved the instructor's dilemma of how to plan course content with little prior knowledge of the teacher-learners' needs and interests as teachers of mathematics.

Issue Two: Helping All Students Find Their Voice

The important role of conversation in constructivist learning theories explains why it is critical to help all students find their voice. It is through conversation with teachers, co-learners, authors through their texts, and even oneself that new understandings are acquired. The concept of voice—"the use of language to explain, describe, question, explore, or challenge" (Richert, 1992, p. 189)—is embedded in the idea of conversation. "In feminist literature, voice and power are often linked by a conceptualization that either explicitly states, or implicitly implies, that claiming, experiencing, and/or honoring one's voice empowers the individual by putting her in contact with her own intelligence" (p. 196). In the context of learning to teach, Richert defines voice as teachers talking about "what they do, how they think, what they feel, and what they believe" (p. 189). When teachers find their voice they become more aware of what they know and believe about teaching. "They become 'students of education' who can act with intent as they responsibly examine the many complex aspects of their classroom practice" (p. 188).

Teacher educators face at least three dilemmas as they try to empower teacher-learners by helping them find their voices. Each dilemma requires shifting the balance of power. First, teacher educators need to quiet their own voice in the classroom in order to listen for student voices. Encouraging students to listen to themselves, as an authority on their own experiences, is an important part of learning. Second, teacher educators must ensure that all student voices are heard and valued, particularly the voices of women, older students, and minorities because some individuals from these groups may feel silenced by the unfamiliar culture they encounter in schools (Belenky, Clinchy, Goldberger, & Tarule, 1986; Weis & Fine, 1993). A third dilemma for teacher educators is how to support empowered teacher-learners to act on their ideas as they return to their classrooms and school communities.

In a transmission model of teaching teachers speak and students listen. To facilitate student conversations teachers have to relinquish their authoritarian role in the classroom (see chapter on Authority and Facilitation by Robinson). Teachers have to play a less dominant role, while still assuming responsibility for introducing critical course content, motivating students to engage in the process of learning, and establishing policies and procedures to ensure that all voices are heard. Teachers can quiet their own voices and encourage student voices by using teaching strategies that encourage students' active processing of ideas through speaking, writing, and reflection, both individually and in collaboration with others. Teaching strategies, such as reflective and dialogue journals, reading logs, small group discussions and projects, oral presentations with written responses, and co-equal supervision, encourage student conversations with themselves, printed material, and others (e.g., fellow students, faculty, and supervisors).

A second dilemma for teacher educators is how to "level the playing field" so that all teacher-learners feel comfortable in expressing their ideas. Teachers must create learning environments in which individuals feel safe to voice their ideas and establish norms that all students will be expected to contribute their ideas and will be listened to. Many agree that American public schools are based on middle class, Anglo-American values and traditions. For students with similar backgrounds the school culture seems normal and their success in school made easier. Students from dissimilar backgrounds lack the valued "cultural capital" (Oakes & Lipton, 1999), defined by sociologists as the verbal and nonverbal communication skills, knowledge, tastes, and habits students bring with them. For these students the school culture

150 Reframing Teacher Education

seems foreign and their success is made more difficult. In traditional classrooms all students' voices are silenced in favor of the teacher's voice of authority, but students from low income and minority cultures are at a particular disadvantage. To empower all students, teachers must move marginalized individuals back to the center so that they can find their voice and ultimately the power that comes with education. Teachers must not only ask if students are having an opportunity to speak but also if they are allowed to speak on their own terms or only in the modes and language of the majority. At the same time reformers emphasize that they are not suggesting that standards be lowered for minority students. They point out the importance of explicitly teaching rules and codes of the majority culture to ensure the success of minority students. Classrooms based on constructivist learning theories can be very confusing to minority students unless the assumptions, interactions, and expectations are made familiar and clearly stated (Delpit, 1993).

A third dilemma for teacher educators is how to support empowered teachers to act on their ideas in their own classrooms and school communities. The voices of teachers are silenced in many schools by norms of privacy, time schedules, and external standards for teaching and learning (Richert, 1992). Teachers have few opportunities to share their thoughts about the dilemmas of practice. To provide teachers with a forum to develop their voice, Hofstra University developed a Summer Institute for Teachers, founded on an emancipatory approach to knowledge construction (O'Loughlin, 1992). "The purpose of emancipatory teacher education, as Goodman (as cited in O'Loughlin, 1992) explained, is to enable teachers to ask themselves critical questions so that they can construct and enact critical visions of pedagogy that are appropriate to their own contexts" (p. 338). In a discussion of the historical context for constructivism in teacher education, Vadeboncoeur (1997) argues, "the need for emancipatory constructivism in teacher education is urgent if we are to attempt to teach all of our children" (p. 31). In emancipatory constructivism, based on Vygotsky's complete multilevel methodology, "the individual, the cultural context, and the meaning or interpretation of the larger sociohistorical context are integrated" (p. 29). O'Loughlin (as cited in Vadeboncoeur, 1997) notes that "the purpose of emancipatory knowledge construction is a commitment to social change, justice, and responsibility, the reduction of inequality, and the exposure of relationships of exploitation and oppression" (p. 30). In a study of the impact of Hofstra University's Summer Institute for Teachers, O'Loughlin (1992) concludes:

> *The imperative is clear. If we engage teachers in processes of emancipatory knowledge construction, we have an obligation to support them in confronting the political changes necessary to carry out the reconstructed practices in their classrooms. . . . As a contribution to this process, the teachers from the institute and I are getting together this year to found a network of activist teachers so that we can support each other in the transformative work of bringing processes of knowledge construction to our students (p. 343).*

Networks or teacher support groups have been part of other change efforts, like the whole language and writing process curricular change movements. Another way for teacher educators and teachers to support each others' change efforts is to work together in a on-going, mutually beneficial way, which is one of the prime motivations behind the Professional Development School relationships formed by many higher education institutions and public schools.

Examples of Helping Students Find Their Voice. The following example from a summer graduate course at James Madison University illustrates one instructor's successful effort to encourage and support one student in finding his voice. The student approached the instructor after the first class. He explained that he could not read quickly and was concerned about the amount of required reading during the six-week course. He asked the instructor to make her selections among the recommended readings early so that he could balance the course assignments, his inability to read quickly, and his daily commuting schedule. As she began identifying books that were appropriate for his area of interest, she realized that she was looking for books that were quick reads, offering less depth of information, and probably not as challenging in the way that key concepts were addressed. Realizing that she may be responding to issues of bias that she didn't know she had, she began questioning him more about what he was interested in studying to better select readings that would support his personal inquiry.

Class discussions were a regular part of each class of this course and the expectation for all students to participate was made explicit in the opening classes. This particular course included teachers from early, middle, and secondary education as well as special and physical education. Their various perspectives were valuable in helping the group better understand issues of teaching, learning, and curriculum across grades and content areas. The "slow reader" was one of three male students and the only African American in the class. In the first few classes the instructor observed that he rarely spoke in the group and frequently doodled as others were taking notes. From reading his papers and talking to him individually, she knew that he had insights into teaching and learning that other students did not have based on their particular teaching positions. She explained to him privately that his class contributions were critical in helping his peers learn and then tried to structure class discussions that encouraged him to speak out. Cooperative learning techniques such as think-pair-share and jigsaws provided opportunities for this young man to share what he was learning in very small groups. Since reporting out functions was usually rotated among members, he also had opportunities to serve as group synthesizer. As he earned the reputation of "most concise synthesizer" among the class, the teacher was again reminded that learners have many ways to demonstrate what they know when given the opportunity. Class members also noted that this was the first course in which they had heard this student participate so actively.

A second example is illustrated in a required course on supervision for teachers in the Masters of Education program at Mansfield University of Pennsylvania. In this course the instructor consciously encourages students to take charge of their own professional development and to work with others to change their school district's system if they don't like the way they are supervised. A sequence of activities in the course leads students toward empowerment. First, to help teacher-learners find their voices regarding teaching; the course begins with a short reflective paper on influences on students' ideas about teaching. The content of these papers is shared in class, followed by a group activity to define criteria of effective teachers. Next follows several simulations of cycles of clinical supervision, in which students play the roles of teacher, supervisor and student. From these cycles teacher-learners find out what collaborative supervision feels like. Next, a Web-based cooperative learning project helps teacher-learners look at alternatives to traditional supervisory models, including peer coaching, action research, and self-supervision. The project concludes with a role-play of designing a district professional development plan, a requirement of all Pennsylvania school districts. A final individual self-selected project allows teacher-learners to tailor the course to their own goals with more practice in supervision or study of one aspect of teaching. In reporting on her self-selected project, one obviously empowered teacher-learner said, "I 'm never going to allow my principal to observe me without a pre-conference so that I can have an opportunity to tell her what feedback I want on my teaching." This teacher was not trying to sound belligerent, but rather felt empowered to ask her supervisor for feedback that would help her improve her teaching. This teacher had found her voice.

Issue Three: Assessment and Grading of Students' Learning

Assessment and grading of students' learning creates at least two dilemmas for teachers or teacher educators attempting to empower their students. First, it is difficult to convince students that they have more power while their teacher maintains the authority to grade their work. Second, traditional assessment tasks do not match constructivist approaches to teacher education.

Neither students nor teachers can escape the reality of grading, which is a part of our concept of schooling from first grade through graduate school. Grades are important to students because they impact high-stakes, life-changing decisions such as scholarships, entry into and exit from teacher education programs, job opportunities, and graduate school. And yet, grading has a dampening effect on teachers' efforts to empower their students. Teachers seem to be sending mixed messages when they encourage students to assume more responsibility for their own learning while maintaining traditional grading practices. Richardson (1997) notes, "It is difficult for the teacher who is intent upon creating a constructivist environment to get around the problems of authority and control in a setting in which grades are important" (p. 7). The same problem occurs when a supervisor (principal, university supervisor, or cooperating teacher) is charged with both supervising and evaluating teachers or student teachers. As long as the supervisor is perceived to have power over the person observed, it is difficult for the teacher to regard the observer as a teacher rather than an evaluator (Acheson & Gall, 1992).

Generally, teachers and students share common expectations about grading. Students believe that grading is fair if teachers articulate clear expectations and processes, and then follow them with few deviations. Peterman (1997) describes the rebellion she and a colleague faced when they experimented with a more open-ended grading system. Peterman was in her fourth year at her institution, her colleague in his first. To align their grading system with their constructivist philosophy, they eliminated a point system and substituted portfolios with individual end-of-course conferences. Student complaints of unfairness resulted in Peterman's colleague retreating from their experimental methods to save his job and a big drop in her department's assessment of her teaching. Peterman's experience illustrates the personal risks teacher educators may face if they experiment with different methods of evaluation and grading. The adjustments she made in her grading system the following year illustrate a compromise in which the basis of grades were specified more, while students were given some flexibility in how they could demonstrate their understandings related to course topics.

A second dilemma is that traditional methods of assessment do not match a constructivist approach to teaching. That is, they do not empower students to assess their own learning or provide them with choices in demonstrating the variety of understandings that can occur in classrooms using a constructivist approach. Traditionally, teachers assign tasks such as quizzes, problem sets, papers, oral reports, and exams, and infer that learning has, or has not, occurred from students' performance on these tasks. Although students accept this process as objective, it is in fact a rather arbitrary process. Chawszczewski (1999) suggests that assessment is even more complicated when using constructivist approaches because teachers want to assess the processes students are using to construct their knowledge, as well as the final products. Since it is difficult to infer these processes using traditional assessment tasks, he suggests experimenting with portfolios, performance assessments, student self-evaluation, and rating systems as alternative methods. Routman (1994) in discussing evaluation in K–12 classrooms recommends integrating assessments with the teaching-learning process. Many classroom activities provide teachers with assessment information, if teachers develop systems for recording useful information while in the process of teaching. Methods of observation that have been emphasized in qualitative research, supervision of teaching, and early childhood education can be used by teachers and teacher educators to assess students' learning processes. Also, more open-ended learning tasks provide students with opportunities for self and peer assessment and with choices for demonstrating their learning related to course topics. While using alternative assessment methods, however, teachers must still make explicit the rules of grading to avoid criticisms of unfairness (Chawszczewski, 1999; Peterman, 1997).

Examples of Assessment and Grading Practices That Empower Students. The Collaborative Masters Program (CMP) at Georgia State provides a comprehensive example of assessment and grading practices that empower students. During a three-day retreat at the beginning of the program group members talk about the qualities of successful groups they have participated in. They turn this list of qualities into group norms that they agree to live by. These agreements then become part of a program evaluation instrument or rubric. This element of the rubric is called giving "full value" (i.e., living up to the CMP agreements). These agreements become personal as cohort members take something that was generated in the abstract and try to live by it through self-monitoring. These norms are re-negotiated periodically throughout the year. Together, faculty and students ask, "Are these norms still working for us? Have we missed anything? Do we need to change anything on the list?"

The CMP program faculty also collaborate with teacher-learners in designing the other components of the assessment and evaluation program, including the benchmarks, the evaluation rubric, a capstone experience, and the grading process. Benchmarks happen every six to eight weeks. Their purpose is to provide teacher-learners with the opportunity to share their work and receive feedback from a faculty member and three or four peers. Members of benchmark groups are self-selected. Each group designs the benchmark experience by deciding how to use the time allotted. Teacher-learners submit a written summary of their work to all benchmark members prior to a benchmark. These sessions consist mostly of coaching, suggesting, and sharing expertise and experience.

Teacher-learners collaborate with faculty in creating the program evaluation rubric already mentioned with specific behavioral descriptions that relate to each of the CMP program goals. This rubric is designed at the beginning of the second semester of the fifteen-month program, after teacher-learners have had a chance to become familiar with program goals and ideals. After the rubric is designed, teacher-learners plot themselves on each dimension and collect artifacts that document their evaluation. They then share this self-evaluation with a faculty member during a one-on-one conference. With faculty guidance they also distill future goals and brainstorm strategies to obtain these goals. Also during this conference, notes are made about the effectiveness of the rubric and questions about its criteria. After all teacher-learners have had their individual self-evaluation conferences, the rubric is revisited. All comments and questions that stemmed from the initial evaluation sessions are brought to light and the rubric is rewritten. Teacher-learners report that this work session often is extremely productive and meaningful. From their personal experience with the evaluation process, they have a much deeper understanding of evaluation and what makes an effective instrument.

By the end of the program, the capstone, a written piece documenting teacher change, is completed. One aspect of the capstone is called the "journey piece." In this piece teachers document the pathway that they have traveled with regard to change, that is, change in practice, beliefs, knowledge, etc. To enable this process, faculty help teacher-learners do a "subtotaling" (i.e., what do I know now that I didn't know before about teaching, children, and beliefs). These subtotals are completed each month or so throughout the year. A faculty member meets teacher-learners in their classrooms one time per month. They share their journey pieces and receive feedback on their synthesis, reflections, and actions. Subtotals provide a mechanism for synthesizing their work for the capstone.

Another example illustrates a more limited effort to involve teacher-learners in assessment. In two courses at Mansfield University of Pennsylvania, a graduate class on supervision and an undergraduate course on emerging literacy, rubrics are used to both define and evaluate assignments. The rubrics, often developed in collaboration with students, contain criteria to evaluate both the process of learning and the final product. For example, in the supervision course at the beginning of a Web-based cooperative learning project, the whole class develops a rubric to evaluate each small group's research and presentation. Students use the rubric to guide their work and to gather self and peer feedback; the instructor uses the same rubric to evaluate students' learning processes and final products. In the emerging literacy course, rubrics are used to explain two writing assignments, a picture book and a philosophy paper. The rubrics are also used in a multiple step assessment process, including self and peer assessment and instructor evaluation.

CONCLUDING THOUGHTS

This chapter about power and empower is not complete without discussing possible negative reactions to the changes proposed. Like P–12 teachers, teacher educators often ignore organizational and political issues that may impact their work. In our enthusiasm for improving our teaching we may not anticipate others' reactions.

A first caution concerns students, who may react negatively to invitations to share power with their teachers. Many college students have had years of success learning in traditional classrooms and may be comfortable with traditional roles of teachers and students. They are frequently critical of teacher educators who refuse to tell them exactly what they are expected to learn and how they will be graded. Some students may enjoy the opportunity to participate more actively in their college classroom but may remain wary of assuming more responsibility or making choices in the context of a traditional system of grading. In addition, some practicing teachers working in schools promoting a transmission model of teaching may believe that constructivist approaches are impractical in their work context.

A second caution concerns the reactions of faculty colleagues or administrators. Teacher educators may feel uncertain about how much power to share with students especially if they work with colleagues who do not embrace their constructivist philosophy. Teacher educators, who share power with their students, can anticipate that a course will not proceed exactly as they envision it. Factors such as students' habits of passivity or their lack of experience or maturity may mitigate against students making good decisions, and thus teacher educators struggle with deciding how much control to give to students. Some teacher educators may have legitimate, self-serving concerns; such as the impact experimental teaching methods may have on their own tenure and promotion. They may worry that others will view them as less competent if they deviate from the traditional teacher role. For example, it is traditionally assumed that some students will do poorly if faculty maintain high standards, and some faculty speak with pride if students regard them as "tough" graders. By contrast, if a constructivist approach results in all or most students earning high grades, faculty may worry that it appears that they have lowered standards rather than simply taught well. Also, teacher educators may be concerned about students' evaluations of their teaching since in most institutions students' opinions are used as indicators of good teaching in the tenure and promotion processes. Since students have due process rights, faculty must also be able to defend their grading procedures before their peers. Finally, faculty may find that sharing power with students is more time consuming. Although many colleges and universities state that teaching is of paramount importance, many tend to promote more rapidly those that publish. Using constructivist approaches to teaching and assessment may exacerbate the problem many faculty have with finding time to write about their teaching and research.

A final caution concerns the compatibility of constructivist approaches with higher education institutions and P–12 schools as they are currently structured. Schools and higher education institutions are hierarchical organizations with an emphasis on competition between individuals, both students and faculty. Structures of domination and control have been considered the backbone of efficient organizations for several centuries. Constructivist approaches, however, emphasize community and collaboration. Richardson (1997) notes that cognitive constructivist approaches with a focus on individualism have been more readily accepted in schools than Vygotskian sociocultural approaches. "Perhaps the reason for this is that such programs [based on Vygotskian theories] could not really be developed within schools as they exist today. Thinking of learning as a sociocultural process and teaching with conscious moral intent would require rethinking the nature of communities within and outside the school, as well as radically altering power relationships" (Oakes & Lipton, 1999, p. 11). "Sociocultural theories threaten those who want schools to represent only one culture's view of the world—only one group's way of knowing. These theories also call into question traditional teaching practices such as lecturing and having students work alone" (p. 78).

These cautions are offered not to discourage teacher educators from sharing power with teacher-learners, but rather to remind teacher educators and teachers that teaching is viewed as a political activity, especially when teaching is focused on empowering learners to construct knowledge and to act on their new understandings.

REFERENCES

Acheson, K. A., & Gall, M. Damien. (1992). *Techniques in the Clinical Supervision of Teachers: Preservice and Inservice Applications.* New York: Longman.

Belenky, M. F., Clinchy, B. M., Goldberger, N. R., & Tarule, J. M. (1986). *Women's Ways of Knowing: The Development of Self, Voice, and Mind.* Stockbridge, MA: Basic Books.

Chawszczewski, D. (1999, April). *Grading and Constructivist Teaching.* Paper presented at the annual meeting of the American Educational Research Association, Montreal, Canada.

Delpit, L. D. (1993). The Silenced Dialogue: Power and Pedagogy in Educating Other People's Children. In L. Weis & M. Fine (Eds.), *Beyond Silenced Voices: Class, Race, and Gender in United States Schools* (pp. 119–139). Albany, NY: State University of New York Press.

Goodman, J. (1992). *Elementary Schooling for Critical Democracy.* Albany, NY: State University of New York Press.

Guyton, E. M. (2000). Powerful Teacher Education Programs. In J. D. McIntyre & D. M. Byrd (Eds.), *Teacher Education Yearbook VIII: Research on Effective Models for Teacher Education* (pp. ix–xii). Thousand Oaks, CA: Corwin Press.

Hall, G. E., & Hord, S. M. (1984). *Change in Schools: Facilitating the Process.* Albany, NY: State University of New York Press.

Jarvis, P. (1997). Power and Personhood in Teaching. *Studies in the Education of Adults, 29*(1), 82–92.

Knowles, M. (1990). *The Adult Learner: A Neglected Species.* Houston, TX: Gulf Publishing.

Lambert, L., Walker, D., Zimmerman, D. P., Cooper, J. E., Lambert, M. D., Gardner, M. E., & Slack, P. J. Ford. (1995). *The Constructivist Leader.* New York: Teachers College Press.

Lortie, D. C. (1975). *School Teacher: A Sociological Study.* Chicago, IL: University of Chicago Press.

McNeil, L. M. (2000). Creating New Inequalities: Contradictions of Reform. *Phi Delta Kappan, 81*(10), 728–734.

Mayer-Smith, J. A., & Mitchell, I. J. (1997). Teaching about Constructivism: Using Approaches Informed by Constructivism. In V. Richardson (Ed.), *Constructivist Teacher Education: Building a World of New Understandings* (pp. 129–153). Washington, DC: The Falmer Press.

Moll, L. C., & Greenberg, J. B. (1990). Creating Zones of Possibilities: Combining Social Contexts for Instruction. In L. Moll (Ed.), *Vygotsky and Education: Instructional Implications and Applications of Sociohistorical Psychology* (pp. 319–348). New York: Cambridge University Press.

Oakes, J., & Lipton, M. (1999). *Teaching to Change the World.* Boston: McGraw-Hill.

O'Loughlin, M. (1992). Engaging Teachers in Emancipatory Knowledge Construction. *Journal of Teacher Education, 43*(5), 336–346.

Payne, K. E., & Cangemi, J. P. (1998). Power and the Esteemed Professorate. *Education, 118*(3), 394–406.

Peterman, F. (1997). The Lived Curriculum of Constructivist Teacher Education. In V. Richardson (Ed.), *Constructivist Teacher Education: Building a World of New Understandings* (pp. 154–163). Washington, DC: The Falmer Press.

Richardson, V. (1996). The Role of Attitudes and Beliefs in Learning to Teach. In J. Sikula (Ed.), *Handbook of Research on Teacher Education* (pp. 102–119). New York: Simon & Schuster Macmillan.

Richardson, V. (1997). Constructivist Teaching and Teacher Education: Theory and Practice. In V. Richardson (Ed.), *Constructivist Teacher Education: Building a World of New Understandings* (pp. 3–14). Washington, DC: The Falmer Press.

Richert, A. E. (1992). Voice and Power in Teaching and Learning to Teach. In L. Valli (Ed.), *Reflective Teacher Education: Cases and Critiques* (pp. 187–197). Albany, NY: State University of New York Press.

Routman, R. (1994). *Invitations: Changing as Teachers and Learners K–12* (2nd ed.). Portsmouth, NH: Heinemann.

Teets, S. T., & Starnes, B. A. (1996). Foxfire: Constructivism for Teachers and Learners. *Action in Teacher Education, 18*(2), 31–39.

Vadeboncoeur, J. A. (1997). Child Development and the Purpose of Education: A Historical Context for Constructivism in Teacher Education. In V. Richardson (Ed.), *Constructivist Teacher Education: Building a World of New Understandings* (pp. 15–37). Washington, DC: The Falmer Press.

Valli, L. (Editor). (1992). *Reflective Teacher Education: Cases and Critiques.* Albany, NY: State University of New York Press.

Wasserman, S. (1990). *Players in the Primary Classroom: Empowering Children through Active Learning.* New York: Teachers College Press.

Weis, L., & Fine, M. (Eds.). (1993). *Beyond silenced voices: Class, race, and gender in United States schools.* Albany, NY: State University of New York Press.

Wiggins, G., & McTighe, J. (1998). *Understanding by Design.* Alexandria, VA: Association for Supervision and Curriculum Development.

Wigginton, E. (1975). *Moments: The Foxfire Experience* (ERIC Document Reproduction Service No. ED120089).

Wigginton, E. (1989). Foxfire Grows Up. *Harvard Educational Review, 59*(1), 24–49.

Professional Background: Teresa Harris

Like many of my colleagues, I've considered myself a constructivist because I read Piaget, linked field experiences to education classes, and employed a workshop approach in my classes. During the time that I worked with the Commission that created this document, I began to critically reflect on what it meant to be a constructivist teacher educator. Reading as I wrote my own chapter, reading the work of my new colleagues, talking and listening respectfully as we sounded out ideas and beliefs provided me new ways of thinking about constructivism.

However, when we decided to provide examples from our own work with students I had to reconsider what I was really doing with my university students. Hearing what my colleagues were doing in their courses provided me with both the encouragement and the vision for what I might accomplish. I've reconsidered the importance of student voice, authentic engagement with course content, and what it means to use the best practices I advocate for my students. Planning for an undergraduate methods course, team teaching with my colleagues, challenging advanced graduate students is more challenging than ever before. But with the increased demands associated with practicing what I preach, my students and I have learned far more than I dared imagine.

Critical Thinking and Multiple Perspectives in Constructivist Teacher Education

Teresa Harris

It is the nature of people to think, constructing understandings based on their lived experiences. However, the human mind spontaneously experiences itself as in tune with reality, accurately observing and recording those experiences. It takes a special intervening process to produce the kind of self-criticalness that enables the mind to effectively and constructively question its own creations. For teacher education students, the many years they have spent as students in countless classrooms have provided opportunities for them to construct understandings of knowledge and what it means to know a variety of academic subjects as well as how this knowledge can be taught to learners. Unfortunately their conceptual understandings of academic content knowledge is not always accurate (Barton, 1997; Carpenter, Fennema, Peterson, Chiang, & Loef, 1989; Driver, Guesne, & Tiberghien, 1985; Gardner, 1991) and conceptions of teaching and learning may be based more on traditional models than current research (Lortie, 1975). As our individual students come together in our own classrooms, they frequently experience surprise at the different perspectives other students bring with them as well as the constructivist methods that we employ. The dialectical interplay between thinking critically about their own positions and then critically considering the multiple perspectives of others allows our teacher-learners to construct new, more comprehensive understandings of knowledge and what it means to know.

To rationally consider one's own understanding in light of the understandings of others suggests a moral dimension of constructivism. The tools of critical thinking allow us to question what is knowledge from the vantage point of other perspectives. No single definition is considered adequate until others are examined with the same scrutiny and rigor. This suggests that the multiple positions and perspectives from the powerful as well as disenfranchised, the experienced as well as the novice, the worldly as well as the provincial, must be examined and reflected upon. Based on both critical thought and reflection, action is then taken. As our teacher education students think critically about their own perspectives and the perspectives of others and then reflect on what teaching and learning means for all students in P–12 classrooms, they are guided by a moral purpose to teach students to read both the word and the world (Wink, 2000).

While the skills of critical thinking allow us to think deeply, an examination of multiple perspectives broadens the scope of our thinking to take into account the varying ways that people construct knowledge. When considering this side of the dialectic, we must consider the various perspectives people hold regarding education and what is means to teach and learn. Culture, language, race and class influence perspectives on what counts as knowledge and how learners come to know both inside and outside the school walls. In addition, we have to remember that the very content we teach reflects various perspectives across time and place.

This chapter examines what it means to think critically in light of the multiple perspectives others hold towards teaching and learning. Grounded in the work of Piaget and Vygotsky, it begins with a discussion of what it means to know as an individual and as a member of a group. The next section focuses on the key features associated with critical thinking: specific skills, application of skills, and critical spirit. Following this is a discussion of five principles of learning as they reflect an understanding of the multiple perspectives students bring into classrooms. The final section includes a variety of examples of how this dialectic is being put into practice in teacher education programs.

A Critical Perspective

For Piaget (1977), knowledge is constructed by individuals as they act on the objects within their environments. Through acts of assimilation and accommodation in response to contradictory experiences that create disequilibrium, individuals test their theories of how the world works. If the current theory works—fine. However, if the theory doesn't answer the question, the individual may choose to ignore the discrepancy and continue operating under the same working theory. Or, the individual may hold competing theories but state specific conditions for which each theory is appropriate. Finally the individual may construct a new, more encompassing theory that addresses the contradiction. It is important to note that the discrepant event that evokes the disequilibrium for any given individual is also a construction of the individual since, according to Piaget, the events in and of themselves are not discrepant. The discrepancy lies in the relationship between or among the individual's competing theories or interpretations of events (Fosnot, 1996). When teacher-learners are presented with a beaker of ice, a thermometer, and rock salt, they readily predict that the temperature of the ice is around the freezing point. However, when asked to predict the change in temperature when rock salt is added, some students will predict an increase while others will predict a decrease in temperature. For those students predicting an increase in temperature, disequilibrium is evidenced as they watch the mercury descend. Puzzled by this unexpected result, they begin to reason out loud. Many students talk about seeing chemicals on highways leaving puddles, suggesting they believe those chemicals heated the snow or ice sufficiently to create the resulting change in matter. Pondering other possibilities, like chemicals decreasing the temperature of the road, or considering other examples, like adding rock salt to ice when making ice cream, shifts their attention in ways that allow them to examine competing theories to explain the temperature decrease.

While Piaget focused his attention on contradiction and equilibration within the individual, Vygotsky (1986) focused his attention on the dialectical relationship between the individual and the social world. For him, individuals spontaneously construct concepts as they reflect on their everyday experiences. Scientific concepts are constructed from the interactions between a less mature learner and a more mature learner. The meeting of spontaneous concepts and the scientific concepts occurs as the adult interacts with the child in the child's zone of proximal development which is bounded by the actual and potential levels of development. According to Vygotsky, "the most effective learning occurs when the adult draws the child out to the jointly constructed 'potential' level of performance" (as cited in Bickmore-Brand, 1993, p. 49). To support development within the zone, Wood, Bruner, & Ross (1976) have noted that adults scaffold experiences so that the young learner has the assistance needed to successfully meet the challenges inherent in the experiences. Bodrova and Leong (1996) point out that the developmental accomplishments that result from these interactions between children and adults are outgrowths of these social situations that include both the social contexts in which the experiences occur and the ways children react to these contexts. In returning to the ice and rock salt example, we note the teacher-learners' are most likely to change their inadequate theories related to temperature change when they engage in conversations with their more knowledgeable peers about what is happening and why. When left to figure things out for themselves, many students are successful. However, it is the reflection on the phenomenon in conjunction with more mature learners that leads to the construction of the most accurate scientific concepts.

So, while thinking is a uniquely individual act that occurs within each person, the multiple perspectives provided by the social interactions individuals have with others is also critical. Fosnot (1996) points out that, "We cannot understand an individual's cognitive structure without observing it interacting in a context, within a culture. But neither can we understand culture as an isolated entity affecting the structure, since all knowledge within the culture is only, to use Cobb's terminology, 'taken-as-shared'" (p. 24).

Since people are thinking beings, and their thinking develops into increasingly mature forms through development and interactions with others, what makes some thinking critical and other thinking uncritical? At the heart of critical thinking is the reflective questioning of common beliefs and explanations by carefully distinguishing beliefs that are reasonable and logical from those that lack adequate evidence or rational foundation to warrant belief (Paul, 1990). Some critical theorists focus their definitions around skills and dispositions while others have focused their attention on rationalism and absolutism. For example, Paul (1990) states, "Critical thinking is disciplined, self-directed thinking which exemplifies the perfections of thinking appropriate to a particular mode or domain of thinking." (p. 33). Siegel attends more closely to reason assessment and the critical spirit in his definition. For him, "Critical thinking involves skills and abilities which facilitate or make possible the appropriate assessment of reasons; it involves dispositions, habits of mind, and character traits as well. (p. 2). A transformative vision of critical thinking, termed constructive thinking, has been proposed by Thayer-Bacon (2000). Examination of the contributions from gender theories, difference theories, and radical feminist theories, Thayer-Bacon highlights the importance of developing personal voice in emotionally safe environments that allow each person the freedom to speak and be heard. Her constructive thinking model is based on the assumption that "knowers are social beings who cannot be separated from what is known; it is also supported by an assumption that knowers are not disembodied minds but are people whose minds are directly connected to their bodies, as one bodymind" (p. 135).

As Lewontin and his colleagues (as cited in Fosnot, 1996) suggest, a dialectic exists between the thinking of the individual and the society in which the thinking occurs. Paul (1990) notes the purposes critical thinking plays within a given social group.

> *It comes in two forms. If the thinking is disciplined to serve the interests of a particular individual or group, to the exclusion of other relevant persons and groups, I call it* sophistic *or* weak sense *critical thinking. If the thinking is disciplined to take into account the interests of diverse persons or groups, I call if* fairminded *or* strong sense *critical thinking (p. 33).*

Strong sense critical thinking, then, is an ability to question deeply one's own framework of thought, to reconstruct the strongest versions of points of view and frameworks of thought opposed to one's own; and to reason dialectically to determine when one's own point of view is weakest and when an opposing point of view is strongest (Paul, 1990). For an individual, thinking critically goes beyond the development of reasoning to encompass the tools that lead to constructive thinking: emotions, intuition, and imagination. When teachers employ a dialogical style of teaching, they help students learn how to express their personal voices as well as develop their abilities to communicate with, and relate to, each other. Through the opportunities provided with dialogical teaching, students develop both communication skills and relational skills needed to be better thinkers. As they talk with one another, they can both express their understandings and correct misunderstandings through direct feedback, and in the process learn how to maintain relationships while thoughtfully considering the perspectives of one another (Thayer Bacon, 2000).

Using this definition, a first step is for teacher-learners to have opportunities to examine the ways they each think about teaching and learning using the particular skills associated with critical thinking. Next, they must have opportunities to share their individual thoughts with the members of the class, hearing the perspectives of others and considering their own understandings in light of those other positions. Finally, teacher-learners must reconsider their own positions using the information and arguments shared by others, deciding if they must accept, reject, or modify their understandings in light of the rational nature of the other positions presented in the group. If teacher-learners are taking into consideration the implications of their positions or their understandings related to teaching and learning for the good of all the children they will be teaching, these exercises and assignments are "strong-minded." However, if these class activities do nothing more than maintain the status quo in terms of educational practice or if they favor some groups of learners over others, the activities and the thinking they involve become nothing more than exercises in "soft-minded" thinking.

Key Features of Critical Thinking

Across the various definitions of critical thinking, common elements emerge: skills involved in thinking critically, the ability to apply those skills appropriately to a given question or problem, and the disposition to act in response to one's thinking.

Skills of Critical Thinking. Siegel (1997) has noted that a critical thinker is one with significant skill and ability with respect to the evaluation of reasons and arguments. "A critical thinker must have, then, both a solid understanding of the principles of reason assessment, and significant ability to utilize that understanding in order to evaluate properly beliefs, actions, judgments, and the reasons which are thought to support them" (p. 2). While the skills that permit a person to think critically vary with age and sophistication of the thinker as well as the context of the inquiry and the subject matter competence required to think critically about the topic under study (Fisher & Scriven, 1997), critical thinkers possess "an understanding of and an ability to formulate, analyze and assess the problem under consideration; the points of view involved; the assumptions made; the central concepts involved; the theories used; the evidence, data or reasons advanced; the interpretations and claims made; the inferences, reasoning, and lines of thought; and the implications and consequences involved" (Paul, 1990, p. 34).

Examining the many aspects of any given question or problem demands particular standards for the thinking to be critical. The standards for good thinking include relevance, accuracy, fairness, clarity, precision, specificity, consistency, logicalness, depth, completeness, and significance (Fisher & Scriven, 1997; Paul, 1990). Based on these standards, people are able to interpret and evaluate observations and communications, information and argumentation (Fisher & Scriven, 1997) and to appropriately assess the reasoning one uses for that interpretation and evaluation (Siegel, 1997).

Providing opportunities for our teacher learners to wrestle with the complex issues of education allows them to critically consider the realities of the professional world they are entering and the perspectives held by various stakeholders. Students at New Jersey City University are expected to respond to writing prompts that include, "Do you support the use of school uniforms?" These writing prompts go beyond assessments of writing ability to address students' ability to think critically about current issues.

Application of Skills. From a critical thinking perspective, knowledge is seen as systemic and holistic; the learner thinks through a recursive cycle of synthesis and analysis to examine the whole, take it apart, and then put it back together for further analysis. In the process of thinking about the content, student prejudices, biases, and misconceptions built up through actively constructed inferences embedded in prior experiences, are exposed. Correcting weaknesses in the thinking process itself requires a similar process of experience, critical reflection, and analysis that lead to new cycles of synthesis and analysis.

Since learning is essentially a public, communal, dialogical, and dialectical process, the role of the teacher is to create environments that support the public questioning of ideas and beliefs held by individual learners. The teacher focuses on significant content by raising live issues or real questions that stimulate analysis and assessment of the content. Because an in-depth understanding of content is used as an organizer of learning within and across subject matter domains, students need opportunities to examine the content from and the kinds of questions asked by the various discipline perspectives. Personal experiences that serve as foundations of student understanding are included in the content to be processed since both the student's perspective based on lived experience and the resulting conceptions and "misconceptions" must be synthesized and analyzed as part of the individual's knowledge construction.

However, even within a context of individual thought from interdisciplinary and multidisciplinary perspectives, the communal nature of learning demands the participation of others within the learning community. Teacher educators support their learners' construction of knowledge by providing opportunities for individuals to argue their personal understandings of content and allowing others to respond with their own constructions. From these experiences teacher-learners are challenged to articulate their positions in response to the perspectives of others with similar and different understandings based on their own lived experiences and understandings. As individuals respond to others' challenges to personal understandings and the reasoning behind those understandings, everyone within the community develops greater skill in identifying what is known and not known. Individuals then become better able to ascertain the inaccuracies in their own thinking as well as in the reasons that they choose to accept or reject alternative positions through these experiences. Recognizing that people bring experiences that are situated in contexts that have emotional meaning that can enrich and impede the ability to understand content from a purely rational perspective, the application of critical thinking skills is a major concern of teacher educators. We must start with the learners themselves and how they understand particular content or issues based on their own experiences, create a safe environment in which to express their unique personal voices, and then expand the conversation to address the many different perspectives various stakeholders hold on any given topic if we are to help learners accept or reject alternatives to their own positions.

One biology professor asked his students to write about an outdoor experience, event or place that had special meaning to them with the intent of helping the students connect to the natural world. This assignment set the stage for a discussion on habitat conservation, the use of natural resources, environmental pollution issues, and the need for environmental regulation. There was great variation among students' responses. Some talked about particular places they went to as children and lamented over changes that had already occurred. Others talked about hopes to return to places or shared experiences of returning and the rekindled memories of family and fun times. With responses in hand, the professor began class sessions addressing scientific concerns related to issues of overpopulation, loss of forest land, crops and orchards to housing developments, overcrowding of park spaces, strip mining, pollution of public waterways. These environmental issues were framed by the question, "What does it mean to you?" as the class discussed being unable to swim in old places or having beaches closed due to sewage spills. Global issues took on new significance as students began to see their own personal experiences were affected.

As they move from students studying content to students preparing to teach content, Berry College students write content autobiographies to discuss their prior experiences with those areas. For example, students are asked to reflect on their experience with school science, scientists, science in the media, and science teachers. They relate their earliest memories through their present experiences to explain what they think the study of science involves.

Critical Spirit

Beyond the skills of critical thinking and the domains to which that thinking is applied, is the inclination of individuals to think critically. Siegel (1997) defines the critical spirit as the attitudes, dispositions, habits of mind, and character traits that lead the person to actually engage in competent reason assessment. Paul (1990) suggests that these dispositions or special "traits of mind" include intellectual humility, intellectual courage, intellectual perseverance, intellectual integrity, and confidence in reason. Siegel's critical spirit and Paul's traits of mind reflect a focus on rational thought as the basis for action. Thayer-Bacon (2000) points out that it is the development of personal voice that moves individuals to, in fact, think and act critically. As she argues for a transformation from critical thinking to constructive thinking, she argues that rather than separating knowers from the known, we must recognize that, in fact, the knower cannot be separated from what is known.

When we teach our students academic content and the methods by which the content can be taught, our students may be inclined to think critically about that content or the effectiveness of the methods, particularly as they recall their own experiences as learners. However, when we focus only on an understanding of content and methods, without considering how the diverse learners in any given classroom may relate to that content and those methods, we are shortsighted in our efforts to educate both teacher-learners and P–12 students. When our own teaching emphasizes content and methods that are best suited for a particular group (e.g., white, middle-class, female student teachers) without recognizing the diversity those students will face in their own classrooms we limit critical thinking to technical reason.

Paul's (1990) concept of strong sense critical thinking moves beyond technical reason to the development of what he calls emancipatory reason. In his view, such reasoning cuts across clear-cut concepts of any given technical domain to move back and forth between opposing points of view. While this position may take into account the interests of diverse people or groups in reasoning, it falls short of effecting real change in educational practices that limit access to opportunity on the basis of race, culture, language, gender, or socioeconomic status.

Critical theorists (Leistyna, Woodrum, & Sherbom, 1996) want to confirm the voices of teachers and students, linking the purpose of schooling to a transformational vision of the future. From this perspective, the critical spirit is one in which students and teachers examine the values, assumptions, ideologies, and interests reflected in bodies of knowledge and representations, link that information to their own experiences, and subsequently pose the kinds of questions that include, "How is knowledge conceived?" and "Whose interests have been advanced by these forms of knowledge?"

MULTIPLE PERSPECTIVES

We come to teaching and learning as people who have experiences that are filtered through our respective cultures and languages, races, genders, and abilities. Having lived in particular historical times and in particular social, economic, and political contexts, we bring those experiences with us as well. Certainly our understandings of teaching and learning reflect those lived experiences and provide the great diversity that is found in classrooms across our country. But our unique experiences don't exist in a vacuum and as our perspectives meet differing perspectives the answers to the essential questions of, "What is teaching and learning?", "Who are teachers and learners?", and "What does it mean to know something?" may be different as well. Joan Wink (2000), in her study of critical pedagogy, points out that "education is rampant with complexities, contradictions, multiple realities, and change. It has taught me that I don't know everything" (p. 14). Teacher educators, preservice and in-service teachers, and students involved in critical teaching and learning must "examine the values, assumptions, ideologies, and interests reflected in bodies of knowledge and representations, link such information to their own experiences, and subsequently pose questions such as, 'How is knowledge conceived? Whose interests have been advanced by these forms of knowledge? How has what we have defined as knowledge changed over time?'" (Leistyna, et al., 1996, p. 5).

Nieto (1999) identified five principles of learning that provide a way to consider multiple perspectives within the theory of constructivism. The five principles of learning are: "learning is actively constructed; learning emerges from and builds on experience; learning is influenced by cultural differences; learning is influenced by the context in which it occurs; and learning is socially mediated and develops within a culture and community" (p. 3). The following discussion focuses on these principles as they support the multiple perspectives of learners in both P–12 and university classrooms.

Active Constructions

Learning as an active construction, a basic principle of constructivism, suggests learner agency. Teachers operating from this perspective see their learners as capable of thinking and reasoning about complex issues and ideas. As a result, instructional practices themselves reflect more complex interactions as students engage in explorations, investigations, and dialogue while teachers serve in a facilitative role. However, too often teaching is no more than the reproduction of socially sanctioned information transmitted to learners as though they were empty vessels. Implicit in the practice of teaching as telling is the notion that learning is mainly habit formation. In this model pre-requisite information is basic to the acquisition of further information that builds up over time to become a body of knowledge. Only learners who possess sufficient ability and experiences to allow them to learn what we have to teach may be viewed as able to benefit from more active, exploratory, investigative experiences. However, learners perceived to be lacking in ability or experiences need to go back to more basic experiences or receive remediation. If we take this position and employ these practices, then we privilege some learners over others, suggesting that we don't really believe that all students can learn due to either a lack of innate ability or the necessary experiential background to learn what we are trying to teach.

When we assume that some learners lack innate ability based on their ability to adapt to our classrooms and when they demonstrate what they know in ways that are inconsistent with our own particular frame of reference, we fail to take into account the different ways that learners construct meaning and express what they know. "Cognitive development is not a static, innate dimension of human beings; it is always interactive with the environment, always in the process of being reshaped and reformed. We are not simply victims of genetically determined, cognitive predispositions" (Kincheloe & Steinberg, 1996, p. 173). If we are not critically considering the unique experiences that shape the learning of our students prior to our receiving them in our classrooms, we fail appreciate the perspectives that they bring to the learning environment.

The critical questions we need to ask ourselves are, "Do we really believe that all students construct knowledge for themselves or do we believe that some students need us to tell them information or provide them with particular skills before they can construct understandings? At what point can these students begin to actively construct meaning?" At issue here may be the incongruence between our own perspectives on what it means to know something and the perspectives of our learners. If we believe that all learners are capable of generating wonderful, powerful ideas (Duckworth, 1996; Meier, 1995) the questions we invite them to ask and consider change dramatically as we reflect on "How do we know what we think we know? Whose viewpoint are we viewing? How is one thing connected to another? How else might it have been? And, finally, what difference does it make?" (as cited in Nieto, 1999, p. 5–6).

These are the questions I asked my graduate students in the JMU course, Teaching, Learning, and Curriculum. These teachers were pursuing a degree in Educational Leadership and represented early childhood, middle grades, secondary education, special education, physical education and music. The perspectives that were shared throughout the course highlighted their diversity based on gender, race, culture, SES, and age as well as their professional experiences in teaching their respective content to particular populations of students. Observing their interactions in whole class and small group discussions, analyzing points of contention by asking more questions, and sharing additional perspectives from relevant areas of professional literature provided a variety of ways for me as a teacher educator to examine the diverse understandings of these teacher-learners. To summatively assess what had been learned in the course, I asked the students to design a final synthesis project that would capture what they understood about teaching, learning, and curriculum. While the traditional final papers were an acceptable response to the assignment, other projects included a simulated lesson based on Joan Wink's (2000) problem posing activity, a collage of teaching-learning-curriculum relationships, and an extended metaphor based on "Life is like a box of chocolates". As the class members listened to the presentations, they were struck by the depth of understanding expressed in the various representations.

Experiences

All too often we say that experience is the bridge between what learners know and what we will teach. This is based on the assumption that all learners have prior experiences upon which further educational experiences can be based. However, our actions don't always match our words as we watch some children enter school prepared for the academic experiences their teachers will provide, while others aren't "ready" because they lack the particular kinds of experiences that make the transition between home and school a smooth one.

In examining the multiple perspectives on what it means to know and the experiences that lead to and support knowing, we must critically reflect on our own positions related to experience and learning. Are we saying that all experiences serve as the foundation of learning or do particular experiences support learning and others "get in the way"? How do we know what learning emerges from and builds on experience? Is some learning more valuable than other learning? Is some experience more foundational than other experience? Are there some experiences necessary to prepare students for academic success? Bourdieu (1986) points out the "cultural capital" that some students have and Delpit (1995) speaks of the "culture of power" in which some children are reared. Both authors are referring to the fact that while some children grow up in a culture that privileges them to the kinds of experiences that make schooling a successful enterprise, other children have never "explicitly learned the rules of the game for academic success" (Delpit, 1995). When examining constructivism through the lens of multiple perspectives, the focus needs to be on what children do have rather than what they do not have. Teacher attitude towards students' identities, previous knowledge, and experiences relates directly to the kinds of practices and climate they create for learning (Rios, 1994). Educators need to accept as valid the kinds of knowledge and experiences students bring with them to school. Teachers then proceed to build on students' experiences and introduce them to modes of being and acting in the world that are new to their experience. Grumet (1992) concludes that it is the relation, "the dance between the student's experience and knowledge", that separates education from training or indoctrination (p. 181).

Do we believe all learners have experiences or does our valuing of particular kinds of experiences support some learners and disenfranchise others? The challenge in teacher education is to challenge our students to think critically about their own presuppositions and reflect on the ways they can identify learners' experiences and use them as a starting point for providing other experiences that build understandings as well as provide the cultural capital that will allow them to participate as informed citizens in a democratic society.

Cultural Differences

While learning is influenced by intra-individual differences, it is also affected by cultural differences. These differences affect how minds work within the cultural, economic, social, and political contexts in which individuals are situated. Styles of learning as they initially appear in child rearing practices and as they become generalized in family and community values provide both individual and cultural identities for learners. It becomes imperative that teachers recognize that cultural orientation towards learning varies. When what is valued within the families of students is in conflict with the Western European notion of independence and learning on one's own rather than a more interdependent approach that values learning through observation, the discontinuity between home and school challenges the very identity of the students.

There are several reasons we appear to have trouble taking the perspective of others in what we value as learning style. The discrepancy we experience between cultural difference and ideals of equality and fair play proves troublesome for some. Others want to avoid the notion of cultural difference as determining learning ability for groups of students. However for some, the failure to recognize the impact of cultural difference on how students go about learning can result in seeing students as deficient in their abilities to learn. "Multiple perspectives on development need to be advanced so that educators move away from a deficit explanation of academic achievement. In order to do this, educators need to begin with a knowledge of the values and the cognitive socialization in the cultures of origin of students (Nieto, 1999, p. 10).

To understand others, we must first know ourselves. This requires exposure to our own traditions to better understand ourselves as well as other traditions so that we may understand the source of the cultural forms embedded within us (Howard, 1999; Kincheloe & Sternberg, 1996). However, our own conceptions of self and others only becomes critical when we also examine the social and historical forces that place these understandings within the social, historical, and political contexts of our particular place and time (Kincheloe & Sternberg, 1996).

Because we all inherit at some level various beliefs, values, and ideologies we must critically examine those traditions rather than merely transmit them; we must examine the current context in which children live and the tools they will need to become active, critical, and responsible citizens. "Critical in this sense, implies that both teachers and students will be able to understand, analyze, and work to affect the sociohistorical and economic realities that shape their lives" (Leistyna et al., 1996, p. 109).

In the process of coming to understand ourselves and our learners we must ask questions, seeking out the conflict inherent in our practice and lived experiences. The very way we detect problems, ask questions, and pursue answers can help us better understand and address the social conditions, cognitive assumptions, and power relations inherent in schooling and that may lead to innovations that promote student insight, sophisticated thinking, and social justice (Kincheloe & Sternberg, 1996). Students in JMU's early childhood program begin their first course by writing an Ecology of Human Development paper as a means for reflecting on their own lives across the four systems. Through a study of themselves within the context of family, community, nation, and international events, they become sensitive to the various influences that culture plays in defining who they are as individuals. Then, as they move into kindergarten classrooms, they are more sensitive the cultural diversity of the children within those classrooms and question more closely the practices employed by their cooperating teachers to support all children's learning.

Context

"The literal meaning of context is 'that which is braided together'" (Kincheloe & Steinberg , 1996, p. 188). Teaching and learning occur in particular contexts that extend beyond the classroom walls and braid together the identities of students with the expectations of schools. Students bring with them the particular identities that reflect their lives outside of school. Those identities are shaped by culture, race, gender, and language as they are situated within social, economic, historical, and political contexts. These factors, taken together create the diverse identities that students bring into the classroom. Within the classroom context are the expectations for academic success as well as the explicit and implicit codes of conduct established by teachers and school personnel. Teachers and learners are faced with the challenge of matching the expectations from inside and outside the school walls to create environments that support both learners and learning. When the context in which students learn is a caring and supportive one, respectful of student identities, students by and large learn (Nieto, 1999). However, the contradiction between cultural expectations and school expectations that define a person's identity can negatively impact one's desire to learn in ways that are considered "acceptable" by the dominant society. It becomes, therefore, imperative that teachers and learners engage in critical dialogues to generate their own ideas and values for the contexts they share rather than merely reproducing the ideas and values of the dominant groups that define schooling. As they reflect on the positions they inhabit and the locations from which they speak, teachers and learners are better able to take responsibility for their beliefs and actions.

Providing a context for what we know moves what learners know from their various perspectives outside of school into the academic conversation. Post-formal educators have begun to acknowledge that contextualization of what we know is more important than the content itself, arguing that "once a fabric of relevance has been constructed, content learning naturally follows" (Kincheloe & Sternberg, 1996, p. 189). Borrowing from Dewey, who points to the importance of the connections the learner is able to make among events, these theorists point to the importance of working with learners to move beyond what they know to connecting that knowledge with "the common experience of mankind" (Dewey, 1916). "Place, in other words, grounds our ways of seeing by providing the contextualization of the particular—a perspective often erased in formal forms of abstract thinking" (Kincheloe & Sternberg, 1996, p. 190).

As teacher educators, we need to discover what our teacher-learners know about teaching and learning and then create situations in which they will be challenged to reconsider their own understandings in light of alternative theories. Students in the early childhood teacher certification program at JMU have multiple field experiences in kindergarten and primary grade classrooms. In seminars and courses they have an opportunity to discuss their experiences in light of developmentally appropriate practices (Bredekamp & Copple, 1998). Many of these students bring their traditional experiences and expectations for learning into their methods courses. However, as faculty model a variety of constructivist approaches and strategies throughout the course of the program, it's not uncommon for us to watch lights come on for students as they connect the value of playful activity to learning. After several weeks in a kindergarten practicum, one student lamented, "When are they going to do something besides just play?" Her inquiry project for this particular term was an observational study of sociodramatic play. As she concluded her presentation to the class at the end of the semester she remarked, "I feel stupid now that I even asked that question." After completing an assignment in a constructivist math methods course that involved students in using games and integrating mathematical experiences throughout the day, one student remarked,

"Oh now I get it!" and began including more child-centered activities in his field placements.

Social Mediation and the Role of Culture and Community

"We can't understand an individual's cognitive structures without observing it interacting in a context, a culture . . . [C]ultural knowledge that is assumed to be held by members of the culture is in reality only a dynamically evolving, negotiated interaction of individual interpretations, transformations, and constructions. At most, cultural knowledge can only be assumed, or 'taken-as-shared,' by its members. Yet cultural knowledge is a whole larger than the sum of the individual cognitions. It has a structure of its own that interacts with the individuals who also are constructing it" (Fosnot, 1996, p. 24). Given the dialectical relationship between the individual and culture, teasing out the multiple perspectives of teachers within their cultural frames of reference and the diversity of students' cultural frames of reference becomes increasingly challenging if the goal is to educate all learners.

Vygotsky recognized that development and learning are mediated by culture and society. From a Vygotskian perspective, "if learning can be influenced by social mediation, then conditions can be created in schools that can help most students learn" (Nieto, 1999, p. 15). To create these conditions, we need to start with an understanding of Vygotsky's zone of proximal development or ZPD. According to Vygotsky (1978), the ZPD is "the distance between the actual developmental level as determined by independent problem solving and the level of potential development as determined through problem solving under adult guidance or in collaboration with more capable peers" (p. 86). Teachers must, therefore, understand the differences between home and school culture, language, and communication patterns to meet the needs of all learners within their respective zones. Without this understanding, children with discontinuous patterns of learning are more likely to be perceived by teachers as slow or culturally deprived, leading teachers to assume that these children are incapable of learning when in fact the home and school definitions of "learning" may be the real difference.

Teachers need to first examine the multiple social contexts in which their students live and the ways those contexts help shape student performance. Bartolome suggests that this examination is actually a process of developing a "deepening awareness of the sociopolitical and economic realities that shape the lives of learners. It is the process by which teachers come to better understand possible linkages between the broader political, economic, and social variables and learners' academic performance at the classroom level to efficiently create, adopt, and modify teaching strategies that simultaneously respect and challenge learners from diverse cultural groups in a variety of learning environments" (1996, p. 235). Within this context, no perspective is privileged over another, but the guiding focus is on social justice and the way unequal power relations in school and society destroy the promise of democratic life (Bartolome, 1996).

In reviewing culturally responsive teaching strategies with culturally diverse groups of learners, Bartolome (1996) found that more important than the strategies themselves were the equalizing of power relations between teachers and learners as they worked together to implement the strategies. For example, Bartolome points out that teachers in the Kamehameha Education Project learned to recognize, value, use, and build on students' prior knowledge and skill to create a comfort zone in which the learners could successfully demonstrate their competence as learners. As teachers saw their students' progress, they began to question their own views of subjugated students and to employ strategies that allowed them to work with their students in more equitable and meaningful ways. However, when the project strategies were transported to other student populations, the same positive student results did not occur (Vogt, Jordan & Tharp, 1987), suggesting that more than the practices themselves accounted for student success (Bartolomem, 1996).

Developing case studies of learners from a variety of social contexts provides teacher learners with opportunities to examine the diverse realities that affect students' lives. As teacher educators model culturally responsive teaching strategies (Gay, 2000) and strategic teaching (Jones, Palinscar, Ogle, & Carr, 1987) in methods courses they provide tools teacher learners can take into their own classrooms to meet their students' learning needs. Finally, as teacher learners are able to work collaboratively with cooperating teachers and university supervisors to reflect on teaching practices, the equity that may develop across the three roles may create the comfort zones teacher learners need to demonstrate their own competence as beginning teachers.

The Process of Learning and Teaching

"In examining the social construction of knowledge, values, and inter-action across 'difference', the idea is not for teachers to be abusive by silencing students or placing their identities on trial. Instead, the process is to be unsettling only to the degree that it forces all of those involved to recognize their role in accepting and perpetuating oppres-sion of any kind. Critically examining their own perspectives enables everyone to avoid the debilitating ramifications of relativism in which any and all positions and practices are equally acceptable, that is, they are simply different. The critical reflection, debate, and negotiation in such dialogue affords the necessary conditions for all classroom partic-ipants to act as knower, learner, and teacher, and to reach beyond their own boundaries. This in turn creates space for a more critical and dem-ocratic exchange of ideas" (Leistyna, et al., 1996, p. 198). According to Bruner (1996), when learning is thought of as coming from reflections and discourse, dialogue is favored as a pedagogical approach. Teaching becomes more complex when learning is based on the idea that all stu-dents have the ability to think and reason. Rather than transmitting important knowledge to students that may reflect a single, frequently privileged perspective, this form of pedagogy suggests that teachers work with students so they can reflect, theorize, and create knowledge.

PROGRAM EXAMPLES

Critical thinking involves the reflective questioning of common beliefs or explanations. Through this reflective questioning, students examine their own perspectives in light of other perspectives, employ the skills of critical thinking to analyze arguments and discrepancies in logic, and reconstruct personal understandings that reflect the strongest rationales. Students in James Madison University's (JMU) early childhood education program begin examining their own perspectives as they consider how the various contexts of gender, culture, race, age, social class, religion, nationality, and family structure in which they live have contributed to their uniqueness. In the assignment, "Telling Our Stories", students then share their own stories of becoming aware of who they are, especially as they confront the differences between themselves and others. Through this experience, students begin a public conversation about prejudices they've experienced and held. Through the telling of personal stories, students explore "self" as the object of another's prejudice or stereotyping.

Based on readings of prominent critical theorists such as Maxine Greene and Henry Giroux, teachers in Georgia State's Collaborative Master's Program (CMP) engage in a conversation about how the issues raised by these authors have been personally experienced. Personal reflection on oppression as students have experienced it serves as the foundation for their informal presentations to the group. Some presentations reflect deeply personal issues for teachers and their classrooms and these serve to help students move beyond accepting the status quo to question the bigger issues related to oppression and inequality in our society.

Another way CMP students critically examine who they are as teachers is through personal pedagogy papers. To make the "-ism's" more personal, in this assignment students must examine the various historical-philosophical traditions as they articulate who, what, and why they are in the world. Teachers approach these tasks in a variety of ways including looking at policies in their schools to see what the philosophical underpinnings are; writing and administering a questionnaire that gets at parental perspectives on a variety of learning issues; collecting articles from the popular press concerning educational issues and trying to decipher what "-isms" are motivating the article. Through this experience teachers analyze various perspectives as they are represented in the broader community to expose any biases and misconceptions that may be represented within the documents. From these multiple perspectives, students then critically reexamine their own statements and reasoning for bias that was not previously apparent.

Personal awareness, reflection, and critical examination of one's own beliefs and experiences are starting points for examining multiple perspectives. Engaging in conversations to hear the experiences of other students as well as critical examination of theoretical perspectives broaden students' awareness of diverse experiences that can impact teaching and learning. The next step for many teacher education students is to work with learners who are different from themselves.

The collaboration among JMU's middle grades faculty from literacy, special education, and multicultural education has resulted in a course that allows students to explore issues of diversity and literacy education through adolescent literature. Teacher-learners begin by reading *Tangerine* (Bloor, 2001), a contemporary novel that includes varied issues such as economic diversity, special needs, and cultural difference. Next, they examine diversity in a historical context, using group studies of books about the Holocaust, the Great Depression, and the Civil Rights movement. In groups of 4–6, these teacher-learners continue with a focused area of study in contemporary literature on Latina/o issues, conflicts between cultures, gay and lesbian issues, African American families, or poverty and the homeless. Finally, with a partner, they select 2 books from a list of fiction about special needs issues. As a result of this experience these teacher-learners are able to explore their own types of personal diversity and consider their own racial identity. They reconsider prior assumptions and reflect on their general lack of knowledge in many of the areas of study. Their concurrent field experiences provide a way to reflect directly on the literature and classroom connections to the issues being raised. The approach across disciplines encourages them to try to make sense of their own professional stance on diversity issues in their own classrooms.

Students at Mills College read and consider multiple perspectives regarding how children learn, ways to teach literacy, and how to judge the content and appropriateness of literature. The goal is not that students have one idea about the best way but that they become independent thinkers about questions of education, pedagogy, content, instruction, and who have sufficient knowledge and experience to consider more than one perspective in order to take a critical stance toward their own practice and ideas. The evidence of this ability is available overwhelmingly in their final portfolio projects that mark the end of their first year in the program and also in their final research projects.

To provide field experiences that offer greater diversity than the local classrooms typically provide in the Shenandoah Valley of Virginia, students in JMU's Early Childhood Education participate in a service learning project. Through this 10-hour experience students work in settings with individuals or groups of people whose values, lifestyles and overall life experiences are different from their own. Students choose among work as drivers for patients with AIDS, Big Brothers-Big Sisters, children living in the local homeless shelter, or with ESL or special needs children. Journals kept during this experience are shared throughout the semester as yet another perspective on teaching and learning in diverse settings beyond the classroom.

Unlike the transmission model of education that privileges particular perspectives to the exclusion of other relevant perspectives, an individual working from a critical framework examines multiple perspectives with an open mind and evaluates those perspectives based on critical thought, weighing the evidence and making reasoned decisions. Particularly for teacher-learners who are the product of a transmission model of education, the opportunity to work with classroom teachers who model the examination of multiple perspectives to inform practice is an essential experience.

Cooperating teachers in the Georgia State University undergraduate program model their value of others' perspectives to inform practice as exemplified when one student teacher in the program received encouragement from her cooperating teacher to visit another classroom to see how learning centers were being used. This particular cooperating teacher went beyond offering the student the opportunity to examine another perspective when she went on to comment, "I look forward to learning from you," demonstrating her willingness to consider the novice's experience as a valid source of information for herself.

The multiple perspectives of students, professors, and classroom teachers come together in JMU's Middle Grades Education program. A team approach that includes a faculty member from reading, special education, and middle grades education work together with classroom teachers to link university classes to field experiences so that students can learn first hand about collaboration and how to meet the diverse needs of middle grades learners. During the first semester of the program, teacher-learners observe students in inclusive classroom settings. Observations and questions that are recorded in journals serve as the starting point for discussion in their university classes on diversity and characteristics of special needs learners.

In the following semesters students continue field experiences in inclusive settings, working with cooperating teachers to develop and teach lessons that respect the diverse needs of their learners. Throughout this experience, students read the relevant professional literature, discuss their observations and experiences with peers and university faculty, and reflect on their teaching with classroom teachers. As a result of this critical thought, students are increasingly able to think like teachers, explaining what they are doing and justifying their actions based on their examination of the multiple perspectives that inform teaching. As they enter the profession, they are better able to use their constructed understandings based on critical reflection in powerful ways to communicate their beliefs to more experienced colleagues.

CONCLUSION

The critical thinking/multiple perspectives dialectic reminds us that neither is sufficient to inform practice. We can think critically about many things; however, if there is no higher purpose for our thinking beyond the contemplative act, it is weak-minded. We may accept that there are multiple perspectives among teachers and learners, but if we fail to take those perspectives into account in ways that guide our interactions with others, we continue to perpetuate situations in which many learners become alienated from schooling and society. As we critically reflect on the multiple perspectives evident in both the content we teach and the learners in our classes, we are better able to move our society towards democratic action that empowers all its citizens.

In reflecting on her role as a teacher and teacher educator Joan Wink said, "I must continually challenge my long-held assumptions; let practice inform my theory; continually build theory that informs my practice; find new answers for new questions; grapple with multiple ways of knowing, listen, learn, reflect, and act . . . The trick is to learn from the contradictions, from the change, from the opposite . . . all of us need to reflect critically on our own experiences and those of others. Then, we need to connect these new thoughts to our own life in new ways" (Wink, 2000, p. 15). We, as teacher educators must begin by recognizing our own ideological inheritance and its relationship to our own beliefs and value structures, interests, and questions about our professional lives. To think about our own thinking involves understanding the way our consciousness is constructed and appreciating the forces that facilitate or impede our accommodations. We are never content with the ideas we have constructed regarding teaching and learning but rather, engage in an ongoing conversation with ourselves (Kincheloe & Sternberg, 1996).

The process we employ to move beyond where we currently are to where we long to go requires critical reflection of our current position, leading us to see beyond the obvious, to discover what is hidden or omitted, and question why. It requires an imagination to transcend the surface and move beyond realities to what might be (Greene, 1996; Kincheloe & Steinberg, 1996). For example, the multiple perspectives from

> "[f]eminist theory, Afrocentrism, and Native American ways
> of knowing have raised our consciousness concerning the role
> of emotion in learning and knowing . . . Self knowledge lays the
> foundation for all knowledge in these traditions, and a unified
> process of thinking has moved these traditions to appreciate the
> continuum of logic and emotion, mind and body, individual
> and nature, self and other" (Kincheloe & Sternberg, 1996, p.
> 185).

"As we critically consider the diverse ways of knowing, we move beyond simplistic, literal interpretations of what it means to know based solely on our own perspective towards a more holistic, integrated conception of knowledge based on multiple perspectives of others. Teachers who employ this constructivist process will be far better equipped to 'read' their classrooms and the requirements of educational bureaucracies. Such teachers will be prepared to articulate the contradictions between society's educational and social goals and the realities of school practice" (Kincheloe & Sternberg, 1996, p. 188).

REFERENCES

Bartolome, L. (1996). Beyond the Methods Fetish: Toward a Humanizing Pedagogy. In P. Leistyna, A. Woodrum, & S. A. Sherblom (Eds.), *Breaking Free: The Transformative Power of Critical Pedagogy* (pp. 229–252). Cambridge, MA: Harvard Educational Review.

Barton, K.C. (1997). Bossed Around by the Queen: Elementary Students' Understanding of Individuals and Institutions in History. *Journal of Curriculum and Supervision, 12*(4), 290–314.

Bickmore-Brand, J. (1993). *Language in Mathematics.* Portsmouth, NHY: Heinemann.

Bloor, E. (2001). *Tangerine.* NY: Scholastic Books.

Bodrova, E., & Leong, D. J. (1996). *Tools of the Mind: The Vygotskian Approach to Early Childhood Education.* Englewood Cliffs, NJ: Prentice Hall, Inc.

Bourdieu, P. (1986). The Forms of Capital. In J. G. Richardson (Ed.), *Handbook of Theory and Research for the Sociology of Education* (pp. 241–248). Westport, CT: Greenwood Press.

Bredekamp, S., & Copple, C. (Eds.). (1998). *Developmentally Appropriate Practice in Early Childhood Programs* (Rev. ed.). Washington, DC: National Association for the Education of Young Children.

Bruner, J. (1996). *The Culture of Education.* Cambridge, MA: Harvard University Press.

Carpenter, T.P., Fennema, E., Peterson, P.L., Chiang, C.P., & Loef, M. (1989). Using Knowledge of Children's Mathematics Thinking in Classroom Teaching: An Experimental Study. *American Educational Research Journal, 26*(4), 499–531.

Delpit, L. (1995). *Other People's Children: Cultural Conflict in the Classroom.* NY: The New Press.

Dewey, J. (1916). *Democracy and Education.* NY: Free Press.

Driver, R., Guesne, E., & Tiberghien, A. (Eds.) (1985). *Children's Ideas in Science.* Philadelphia, PA: Open University Press.

Duckworth, E. (1996). *The Having of Wonderful Ideas.* NY: Teachers College Press.

Fisher, A. & Scriven, M. (1997). *Critical Thinking: Its Definition and Assessment.* Point Reyes, CA: Edgepress.

Fosnot, C. T. (1996). *Constructivism: Theory, Perspectives, and Practice.* NY: Teachers College Press.

Gardner, H. (1991). *The Unschooled Mind: How Children Think and How Schools Should Teach.* NY: Basic Books.

Gay, G. (2000). *Culturally Responsive Teaching: Theory, Research, and Practice.* NY: Teachers College Press.

Greene, M. (1996). In Search of a Critical Pedagogy. In P. Leistyna, A. Woodrum, & S. A. Sherblom (Eds.), *Breaking Free: The Transformative Power of Critical Pedagogy* (pp. 13–30). Cambridge, MA : Harvard Educational Review.

Grumet, M. (1992). The Curriculum: What are the Basics and are We Teaching Them? In J. Kincheloe & S. Steinberg (Eds.), *Thirteen Questions: Reframing Education's Conversation.* NY: Peter Lang.

Howard, G. R. (1999). *We Can't Teach What We Don't Know: White Teachers, Multiracial Schools.* NY: Teachers College Press.

Jones, B.F., Palinscar, A.S., Ogle, D.S., & Carr, E.G. (1987). *Strategic Teaching and Learning: Content Instruction in the Content Areas.* Alexandria, VA: ASCD.

Kincheloe, J. L., & Sternberg, S. R. (1996). A Tentative Description of Post-Formal Thinking: The Critical Confrontation with Cognitive Theory. *Harvard Educational Review, 63,* 296–320.

Leistyna,P., Woodrum, A., & Sherblom, S. A. (1996). *Breaking Free: The Transformative Power of Critical Pedagogy.* Cambridge, MA: Harvard Educational Review.

Lortie, D. (1975). *Schoolteacher: A Sociological Study.* Chicago: University of Chicago Press.

Meier, D. (1995). *The Power of Their Ideas: Lessons from a Small School in Harlem.* Boston: Beacon.

Nieto, S. (1999). *The Light in Their Eyes: Creating Multicultural Communities.* NY: Teachers College Press.

Paul, R. W. (1990). *Critical Thinking: What Every Person Needs to Survive in a Rapidly Changing World.* Rohert Park, CA: Center for Critical Thinking and Moral Critique.

Piaget, J. (1977). Equilibration of cognitive structures. New York: Viking.

Rios, F. (Ed.). (1994). Teacher thinking in cultural contexts. Albany: State University of New York Press.

Siegel, H. (1997). Rationality redeemed? Further dialogues on an educational idea. NY: Routledge.

Thayer-Bacon, B.J. (2000). Transforming critical thinking: Thinking constructively. NY: Teachers College Press.

Vogt, L.A., Jordan, C., & Tharp, R.G. (1987). Explaining school failure, producing school success: Two cases. Anthropology & Education Quarterly, 18, 276–286.

Vygotsky, L.S. (1978). Mind in society. Cambridge, MA: Harvard University Press.

Vygotsky, L.S. (1986). Thought and language. Cambridge, MA: MIT Press.

Wink, J. (2000). *Critical Pedagogy: Notes from the Real World* (2nd ed.). NY: Longman.

Wood, D., Bruner, J., & Ross, G. (1976). The Role of Tutoring in Problem Solving. *Journal of Child Psychology and Psychiatry, 17,* 89–100.

Learning and Development in Constructivist Teacher Education

Paul Ammon and Linda Kroll

It is obvious that becoming a teacher involves a great deal of learning, and that becoming a *good* teacher is a long-term process, indeed, some would say a life-long process. Most likely that is why we speak not only of "learning to teach" but also of "teacher development." Learning and development are both frequently used terms in discussions of constructivism as well. On the one hand, constructivism is often identified as a theory of learning (e.g., Fosnot, 1996). On the other hand, constructivists from whom educators have drawn most heavily in recent years—Piaget and Vygotsky—are generally considered to have proposed theories of development. Learning and development are both processes of change in knowledge, but are they different processes, and if so, how are they related to each other? From a constructivist standpoint, these are not questions about what learning and development "really are", but about how it would be most useful for us to conceptualize what they are and how they are related. We begin this chapter by considering the nature of learning and development as processes entailed in the construction of knowledge. Then, after taking a closer look at the various kinds of knowledge teachers need to construct, we discuss from a theoretical standpoint how learning and development might come together in the construction of such knowledge. Finally, we describe some of the ways in which learning and development can be fostered together in teacher education practice.

THE NATURE OF LEARNING AND DEVELOPMENT

There is general agreement, both in formal theory and in everyday discourse, that learning refers to a kind of change that comes with experience, while development refers to a kind of change that comes with the passage of time. Beyond that, neither theorists nor practitioners have yet to achieve any real consensus on the nature of learning and development, and consequently their positions on the relationship between the two have covered a considerable range as well. At one extreme is the view that development refers to gradual changes that occur entirely independent of learning—changes that nonetheless influence what and how individuals can learn from experience at a given time (Gesell, 1940). At the other extreme is the view that development itself is essentially a result of cumulative learning, as many instances of learning add up over time to produce the kind of change that seems developmental (Bijou & Baer, 1961).

These contrasting positions on the relationship between learning and development carry very different implications for education in general. The first implies that efforts to foster learning of a particular kind must sometimes be postponed until the necessary readiness has developed. The second position implies that development simply will not occur without further learning, so it is imperative that we do something to foster learning now, instead of waiting until later. From this second point of view, waiting for readiness can impede the learner's progress and can have negative effects on motivation by not challenging the learner enough. However, the problem with this position from the first viewpoint is that premature pressure to learn can result in superficial learning and can have negative effects on motivation by challenging the learner too much. In either case, there is genuine concern with preparing learners for what lies ahead in the future, but there is disagreement on how best to do that.

Differences between Learning and Development

Both of the positions outlined above on the relationship between learning and development find support in research and practice, suggesting that there is some wisdom in each of them. Therefore it seems important that we seek to reconcile them as best we can. Toward that end, we now examine more closely how the terms "learning" and "development" are generally used. Despite the lack of consensus on how these terms should be defined, there is nevertheless a general tendency—both in formal theory and in everyday discourse—to locate learning and development at different points along each of three dimensions.

The first dimension, which we have already mentioned, has to do with whether change is *short-term* or *long-term.* That is, we think of learning as something that can at least begin to happen in a matter of minutes, or even seconds, whereas talk about development is usually restricted to changes that come about over periods of months or years. Second, to the extent that we are talking about changes in knowledge that are quite *specific,* we tend to refer to them as instances of learning, whereas more *general* changes, e.g., in ways of thinking or of understanding a whole domain of experience, are seen as instances of development. And, third, we also tend to see learning and development as having different origins or sources: learning comes more from sources that are *external* (such as explanations, modeling, or corrective feedback) whereas the sources of development are more *internal,* and are therefore harder to specify (but see below).

While each of the three dimensions—short versus long-term, specific versus general, and externally versus internally driven—seems useful for distinguishing what people tend to mean by learning versus development, each also poses problems for differentiating between these two kinds of change with absolute clarity. For one thing, we are talking here not about categorical distinctions, but about continua, so it is not clear exactly where along each continuum learning shades into development, and many changes seem to fall somewhere in the middle of a given continuum, rather than at one pole or the other. If it takes a student teacher several weeks to get a handle on asking students productive questions, is that a case of learning or development? Furthermore, while the three dimensions may be correlated with each other to some extent, they are not completely correlated, so that a change may seem developmental on one dimension but not on another. For example, it may take a teacher years to construct a particularly effective teaching strategy (a long-term change, which implies development), but the strategy may apply only to one kind of situation in the classroom (a specific change, which implies learning).

From a constructivist point of view, the external-internal dimension seems especially problematic. If we see the primary source of change as internal, then it seems we must be talking about some version of nativism. On the other hand, if the primary source is external, then it seems we must be subscribing to some version of empiricism. As we have seen in Chapter 1, though, constructivists generally hold that knowledge cannot be reduced to that which comes primarily from inside or to that which comes primarily from outside. In fact, changes in knowledge are never just internally or externally caused, since internal and external factors interact from the beginning of life. Consequently, both are always implicated in what individuals bring with them "internally" to a new situation, and in what the individual makes of the "external" situation. Nevertheless, it does seem useful, in differentiating development from learning, to cite as developmental the kinds of changes in which an especially important part is played by sources that are relatively independent of specific encounters with the external world, either past or present, and might therefore be called internal.

Organization and Progressive Systemic Change

It seems useful to distinguish two kinds of internal sources involved in developmental change. First, some changes reflect organic growth of the sort that is generally known in the study of human development as "maturation," such as the build-up of myelin sheaths around neurons during childhood, which increases the speed of neural transmission and makes more advanced brain function possible (Diamond & Hopson, 1998/1999). Maturation appears to figure importantly in the kinds of developmental changes that occur from birth through adolescence, when organic growth is extensive.

But further organic change after adolescence normally does not seem as significant as a causal factor in development until old age. Thus, if maturation were the only internal source of the changes we call developmental, it would seem inappropriate to talk about "adult development." Yet many of us think adults can undergo long-term, general changes that we would want to call development. Indeed, references to "teacher development" seem as common in today's educational literature as references to "learning to teach." In the absence of substantial contributions from further maturation, we can still attribute such changes in adulthood to a second kind of internal source, which has generally been called "organization." In fact, organization (and reorganization) can be seen in all developmental change, throughout the life span, whether maturation is implicated or not. Organization is the more or less continuous process by which we coordinate and integrate specific experiences. While it is influenced by those experiences, the process of organization itself is not entirely determined by experience, just as it is influenced but not determined by organic maturation when that occurs. Both maturation and experience open up new possibilities with regard to the forms of knowledge that can be constructed, but organization is necessary for those possibilities to be realized.

The concept of organization leads quite naturally to the notion that development is concerned with changes in knowledge *systems*, i.e., with changes in interrelated concepts and skills which, taken together, represent the learner's current understandings with regard to whole domains of experience. The idea of systemic change, in turn, seems consistent with the idea that developmental changes take time and are quite general, in the sense that they emerge gradually and are manifested in many different but related ways. But what is it that leads to systemic change? What drives the process of organization and reorganization, if it is not just the opening up of new maturational possibilities and/or the occurrence of specific experiences? Theorists in the tradition of Piaget have generally proposed that we humans have a natural tendency to organize our knowledge in ways that work best for us, in the sense that they enable us to make the best use of our organic possibilities and past experiences to respond adaptively to a wide range of new situations. In order to perform this adaptive function well, our knowledge systems also tend toward internal consistency, so that they don't give us contradictory ideas about how to proceed. Put another way, our ultimate goal is to construct internally consistent theories that account for as much of our experience as possible, so that we have the soundest possible basis for our future actions. While this goal is attained only in very limited ways during the early stages of development, and may never be attained entirely, it can at least be approached through a series of successive approximations in the kinds of knowledge systems that are organized at different points in the course of development. Thus development is a gradual process of long-term, progressive change, based to an important extent on the internal process of organization and (sometimes) on organic maturation, along with opportunities to learn.

Relational and Motivational Sources of Development in Social Context

The difficulty of distinguishing internal and external sources of development becomes especially apparent when we look beyond the developing individual to consider the social context in which individual development occurs. Development is typically accompanied by changes in the kinds of relationships an individual has with others, and at the same time by changes in the kinds of goals an individual is inclined to strive for. A classic developmental theorist who highlighted these sorts of changes across the life span was Erik Erikson. Erikson (1968) suggested that, during different periods of life, we are especially concerned with such issues as declaring our own autonomy, demonstrating our competence through "industry," establishing our identities (which involve solidarity with some people and distance from others), seeking intimacy with significant others, and promoting the well being of those who follow after us. To the extent that these sorts of changes are relational, they seem to represent external sources of development, in that they entail the expectations, demands, and responses of others. But to the extent that such changes are motivational, they seem to represent internal sources of development, in that they entail interests and emotions that energize and direct our behavior. In any case, relational/motivational changes can have quite pervasive effects on the process of knowledge construction, which is why it seems appropriate to suggest that they are sources of cognitive development, and not just influences on learning, as they surely are as well. Finally, it should be clear that just as relational/motivational changes can bring about systemic changes in knowledge, so too can changes in knowledge systems cause relational/motivational changes.

The relational sources of knowledge construction are highlighted especially in social constructionist theories, which (more or less by definition) hold that knowledge systems are *constituted* through activities undertaken in concert with others. However, if knowledge is held to be constituted *wholly* through social interaction, then the notion seems skewed heavily toward outside-in empiricism and therefore is problematic from a constructivist point of view. On the other hand, if we conceive of internal and social organization as separate but interacting factors, we can maintain the non-reductionist perspective that is central to constructivism. Even though Vygotsky talked about knowledge originating in interpersonal activities and then becoming *intra*personal through a process of internalization, he still acknowledged a "natural line" of development along with the cultural line (Moll, 1994), and spoke of spontaneous concepts which interact with scientific concepts of the sort that we generally acquire through formal education (Vygotsky, 1934/1987). And while Piaget, with roots in biology, might seem to overemphasize what is natural for the individual, his conception of "natural" included interaction with others (Piaget, 1965/1995, 1967/1971), and was characterized by an openness to new possibilities, much as evolution is an open-ended biological process in which environments are as important as genes, and neither is solely responsible for change.[1]

Learning and Development in Becoming a Teacher

With this explication of the concept of development as background, we return now to the question of how learning and development are related, and to the issue of "learning to teach" versus "teacher development." It seems clear that instances of specific, short-term, externally driven changes of the sort that we call learning contribute to general, long-term, internally driven changes of the sort that we call development. At the same time, development influences the meanings that specific learning experiences can have, and therefore it influences what is learned. Thus, in our efforts to promote knowledge construction among teachers, our goals must include both learning and development. The learning of specific skills, strategies, and facts is essential in order for a teacher to act, and the development of broader and deeper understandings is essential in order for teachers to act *effectively* in response to the ever changing challenges they face.

In the discussion so far, we have suggested that learning and development may be differentiated, in part, according to the specificity or generality of the knowledge that is constructed, and we have argued that both specific and general changes in knowledge are essential in the process of becoming a good teacher. We turn now to a closer look at the nature of the knowledge that teachers need in order to teach well, before going on to a discussion of how learning and development interact as teachers construct the knowledge they need.

THE NATURE OF KNOWLEDGE

When we think about learning and development, we have to consider the nature of what is learned and what develops. Within a constructivist perspective on learning and development we have to consider what is constructed; what is the nature of knowledge? And within the context of teacher education we have to think about what we want prospective teachers to learn; are there different types of knowledge that teachers need? Such questions lead us to consider the nature and kinds of knowledge and knowing, in general and within teacher education.

Within the constructivist view there is a range of perspectives on the nature of knowledge, where it resides, and how it changes or is acquired. Depending on one's view of the role of the learner and the nature of development, the nature of knowledge can be defined in a variety of ways. However, it is not "a picture of reality." The more behaviorist, transmission view of knowledge is challenged by a constructivist view of learning. This is not to rule out any sort of mental representation that might be considered a "picture." The point is that such representations are not copies of what is "out there," but, rather, are mental constructions that represent one's own understanding at a particular moment in time. Von Glasersfeld puts it succinctly, ". . . what we call knowledge does not and cannot have the purpose of producing representations of an independent reality, but instead has an adaptive function" (Von Glasersfeld, 1996, p. 3). While Von Glasersfeld considers learning and development as processes of self-organization, Rogoff (as a representative of the sociocultural perspective on constructivism) considers learning and development as "participatory appropriation" where the learner gradually moves from the periphery of an activity to the center of the activity by gradually taking more and more responsibility for it (Rogoff, 1995). Knowledge lies within the activity and is seen as a local form of interaction or participation. In both cases, knowledge is seen both as a process and as an object that changes or is reconstituted, rather than as something to be acquired and held. It is more a way of being in the world that allows the learner to be an active participant (whether one takes a more cognitive or more sociocultural view of it).

Types of Knowledge: Conceptual, Procedural, and Metacognitive Knowledge

Others have looked at learning and development as the construction of more than one type of knowledge. For lack of more precise terms one could refer to two basic varieties of knowledge as conceptual or propositional, on the one hand, and practical or procedural, on the other (Chang-Wells & Wells, 1993). Conceptual knowledge can be described in linguistic propositions; it is sometimes referred to as "knowing that" or "scientific knowledge" (Fenstermacher, 1994). If there is such a thing as "factual" knowledge, it fits in this category. Procedural knowledge is knowledge of routines, procedures, and strategies; sometimes it is referred to as "knowing how." In differentiating types of knowledge, Chang-Wells and Wells describe knowledge not as an object but as "a mental state—the state of understanding arrived at by learning, that is, through the various constructive processes involved in coming to know" (Chang-Wells & Wells, p. 58). Both conceptual and procedural knowledge can be conceived of in this way. However, the distinctions between conceptual and procedural knowledge are significant in that some "thing" can be known in one way and not the other. Each form of knowledge has different strengths; e.g. conceptual knowledge may lead to generalization possibilities while procedural knowledge may lead to automaticity in the use of this knowledge. In addition, Chang-Wells and Wells identify a third type of knowledge, metacognitive knowledge, as "knowledge about one's own mental processes and the control of these processes to achieve one's intended goals" (Chang-Wells & Wells, p. 59). Metacognitive knowledge not only controls what knowledge is used when, but also helps determine what knowledge needs to be learned.

Chang-Wells and Wells (1993) use the notions of conceptual, procedural, and metacognitive knowledge in analyzing the learning that occurs among students in an elementary classroom, but the same notions seem relevant to the learning that teachers do as well. For example, in managing and organizing her classroom, a teacher calls on all three kinds of knowledge. She has conceptual knowledge about different possibilities at both physical and social levels (e.g. desk organization, working groups), and regarding the learning and moral goals associated with each possibility. She has procedural knowledge of how to organize and manage a classroom. However, how coordinated or related each of these kinds of knowledge is, or how related each of these kinds of knowledge is to the other is the result of her metacognitive knowledge regarding her thinking about classroom organization. Thus, metacognitive knowledge helps the teacher coordinate, differentiate and integrate her knowledge with regard to particular content, regardless of whether it appears as conceptual or procedural knowledge. The use and coordination of all three kinds of knowledge leads to (hopefully) what the teacher will regard as "successful" classroom organization.

Fenstermacher (1994) addresses the question of what constitutes teacher knowledge from the perspective of how both teachers and researchers learn about educational practice, identifying the messiness of trying to differentiate between formal (or propositional or conceptual knowledge) and practical (or procedural knowledge; knowledge that is derived from action and reflection in and on action [Schön,

1983]). He demonstrates that teachers must coordinate conceptual knowledge (with regard to subject matter and pedagogical methodology) with practical knowledge situated in the pedagogical moment. (This conception is reminiscent of and owes something to Shulman's [1986] concept of pedagogical content knowledge.) Differentiating in an instance of practice what action is based on conceptual knowledge and what is based on practical knowledge is an exercise to understand better the knowledge base of that practice. In reality all kinds of knowledge are coordinated and come into play. For example, in teaching a reading lesson, the teacher must coordinate conceptual knowledge about the development of reading, child development and learning, and pedagogical methods for the teaching of reading, with his/her practical knowledge of the children in the reading group, and their particular cognitive, social and emotional strengths and needs, thus relating specific knowledge of particular children to general knowledge about child development. In addition, she must consider other management and organizational issues to keep the rest of the class engaged in meaningful learning activities. While all of this coordination may not happen in each lesson, for the teacher to consistently teach well, all of it must be coordinated at one time or another.

As demonstrated in this example, the multiple-task nature of teaching requires a moment-to-moment coordination of conceptual and procedural knowledge. Conceptual knowledge (such as knowledge of literacy development coupled with knowledge of how children learn) seems especially important for the non-routine aspects of teaching. Without it, the teacher may apply "old" procedures that do not fit very well (e.g., "one size fits all" literacy programs), procedures derived from the more intuitive "common knowledge" that develops as a result of unreflected upon experience. Of course, the teacher's conceptual knowledge itself may not always be adequate either, which is why we are interested in fostering its development toward more powerful forms of understanding. To the extent that any type of knowledge is organized into a system it can (potentially) develop from less to more powerful forms.

Piaget (1974/1976, 1974/1978) addressed the question of the nature of knowledge by investigating how we are conscious of and understand the knowledge we use. He posits three levels of developing consciousness: action, cognizance, and conceptualization. At the action level one makes an attempt to solve a problem. Depending on the nature of the problem, one may succeed, yet may not be able to explain or be conscious of how one solves the problem. At the cognizance level, understanding of the problem is represented at a global level; the important variables may be identified conceptually, but how to coordinate them is still a process of trial and error. At the conceptual level, the problem-solver can reflect on and coordinate the different aspects of the problem. For example, in looking at children's understanding of what makes a good story, their responses change as their ability to tell stories and understand stories develops (Kroll, 1980). At the action level, when they are asked the question what makes a good story they begin by giving an example of their favorite story and then retelling that story. Questions which ask them to analyze parts of a story or essential elements are answered by a continuation of the retelling. At a second level, one which might be described as a cognizance level, they respond to the question of what makes a good story by referring to specific parts or phrases that are contained in a story (once upon a time, happily ever after). At the conceptual level, young storytellers respond that good stories have a moral or a lesson to teach us, that we can learn from stories. This final level is a much more complete and sophisticated notion of story.

Such levels of consciousness in knowing seem to be useful in considering the knowledge necessary for teaching. While there are some examples of knowledge that can be perfected at the action level of understanding, (learning to drive a car is a good example) most knowledge is not flexibly usable until the conceptual level, particularly when one thinks about knowledge that requires both action and reflection, such as teaching. To return to our literacy teaching example, volunteer tutors are often given an action-level way of proceeding when working with individual students. Thus, they get pretty good at figuring out how to engage their tutees using literature or worksheets that have been provided by someone else. Student teachers often begin in this way as well. However, as they gain experience and reflect on the processes they are using with the student, in coordination with whatever instruction they may be receiving at the college regarding the teaching of literacy, they begin to make connections between particular assessment results and the instruction they prescribe. What they try may still be at the level of trial and error—"let's see if this text or this activity will help the child move forward." This could be seen as a cognizance level. Finally, at the level of conceptualization, the teacher coordinates her assessment with a well-conceived literacy program that is both developmental and flexible, coordinating an understanding of literacy development with current knowledge of individual differences. What is critical here is the growth of not only conceptual and procedural (or practical) knowledge, but also the development of metacognition with regard to knowledge about literacy teaching.

Piaget's model of achievement at the action level that is constantly improved or restructured by reflections and coordinations at levels of cognizance and conceptualization seems like it might be helpful in thinking about what constitutes learning and development in a teacher education program. For example, student teachers need to develop an understanding of classroom management. They need to move from an interpretation of classroom management as controlling children's actions to one of organizing the environment and instruction to take advantage of children's individual differences toward their most optimum learning. One student teacher set for himself the problem of managing a few very active five and six year old boys. His initial notion was to find ways to curtail their bothersome (to him) behavior during circle time. He then began to think of how to take advantage of their tendency to wiggle to enrich his curriculum. Finally, he came to a balance of actions that took advantage of their individuality when it could benefit everyone in the group and helped them to curtail this tendency when he felt it was detrimental to their understanding of a particular activity. While this balance did not always manifest itself as he would have liked, it did represent a conceptualization level in consciousness of the complexity of classroom management, and an organized way to coordinate the conceptual and procedural knowledge he was constructing with regard to classroom management. Thus, in thinking about the student teacher's learning and development, the notion of "situated knowledge" where particular and general understandings are coordinated within the context of the activity can also be helpful in thinking about how he made both moment to moment and day to day decisions about what he did (Putnam and Borko, 2000). Again, we can see that knowledge is both a "thing" and a "process" that includes knowing what one knows and how one knows as well as *acting* on what one knows.

Domains of Knowing

Another way of thinking about knowledge is to differentiate between *domains of knowing*. Typically, in complex, integrated fields of study or expertise, such as teaching, the knowledge one employs is derived from different knowledge systems that correspond to different domains of experience. Domains can be distinguished primarily by the different sets of issues or core questions they engender. Within each domain of knowing we find conceptual, procedural, and metacognitive knowledge. Thus, in considering teacher knowledge, possible domains could include (but not be restricted to) subject matter knowledge, pedagogical knowledge, and moral knowledge. (In discussing these particular domains of knowing, we do not intend to exhaust the domains relevant to learning to teach. For example, another possible domain is that of self-knowledge: "Who am I as a teacher?"; "Who am I as a learner?"; "How does my concept of teaching itself coincide with my own actions in the classroom?")

Subject Matter and Pedagogical Knowledge. Teachers need knowledge about the discipline(s) they teach. Such knowledge involves understanding not only the "facts" of the discipline, but also its organization, its application, and what one knows or does not know within the discipline. Thus, conceptual, procedural, and metacognitive knowledge are all part of subject matter knowledge.

Teachers also need pedagogical knowledge, knowledge about specific instructional techniques, about curriculum construction, about how people learn. This, too, has conceptual, procedural, and metacognitive components. To actually teach, however, teachers must coordinate their subject matter knowledge with the different aspects of pedagogical knowledge. And this coordination must occur in conceptual, procedural, and metacognitive realms.

For some teachers (and many other adults), however, subject matter such as mathematics and literacy may be known in largely procedural terms (e.g. how to compute answers to arithmetic problems), because that is how the teachers were taught it themselves and that is how they *use* it now as adults. Consequently, teachers may not at times think conceptually about the subject matter they are teaching. For example, they may see learning arithmetic mainly as mastering a set of algorithmic procedures or learning to read essentially as mastering decoding skills. Becoming a teacher who can teach for understanding may require supplementing one's own procedural knowledge with greater understanding of a subject as conceptual knowledge. Teachers must also integrate their conceptual knowledge of the subject matter with their conceptual knowledge of human learning and child development, and with conceptual knowledge about achieving equity in outcomes and opportunities, to construct pedagogical content knowledge. (Here we anticipate how the moral domain of knowledge comes into play.) With this understanding in place, beginning teachers can then integrate pedagogical content knowledge with their general knowledge of pedagogy (for example, classroom management, which also includes notions of equity) to construct methods to enable their students to construct their own conceptual knowledge of the subject matter. The ultimate goal of this process is that young students, with the help of their teachers, will construct their own newly developed conceptual knowledge which they can then use to understand the content, and procedural knowledge which will produce the automatic procedures we all use when we read to learn or figure to understand the world mathematically and scientifically, which will then allow them to continue to act on and learn new content!

Moral Understandings. In addition to the disciplines and pedagogy as domains of knowledge, teachers need to coordinate their moral understandings with their content and pedagogical knowledge. The conceptual understanding of the inherently moral nature of every act of teaching is a specific part of the moral domain of knowledge. The moral imperative of creating classroom situations that enable all students to learn to their full potential both drives the teacher's purpose and requires an understanding of the moral and political nature of teaching. In the interest of promoting social justice through an excellent and more equitable educational system, teachers must integrate their understandings within the moral domain with the other content and procedural knowledge characteristic of more traditional subject matter. And, as with subject matter, differentiating and integrating conceptual and procedural knowledge within this domain is not so obvious. The idea of social justice, equal access and opportunity, and the achievement of excellent goals for all are "Big Ideas" (Schifter & Fosnot, 1993) in many senses. They have conceptual components constructed out of moral concepts about people's rights and the responsibility of a system of government or education to recognize everyone's rights. In addition, within these Big Ideas teachers construct an understanding of the difference between theory (or the ideal—what ought to be, based on these moral concepts) and practice (or what individuals actually experience). For teachers, this conceptual knowledge must be constructed and then coordinated with action at a system-wide and classroom level. Conceptual knowledge contributes to the construction and reconstruction of procedural knowledge and vice versa. Both will change as individuals reflect on the results of their actions. For example, knowing that interest in reading is partially generated by reading about familiar topics results in a diverse selection of literature, depending on who is in the classroom. Thus, subject matter knowledge (about literature) is coordinated with moral understandings based on notions of equity. What literature to use when and how to use it is a messy process to understand, but it is monitored by metacognitive knowledge.

Conclusion

An essential question for teacher educators, then, is how can teacher education programs foster and support the construction of conceptual, procedural, and metacognitive knowledge in the various domains relevant to teaching. In order to answer this question, we will look at how these kinds of knowledge are constructed in preservice teacher education and once teachers begin their employment in classrooms. How do teachers learn and what does teacher development look like over the short and long term? In examining teacher development and learning we then suggest what teacher education programs, based on principles of constructivism, can do to foster and support the construction of teacher knowledge in all its forms.

TEACHER KNOWLEDGE, LEARNING, AND DEVELOPMENT

It should be clear from the preceding discussion that, in our efforts to promote teacher learning and development, we must proceed on several different fronts. First, we must address a teacher's need for different types of knowledge, including conceptual, procedural, and metacognitive knowledge. Second, we must address the teacher's need for knowledge in various domains, including those having to do with subject matter, pedagogy, and morality. Finally, we must address the teacher's need for facility in coordinating the multiple types and domains of knowledge that come into play when the teacher engages in such activities as lesson planning, classroom management, and the assessment of student learning. While real progress on each of these fronts requires a lot of teacher learning, it requires teacher development as well. The question we turn to now is how, in principle, to help teachers construct the knowledge they need in ways that are attentive to both their learning and their development. Then, in the final section of this chapter, we will consider how principle might be put into practice in programs of teacher education.

The Need to Focus on Development as Well as Learning

Teacher educators, like teachers in general, are probably inclined to focus more on learning than on development. For some, this bias may reflect the belief that development cannot be influenced by specific learnings and therefore lies beyond an educator's control (consistent with a nativist view of development). For others, it may reflect the belief that development can be influenced entirely through specific learnings and therefore does not need to be treated as a separate issue (consistent with an empiricist view of development). However, even when development is understood as different from but thoroughly intertwined with learning, the here-and-nowness of specific learnings, and the immediate need for them in the process of becoming a teacher, may lead to a neglect of development, and to missed opportunities to promote it.

A concern with development is important because it leads us to take a long view on the goals of instruction—to focus not only on helping teachers do as well as they can in the classroom right now, or on preparing them for better teaching in the near future, but also on what we want them to be like much later, as experienced, expert teachers. Because it is impossible to anticipate all the particulars of a teacher's work in the distant future—the who, what, and where of her teaching— taking a long view shifts the focus from such particulars to broader understandings that will enable the teacher to comprehend the particulars of her work in productive ways. However, long-term goals are "at risk" in teacher education programs because the pressure of great need and little time puts the emphasis on short-term goals, and because it is possible to attain short-term goals without also doing what we can, at the same time, to promote long-term goals as well. A teacher who seems reasonably well prepared for her first year of teaching may improve rather little after that and never reach the kind of expertise one would hope for from a constructivist point of view. While future development generally requires continued support, teachers are more likely to create and take advantage of opportunities for further development if a foundation for it has been laid in their earlier preparation.

Along with a forward-looking concern for a teacher's development in the future, it is also important for us to consider the extent of the teacher's development to date, because of its relevance to both the learning and the further development we are trying to foster. With respect to learning, there is so much for teachers to know that we often try to pass a lot accumulated knowledge on to them by showing and telling. There is no question that showing and telling can be quite helpful, but we must remember that it is never just a matter of experts transmitting their knowledge to novices, because learners always construct interpretations of what they see or hear. Consequently, information may not be understood the way it was intended. Breakdowns in communication between teachers and learners sometimes become apparent when learners are asked to act on what they have been taught. If teacher-learners do not perform in response to our instruction the way we hoped they would, we often provide corrective feedback. Sometimes we then check to see if their performance has improved, but sometimes we don't—perhaps because of limited resources or the feeling that there is so much to cover and so little time to do it. In effect, then, we are hoping that our feedback will lead to improved performance in the future, but we are neglecting the possibility that even our feedback may be interpreted differently by the learner. Thus in order to effectively promote the learning that seems important to us in the moment, we must try to get in touch with the interpretive frameworks that teacher-learners are bringing to bear on the information we are providing them, i.e., the knowledge systems they have already constructed through their development to date.

Getting in touch with a teacher's interpretive systems is as important for fostering future development as it is for promoting present learning. If we think of development as knowledge change that is systemic, then in order to foster development, we must address the nature of the present system. That is, we must see to it that teacher learners are actively using their current understandings of the "big ideas" at the core of the relevant knowledge systems, and we must help them push their understandings further, so that over time the entire system is transformed. We can assist teachers in this developmental process either directly, by means of our own interactions with them, or indirectly, by engaging them in productive interactions with others—peers, books, web sites, and so on.

Sometimes "pushing further" simply means extending the use of current understandings to more and more situations. This sort of "horizontal" development helps learners become accomplished in their current ways of thinking. Consolidating a recently constructed knowledge system is an important precondition for subsequent "vertical" development to a still higher level of understanding, because development is hierarchical, and elements of lower levels are included in higher levels. Horizontal development also helps learners discover the ways in which their current knowledge systems fall short of being internally consistent and externally adaptive. From a Piagetian point of view, increasing awareness of these limitations produces a sense of disequilibrium, leading learners to question the adequacy of their current understandings and to search for more adequate alternatives.

When learners have become accomplished at their current ways of thinking, and when they have also begun to discover their limitations, "pushing further" can focus more on vertical development. For example, we might try to facilitate the learner's vertical development simply by suggesting a more advanced way of understanding. Suggesting solutions to problems is not inconsistent with constructivism, so long as it is understood that learners must necessarily respond in their own ways, either accepting or rejecting what is suggested, and understanding it either as intended or in some other way. Consequently, suggestions seem most likely to foster development when they reflect a new way of understanding that is only slightly more advanced, and the learner is able to comprehend what is gained by thinking in this new way. Otherwise, we may be providing incomprehensible answers that are not yet meaningful for the learner, and the result may be superficial learning rather than true development.

From a constructivist perspective, any form of direct instruction, including modeling, is basically a matter of suggesting possibilities for the learner to consider. However, for the kinds of complex and abstract understandings entailed in teacher development, it seems clear that language serves as the principal medium by which possibilities are suggested in teacher education. It also seems clear, given how facile adults generally are in repeating what they have heard, that teacher educators may easily overestimate the extent to which verbally conveyed suggestions have actually been understood and incorporated as intended. Piaget (1935 & 1965/1970b), himself, cautioned educators against "verbalism, that dismal scholastic fact—a proliferation of pseudo-ideas loosely hooked onto a string of words lacking all real meaning" (p. 164). On the other hand, Piaget also acknowledged the essential roles of language (1967), social transmission (1970a), and cooperation with others (1965/1995), in the development of knowledge. Moreover, Piaget's clinical method offers a way of interacting with others in interviews that probe beneath the linguistic surface of what they say to reveal what sorts of understandings they have actually constructed (Ginsburg, 1997). Followers of Vygotsky, with such notions as the transformative power of speech as a tool (1978) and the value of direct instruction in scientific concepts (1934/1987), might seem more optimistic about the possibility of inducing development through talk about higher-level understandings. Even so, Vygotsky's notion of a Zone of Proximal Development (1978) suggests an upper bound on what is possible along those lines. Thus, within limits, both of these constructivist theories point to the possibility of actively fostering development through language and other means.

Fostering Learning and Development Together: Parts, Wholes, and Coordinations

To return to the question of how to promote both teacher learning and teacher development, and to risk stating the very obvious, it seems that the key is to promote them together, i.e., in a coordinated fashion. If we think of developing knowledge systems as "wholes," and of the learnings that contribute to and are organized within them as "parts," then three types of coordination are suggested: part-part coordination, part-whole coordination, and whole-whole coordination. By analyzing a single example of teaching practice below, we will illustrate these different kinds of coordination in relation to each other, and in relation to different types and domains of knowledge. In the process, we will also illustrate the incredible complexity of teaching, of the knowledge that it requires, and of the learning and development that must be fostered in order for teachers to attain that knowledge.

A particularly challenging aspect of teaching practice for many new teachers is making smooth transitions from one instructional activity to another. Not only is there the goal of keeping the time between activities brief and orderly, but there is also the goal of ending one activity and beginning another in a way that enhances the learning that both activities are intended to promote. To the extent that the teacher wants her curriculum to be integrated, transitions also provide opportunities for students to make connections between different domains of learning. In addition, the time between activities can be approached as a learning experience itself—one that is part of the "hidden" curriculum having to do with the development of social skills and personal responsibility. In fact, transitions often reflect the general "culture" of the classroom—at least by default, if not by design—so another goal may be for each transition to reflect the way of living and learning that the teacher wants to foster in general.

On the face of it, the knowledge that enables a teacher to make a smooth transition is procedural, as it entails a series of steps for ending one activity and beginning the next. To be concrete, suppose we are in an elementary school classroom where there is typically a transition from reading self-selected literature with partners to meeting as a whole class for a "mini lesson" on some aspect of writing at the beginning of writers' workshop. Toward the end of the partner reading session, the teacher warns the students that reading time will end in five minutes and suggests that each pair of partners come to a convenient stopping place—the end of a page or chapter—and then have a brief discussion of what they have read. The teacher then tells the students when there is only one minute left and reminds them how they are to end their work with their partners. When reading time is over, the teacher asks the students to put the books they have been reading back on the shelves, and then to gather in a circle on the rug in the front of the classroom. With younger children the teacher might then initiate a song—one which is familiar to the students, and which serves as a clock for the transition in that the students know they are to be ready for the next activity by the end of the song. With older students, the teacher might accomplish this by means of a countdown or some other device. Once the students are seated in a circle on the rug, the teacher then takes a moment to have the students share their reflections on how well they worked with their partners while reading, and why their partnerships did or did not work well. Finally the teacher questions the students about the texts they were just reading and connects some of their responses to the mini lesson she is about to begin on a related aspect of writing.

We might begin a discussion of this transition procedure by thinking of the individual steps as its parts, and of the series of steps as the whole. Clearly the parts need to be coordinated with each other, in the sense that each leads to the next, but they also need to be coordinated with the whole, in the sense that they are only helpful to the extent that they contribute to the overall goals of a smooth transition. This last point reminds us that a procedure can be seen as much more than a simple routine that is carried out in essentially the same way each time it is used. A novice teacher might learn it as a simple routine initially, based on what a more experienced teacher has described or demonstrated, but then it would not yet have the kind of flexibility needed to attain its goals in the face of variability from one occasion to another, as there are changes in the nature of the learning activities, in the students' maturity levels, and so on. That sort of flexibility would require not just the learning of a specific routine but also the development of a whole procedural system over time. Thus, specific routines might be seen as parts of a still larger system.

There are two different (but not mutually exclusive) pathways by which a flexible procedural system for making smooth transitions might develop. First, it might evolve through an extended period of trial and error in which the teacher tries repeatedly to use the original routine, accommodates it to varying conditions, and in effect develops intuitions about how to make the general procedure suit each particular occasion. Although this sort of tacit knowledge may eventually prove to be quite effective in the teacher's own practice, it may take a very long time to develop, and it may never take a form that can be shared with others, in the sense that the teacher can talk about it in ways that enable others to critique and learn from her practice. Furthermore, the extensive practical experience required by this pathway seems especially problematic at the preservice level, where student teachers generally have limited time and opportunity to experiment with classroom management techniques in someone else's classroom.

A second developmental pathway might start from the part-whole coordination noted above, as the teacher reflects on the individual parts of the original routine in relation to its overall purposes. The teacher might engage in this reflection alone or with others, and she might do so as she plans instruction, carries it out, or thinks about it in hindsight. In any case, her reflection is likely to be guided by certain questions: What are all the goals of the transition and how does each step contribute to each of these goals? Is each procedural step really necessary for attaining the goals in the situation at hand? Are there alternative ways of carrying out particular steps—ways the teacher might have learned from other teachers or from her own experience? If so, what are the pros and cons for employing each alternative?

To answer these questions, the teacher must bring other knowledge systems into play. For example, the teacher's conceptual knowledge of subject matter might come into play if she considers the transition in relation to her instructional objectives for the students before, during, and after the transition (and "subject matter" here might include not only reading and writing, but also the sorts of social understandings the teacher hopes the students will develop in learning to work well with partners). The teacher's knowledge of pedagogy is also likely to enter in, as she considers not only particular teaching procedures but also more general concepts regarding her students as learners and the conditions under which they are likely to learn and develop. In addition, the teacher's own moral understandings might be involved as she thinks about the kinds of moral understandings she would like her students to gain, and about the issue of whether her procedure is unfair in any way to any of her students. Since these other knowledge systems must be coordinated not only with the procedure in question but with each other as well, we now have whole-whole coordination, as well as part-whole coordination, in the teacher's thinking.

So, on this second developmental pathway, a teacher constructs a flexible procedural system for making transitions not just by coordinating numerous specific learnings about making transitions but by coordinating several different knowledge systems as well, including systems of different types (e.g., procedural and conceptual) and from different domains (e.g., subject matter, pedagogical, and moral). For teacher-learners to juggle several types and domains of knowledge in this way may at first seem quite daunting, even when facilitated by a teacher educator. Moreover, the resulting knowledge system may still require a certain amount of trial-and-error experience for fine tuning in practice. In the long run, however, this kind of developmental path may offer several advantages. First, if the teacher's direct experiences with transitions are informed by conceptual analyses of what such transitions entail, then the length of time it takes to construct a flexible procedural system from such experiences may be shortened considerably, and the resulting knowledge may be more readily shared with other teachers. Moreover, because knowledge that develops by this route is less dependent on handed down experience, or on one's own experience in conventional teaching situations, it may lend itself more readily to innovation—to teaching in ways that transcend the pedagogical and moral limitations of "business as usual" in the schools. Teaching that transforms and doesn't simply reproduce seems to require high levels of teacher development with respect to multiple types and domains of knowledge, which in turn requires their active use in a variety of contexts. Thus, an additional advantage of a developmental pathway that coordinates many different knowledge systems is that it may advance the development of all those systems. Finally, if teachers also reflect on the coordinations involved in the developmental process itself, and on the conditions that support such coordinations, then they may be able to construct better metacogntive understandings of how to promote their own development as well.

In sum, we could have answered the question of how to help teachers develop as they learn by saying that it generally comes down to raising questions for them to think about in relation to specific procedures and concepts they are learning about or are already using in their practice. We could have gone on to say that the most productive questions to ask are those that lead teachers to reflect on *why* a particular practice in a given situation does or doesn't make sense when considered from a number of different perspectives, including perspectives having to do with the academic and social content to be learned, the ways in which students learn and develop, and the moral imperatives of justice and equal opportunity. However, had we simply answered the "how" question that way, we would have failed to address the "why" question ourselves. In effect, we have answered this why question above by arguing that, from a constructivist perspective on pedagogy, the asking of why questions makes sense because it promotes the use and, therefore, the development of broader understandings that enhance what teachers learn from their experience and how they apply it in their practice. We might add here that one of the long-term goals in raising why questions with teachers is to have them raise such questions more often for themselves, as they begin to internalize (a la Vygotsky, 1978, 1934/1987) the kinds of questions we raise for them. By asking their own why questions, teachers can gain greater autonomy—both individually and collectively—to enhance their own learning and foster their own development.

Teacher Learning and Development in the Pedagogical Domain

As we have seen, a fundamental tenet of constructivism is that efforts to promote learning and development are more likely to succeed if they are grounded in an understanding of learners' current ways of thinking and interpreting experience. As we have also seen, promoting the learning and development of teachers entails several different domains of knowledge. What, then, does teacher development look like in these various domains? What different ways of thinking and interpreting experience are teachers likely to construct in the course of their own development? In general, knowledge systems appear to become increasingly complex as they develop, and various schemes have been proposed for quantifying their complexity in ways that can be applied to any domain of knowledge (e.g., Fischer, 1980; Pascual-Leone, 1970). But quantitative, domain-general ways of characterizing developmental levels seem less useful to practitioners than those that are more qualitative and domain-specific, so the latter is what we will focus on here.

Unfortunately, there are no definitive descriptions of the qualitative changes that adults' understandings might go through in any of the domains related to teaching. Moreover, there probably never will be, as the course of development is likely to vary, at least in its particulars if not in more basic ways, with individual and contextual differences. Thus it behooves teacher educators to study teacher development within the populations and contexts in which they work. However, there are some leads from previous research on what development might look like, especially from studies of adult cognitive development in social, physical, and logicomathematical domains that are relevant but not unique to teaching (e.g., Moshman, 1998). Some of that research has been carried out with samples of teachers (e.g., Sprinthall, Reiman, & Thies-Sprinthall, 1996). Less well researched is development in the one domain that does seem unique to teaching, i.e., pedagogy itself, but one can nonetheless find some leads to pursue there as well (e.g., Calderhead, 1987). Since it is not possible here to explore the available leads on qualitative developmental changes in all of the domains related to teaching, and since the present volume is about constructivism, we will focus only on the domain of thinking about pedagogy, and specifically on the development of constructivist thinking about pedagogy.

Just as constructivism was a fairly late development in the history of thinking about knowledge, and a response to the limitations of earlier conceptions, so, too, it seems to be a perspective that teachers only come to understand (if they come to understand it at all) after working with other ways of thinking about learning and teaching long enough to realize their strengths and discover their limitations. And just as constructivist theory has continued to evolve in recent years, so, too, a teacher's constructivist thinking may undergo further qualitative changes as it continues to develop. Consider again the elementary school teacher in our previous example, who was thinking about procedures for transitions in which children come from some other activity to a circle on the classroom rug. She might have concerns about what is likely to happen when children who have previously had conflicts with each other sit together on the rug. Initially her solution might be to approvingly point out good behavior on the part of others, and to reward good behavior and punish transgressions on the part of the "problem" children. However, as her thinking about pedagogy develops further, she may come to question the wisdom of routinely controlling children's behavior for them by means of such practices, if one of her goals is for them to be able to control themselves. Consequently, her new solution might be to allow the children a lot of space to resolve conflicts on their own, with little or no intervention on her part. Sooner or later, however, she might see that such a laissez-faire approach has resulted in little or no progress on the part of her students! Rather than return to external controls on their behavior, which she also found unsatisfactory, her next move might be to provoke the sort of discussion that would engage her students in thinking together about the consequences of their actions for themselves and for others, and about the way they want life in their classroom to be (Child Development Project, 1996; DeVries & Zan, 1996).

The sequence of teaching strategies employed in this example illustrates part of a more general series of qualitative changes that has been found in the development of pedagogical thinking among teachers prepared in a program that emphasizes a constructivist developmental perspective on teaching (Ammon & Black, 1998; Ammon & Hutcheson, 1989; Levin & Ammon, 1992; 1996). Table 1 provides a very brief summary of five developmental levels, beginning with pre-constructivist notions rooted in empiricism and behaviorism, going on to a preliminary, global, and essentially romantic version of constructivism, and then on to versions of constructivism that are more differentiated and integrated. In the research based on this scheme to date, it has been found that, while a teacher's pedagogical thinking may be at different levels with respect to different aspects and instances of teaching at a given point in the teacher's development, there is nonetheless a predominant level at any one time, and that the predominant level changes through the sequence shown in Table 1. In our example, the teacher's different ways of dealing with behavior problems on the classroom rug correspond, respectively, to levels 2, 3, and 4 of thinking about pedagogy. It is important to note, however, that the teacher's pedagogical thought is not the only knowledge system involved in this example, because the more constructivist solutions to problem behavior that she employed (i.e., those at levels 3 and 4) presuppose a teacher whose development in the moral domain has progressed beyond the idea of morality as submission to authority, to the idea of morality as choosing, on one's own, to do whatever is consistent with the greatest good for the greatest number, given some defensible notion of what is "good." Thus we are reminded that "teacher development" includes more than development in the domain of thinking about pedagogy.

Table 1 may be somewhat misleading in the way it represents developmental levels of pedagogical thinking. It is not the case that more advanced modes of teaching ever replace earlier ones entirely. A teacher who has reached (say) level 4, differentiated constructivism, is—by definition—especially interested in guiding student thinking within particular domains of content, but she is also likely, at times, to show and tell, to model and reinforce, and to provide opportunities for free exploration in hands-on experiences. The difference at this level is that the earlier ways of teaching now play more limited roles, and are not expected to accomplish as much as before. Showing and telling are sometimes effective ways to provide information; modeling and reinforcing are useful in promoting the construction of procedural knowl-

Table 1   Developmental Levels of Pedagogical Conception

Qualitative Level	Learning Comes From:	Teaching Is Essentially:
1. Naïve Empiricism	Experiencing	Showing and telling
2. Everyday Behaviorism	Doing (i.e., practicing)	Modeling and reinforcing
3. Global Constructivism	Exploring	Providing hands-on experience
4. Differentiated Constructivism	Sense making	Guiding thinking within domains
5. Integrated Constructivism	Problem solving	Guiding thinking across domains

*Adapted from Levin and Ammon (1992).

edge; and providing unguided hands-on experience can give both teachers and students insights into the issues that must be addressed through further instruction. In fact these ways of teaching may often serve as means to the end of guiding student thinking toward better understandings. Thus the levels of pedagogical thinking imply not only that a teacher's view of teaching changes over time, but also that it expands to become more inclusive, as suggested by the nested circles in Figure 1.

If a goal of constructivist teacher education is the development of constructivist pedagogical thinking (along with development in related domains of knowledge), then a paramount question for teacher educators is how to foster that development. What kinds of learning experiences can teacher educators arrange to promote the development of constructivist thinking? If more advanced ways of thinking about pedagogy represent attempts to overcome the limitations of less advanced ways, then it seems important for teachers to have experiences that focus their attention on cases in which their lower-level ways of thinking about teaching do not lead to satisfactory results. Along with the question of why a particular teaching method seems like a good idea, an equally important question, given that no method works all the time, is why it doesn't always work. This is a challenging question,

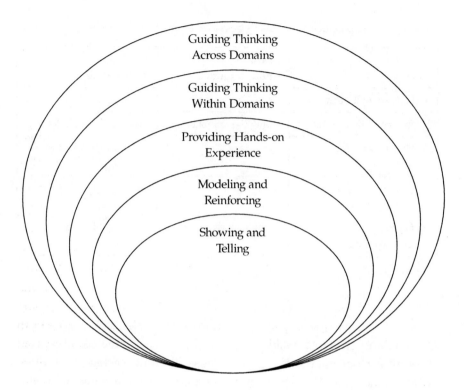

Guiding Thinking
Across Domains

Guiding Thinking
Within Domains

Providing Hands-on
Experience

Modeling and
Reinforcing

Showing and
Telling

Figure 1   An Expanding Conception of Teaching

because any method that teachers persist in using—even just showing
and telling—does work in some ways for some learners some of the
time, so that there are grounds for thinking it is more generally an adequate method. Moreover, when a method *doesn't* work, there are other
ways to explain such failures, without questioning the method itself.
Among the favorite explanations employed by teachers and others
alike are lack of student motivation, or lack of ability, or lack of pre-
paredness for school due to some presumed deficiency in the student's
background. When they serve to perpetuate transmission approaches
to teaching, these explanations based on supposed deficits also serve to
reproduce the social status quo and its inequities. They therefore
underscore the need for teacher learning and development in the social
and moral domains, so that teachers will know about the variety of cul-

tural resources their students do bring to school with them, and understand the need to take such resources into account when planning and evaluating instruction to insure equal access for all students.

As for the limitations inherent in lower levels of pedagogical thinking, they can be summarized briefly in terms of some risks they involve in practice.[2] Teaching by showing and telling alone (level 1) runs the risk of not engaging students actively and productively in the process of knowledge construction, even though it may be sufficiently engaging for some students some of the time. Behaviorist approaches (level 2) entail more activity on the part of students, but the emphasis is on having them perform procedures under the control of the teacher, so there is the risk that they are not given enough autonomy and opportunity to make sense of things in their own ways, and to become independent learners. Student autonomy is much more apparent with global constructivism (level 3), but in trying to give up control, the teacher also risks giving up opportunities to be more active in helping students with their sense making. Students should not be expected to reinvent from scratch all of the more advanced understandings that have already been attained in the cultures they live in. Thus, in keeping with differentiated constructivism (level 4) the teacher needs to show, tell, and ask students just enough about the content of instruction to guide their thinking toward better ways of understanding it, without taking away all of their autonomy as learners. In order to show, tell, and ask just enough, the teacher must have a good understanding of student development within each domain she teaches, so that she can help students understand the content on a level just beyond their present level.[3] Figuring out "where students are" in a given domain and helping them take the next step can be both challenging and rewarding by itself. However, if the teacher focuses exclusively on one domain at a time, she then runs the risk of not preparing students to coordinate multiple knowledge systems in the solution of complex problems—a risk which is finally reduced when integrated constructivism (level 5) becomes the predominant mode of pedagogical thinking.

In addition to helping teachers find the limitations inherent in their current ways of thinking, teacher educators can also employ a variety of means to help teachers transcend those limitations. That is, teachers should not be expected to reinvent more complete understandings of teaching, any more than students are expected to reinvent more complete understandings of what they are learning. Help for teachers can come both from learning about theory and from learning about the practices of others. The key is for new ideas to be treated not as formulas to be followed in some rote fashion, but as possibilities that teachers may or may not appropriate for their own purposes and according to their own understandings. Sometimes a new idea will not be appropriated at all because it requires too much of a stretch from a teacher's current level of understanding. Sometimes it will simply be assimilated to the teacher's current way of thinking and not really understood as a new idea. When that happens, teachers' ways of transforming the new idea can provide a teacher educator with insights into their current thinking. Sometimes teachers will adopt new practices and only later come to understand their possibilities, after working with them and reflecting on them. And sometimes new ideas will be understood as promising ways to answer questions that teachers have been struggling with. When that happens, a new idea will have served as a catalyst for broader systemic change, i.e., for development in teacher thinking and for improved practice. At that point, teachers will need support for extending new ideas to more and more instances, i.e., for horizontal development, until a broad enough foundation has been built for starting the cycle again with a renewed emphasis on vertical development.

So far our discussion of how to foster teacher development along with teacher learning has focused mainly on some general principles. We turn now to the question of putting these principles into practice in actual teacher education programs.

TEACHER EDUCATION: WHAT HAPPENS IN TEACHER EDUCATION PROGRAMS TO FACILITATE TEACHER LEARNING AND DEVELOPMENT?

Most teacher education programs have as their goals specific knowledge content or learning over which teachers must demonstrate mastery. The differentiation of learning and development, as we have defined them here, is not generally a focus. It is our belief that it is only with teacher development in mind that programs can prepare teachers to be agents to change schools for the better, as well as competent to teach in schools as they are now. If the learning and development goals of teacher education are to enable teachers to develop both conceptual and procedural knowledge in different domains, and to develop metacognitive knowledge regarding the construction and coordination of different types and domains of knowledge, then what practices within teacher education can promote these goals?

Preservice teacher education programs generally have two or three components in common. First, all programs have at least one or more field placements or student teaching placements. A second component of teacher education programs is the college coursework all teacher candidates take. While this coursework may vary from program to program and specialty to specialty, all students have courses in curriculum and instruction, the subject matter they will teach, the learning and teaching of literacy, and human development and learning. In addition, some programs include courses that focus on issues of diversity and multicultural education, inclusion of children with special needs, teaching methodology for English Language Learners, and a component addressing the use of technology in education. A third component of many programs is the seminar in which the intersection between the fieldwork and coursework is the focus. This seminar occurs during the same semesters that students are student teaching, and in some cases may be the only college course during that time. These components, fieldwork, coursework, and a reflective seminar are characteristic of most pre-service teacher education programs.

Teacher education does not end with credentialing. Many states require continuing education credits for renewal of credentials, and most teachers seek professional development opportunities during their teaching careers. These programs differ widely, but most are usually designed with the full or part time teacher in mind. Many professional development programs lead to higher degrees in education or to further certification. Whatever the details of inservice teacher education, it generally includes one or more components similar to those we described at the preservice level, i.e. guided fieldwork, coursework or other forms of study, and structured opportunities for reflection.

While this information is probably common knowledge among our readers, it seemed well to set the stage clearly for our discussion. In this section, we examine, within these components, programmatic examples designed from a constructivist perspective to foster teacher learning and development. We will look first at aspects of preservice programs and then see how these aspects are related to further professional development.

Coursework and Other University Sponsored Experiences in Preservice Teacher Education Programs

How coursework in general can enhance teacher learning and development varies widely, depending on the configuration of the program. Is the program an undergraduate or graduate program? Is it a blended program where subject matter and pedagogy are learned simultaneously; or is it a sequential program where pedagogical learning follows the acquisition of subject matter knowledge? How a program is structured is subject to institutional requirements and state credentialing regulations. However, these differences offer us an opportunity to examine a plethora of possibilities in the design and implementation of programs that are effective in preparing teachers. In spite of the difficulties inherent in delineating different "kinds" of knowledge, here we will examine examples of program work that support the development of conceptual, procedural and metacognitive knowledge with regard to teaching.

Subject Matter and Pedagogical Content Knowledge. Although ultimately teachers must use conceptual, procedural, and metacognitive understandings simultaneously, often coursework has traditionally been divided between the three. Thus, some coursework addresses conceptual knowledge within particular disciplines (such as psychology, sociology, mathematics, literature, science and so forth), some coursework addresses methodology of instruction where pedagogy is seen primarily as procedural (ways to teach reading, mathematics, science etc.), and the metacognitive aspects of learning to teach are the focus in the seminar that accompanies the fieldwork assignment(s). However, in programs where learning is seen as a constructive process, such categorization (while it may exist on paper in the form of institutional or state required names of classes) is generally avoided. For example, at Berry College in Rome, Georgia where teacher education is an undergraduate endeavor, the interdisciplinary nature of knowledge is emphasized. "Although there is clear need for understanding of disciplinary content, that understanding must become a part of interdisciplinary thinking. Once we step outside the classroom, there is little in life that narrowly follows disciplines" (Hausfather, 1999). The faculty at Berry envision and are working toward a model in which courses are taught by teams of professors who bring different perspectives to the questions at hand. Related disciplines, such as the pedagogy of reading and language arts and the contents of literature, the arts and humanities are all taught integrating interdisciplinary content knowledge and pedagogical knowledge. Such a model supports in students the development from the outset of understanding regarding the relationship between different contents, and between content(s) and teaching, and of coordinating conceptual and procedural knowledge through metacognition.

At Mills College in Oakland, California, prospective secondary teachers of mathematics and the sciences come into the program with subject matter competency based on prior coursework (according to state guidelines). In spite of this existing expertise, all of them, whether they will be teaching math, life science, or physical science, take subject matter courses in mathematics, biology, chemistry, and physics. Simultaneously, they take curriculum and instruction courses that incorporate and teach about constructivist techniques such as discovery learning and project based mathematics. Guided consideration of how they themselves are learning and relearning subject matter, while they also consider the teaching of the same subject matter, is critical in helping them to construct pedagogical content knowledge. The student teachers must coordinate their reflections on their own learning (metacognition) with what they know about the subject (content knowledge) and what they know about how people learn and how teaching helps them learn (pedagogical knowledge). The juxtaposition of coursework in different areas encourages this coordination. In addition, because they take these courses as a cohort of 15 students, and because they are often required to complete assignments collaboratively, students can raise questions for one another about how these pieces fit together. This collaboration facilitates the construction of coordinated knowledge.

Elementary school teachers teach across the curriculum and, therefore, must be conversant with a broad range of content. Their subject matter preparation generally represents a broad spectrum, and, for the most part, occurs prior to their coursework in pedagogy. (An exception is the already mentioned undergraduate teacher education program at Berry College.) Practices that encourage prospective teachers to reconstruct their content knowledge while constructing pedagogical knowledge can be effective in helping teachers to develop conceptual, procedural and metacognitive knowledge. One way to begin is to ask the students to reflect on their own learning of subject matter. In several programs, autobiography is a technique that both asks students to recall their own learning process and introduces them to the notion that there are multiple ways of learning something. Berry College asks undergraduates to write autobiographies about the learning of science, mathematics, and other content areas. At Mills College, teacher education graduate students who are earning a Multiple Subjects credential are asked to write autobiographies of learning to read and write. Writing and sharing autobiographies both reminds students of where they have been and informs them of the different ways people get to the point of being effective or fairly effective readers and writers.

Reflection on one's own learning can be coordinated with analyses of how children learn. At Mansfield University of Pennsylvania, students study emergent literacy in a class that also satisfies the writing requirement for their degree. As one of the requirements for this class, students correspond with third grade writers. Thus, the students are close observers of and participants in young children's writing development, while they focus on their own current "learning to write (better)" process. In these examples, the metacognitive aspects of reflection on the learning to write and read processes are necessary to connect personal experience with the learning of pedagogical knowledge. Students must reflect on both the conceptual and procedural aspects of learning to write. By closely observing and supporting the writing development of a third grader (through regular correspondence) a student can begin to understand the conceptual issues at stake in a 3rd grader learning to write. Simultaneously, the student is reflecting on and receiving feedback on her own writing. The opportunity for comparison and contrast can lead to disequilibrium and reconstruction of the student's understanding of both what it means to learn to write and of what "good writing" is. This juxtaposition of one's own current writing with that of a 3rd grader also leads to reflection on what the long-term goals are when working with young writers. In addition, as the student reflects on her own writing and her younger correspondent's writing, she constructs procedural knowledge about ways to improve her own writing and procedural knowledge about how to support her 3rd grade friend's writing development. Thus, through the application of reflection and metacognitive knowledge the student constructs more advanced conceptual and procedural knowledge.

Developmental Theory and Constructivism. The study of developmental theory and constructivism is a component of the curriculum in many teacher education programs that profess a belief in a constructivist theory of learning. At Mills College graduate students take an introductory course in which they focus on developmental theory and its relevance for teaching. For the final assignment they must create clinical tasks (like Piaget's clinical tasks) that focus on school-related instructional content (like learning to read, do mathematics, geography etc.). This challenging assignment asks them to construct a theory, using what they have learned about cognitive development, about how children might learn a particular concept. For example, how five and six year olds understand the daily calendar routine presents students with a wonderful opportunity for exploring a child's understanding of seriation, ordinality of numbers, and number patterns. Once they hypothesize a particular set of stages or ways of understanding the concept they have chosen, then students must develop a task and interview to test out their theory. For many of them, this assignment provides them with the aha! moment of discovering new lenses to understand children's thinking. Here, they connect their conceptual understanding of the content they are teaching with their procedural understanding about teaching and doing the content. Many of them also connect this assessment process with Vygotsky's notion of the zone of proximal development, because once they understand what the children do understand, they can think effectively about how to build on the child's current understanding to the understanding s/he can have with the help of a more knowledgeable other.

In the Developmental Teacher Education Program (DTE) at the University of California, Berkeley, students take a similar course in developmental theory. One activity they do that helps them construct their own understanding of Piaget's tasks and stages is teaching one another the formal operations tasks. By teaching these tasks to each other (in a jigsaw fashion) they end up understanding not only their own task, but also several others, and making the generalizations necessary for seeing how formal operations build on and elaborate on concrete thinking. Such an understanding helps them to see where the children they will be teaching are going, to go beyond the notion of expertise in particular problems to looking at conceptual and procedural knowledge that cuts across these problems. In addition, this activity provides opportunities for learning about the value and processes of collaborative learning and teaching.

Another activity/project in DTE is the jointly authored volume on what it means to take a developmental approach to teaching literacy that DTE students write together in their final semester. The goal of this work is to create a document that will be of use to them as they begin their teaching the following year. They must address the needs of both primary and intermediate level teachers, issues of second language acquisition, diversity and all aspects of literacy development including reading, writing, listening and speaking. In this final seminar, students (in conjunction with their professor's expertise and advice) develop the readings and syllabus for the class as they go along. Thus, as questions regarding, for example, the teaching of writing and developmental aspects of learning to write occur, they may decide that everyone should read and discuss a particular article. If a few people are working in one aspect, their professor will guide them to appropriate resources. Such flexibility and individual or group goal setting within a larger common context give them the opportunity to use their newly constructed conceptual, procedural, and metacognitive knowledge with regard to literacy learning and teaching. This assignment also entails opportunities to reflect on and integrate prior coursework and fieldwork. It provides an additional opportunity for collaboration and learning how to collaborate as professionals.

Knowledge in the Moral Domain. Teaching *about* the moral domain of knowledge is not the obvious solution to helping beginning teachers to consider this aspect of the profession. However, consideration of this issue is crucial for a teacher's learning and development. Issues and content from the moral domain can be woven into most of the coursework. It is possible to address this domain directly as well. In DTE, it is taught as the underlying developmental component to thinking about classroom management and organization. Thus, student teachers are asked to consider aspects of social and moral development as they consider the goals and objectives of classroom management.

At Mills College, all credential students take a year long class, *Introduction to the Profession of Teaching Diverse Learners*, that considers big ideas in teaching; major moral issues that go beyond our teaching, but impact our classrooms, including issues of racism, inclusion, curriculum and equity. Students gather for two case conferences in which each student prepares a case around a particular big idea. Each student prepares a story or example which is supposed to be a case of, in one situation, student motivation and, in the other, an ethical dilemma from his/her own teaching experience. They share these stories with one another in small groups, discussing how these cases illuminate the question at hand. The final question of the discussion is supposed to focus on "what is this a case of?", thus considering if these are really cases that are about student motivation or ethical dilemmas. These cases help them to address directly the moral component of teaching, and allow them to exercise their "moral muscles" in a context that is risk free as far as their own students are concerned. Thus, they can consider all aspects of a problem without fear of hurting a particular student, and they are aided in this consideration by the group of students to whom they present their case.

Another forum in which Mills students have the opportunity to confront the moral questions of teaching is in three program-wide all day retreats which are held at the beginning, middle and end of the credential year. Each retreat has its own particular focus, but all fall under the moral domain. For example, in the fall, students come to the retreat for their first opportunity to meet as a credential group. All specialty areas (single subject [either math and science or English and social studies], multiple subjects, or early childhood) come together to form cross specialty cohort groups that will work together in the *Introduction* class discussed above. Students have all read Ladson-Billings' *The Dreamkeepers* (1994) before coming. Part of the retreat is devoted to consideration of the issues raised in this book. Other retreats have focused on equity and access issues for children of color and children with special needs. Spending a long, concentrated amount of time on such questions reminds all of us of how these issues permeate the work we do, whether with P–12 students or higher education students.

The Fieldwork Component and Student Teaching Seminar in Preservice Programs

The most obvious place for students to see the connection of theory (learned at the college) and practice (what goes on in the classroom) is within the field placement. If students are reflective about what they observe and do in classrooms, they can make connections and ask questions that will move them forward in their construction of conceptual, procedural, and metacognitive knowledge. Most teacher education programs at the preservice level require student teachers to keep some kind of reflective or interactive journal to promote this reflective process. These activities are described in the chapter on action-reflection (Bowen, this volume). Student teachers are helped to develop this metacognitive stance by supervisors or professors who respond to the journal writing on a regular basis. The response that supervisors make is a form of scaffolding (to use Bruner's term) toward what one hopes will ultimately be a permanent reflective stance which the teacher can carry on somewhat independently. In one instance in DTE a student wrote an observation and question in her journal, then followed with the comment "OK, Barbara *(her supervisor)*, I know what you are going to ask me." and then answered the question. This is a wonderful example of moving from assisted practice to independent practice à la Vygotsky. A recent Mills College graduate, currently in her first year of teaching, wrote to her former supervisor that she gets up early every day to write in a journal. "The first semester is almost a blur already, but I am in a new routine for this semester that involves waking up at 5:50 to journal for 1/2 hour before school. It is such a good thing." Such reflective practice can help practicing teachers differentiate and coordinate conceptual and procedural knowledge.

However, it is often true that, while the differences seem obvious, the messiness of differentiating conceptual and procedural knowledge is particularly difficult in action on a daily basis. One of the considerations in designing teacher education programs is the observation that when student teaching occurs apart from conceptual and reflective coursework, novice teachers seek to become like their mentor teachers and may lose sight of the conceptual and reflective knowledge they began to learn and develop in their earlier education. The student teaching experience is often seen as paramount in shaping the student's future practice. A constructivist perspective on teacher education seeks to facilitate the reciprocal exchange of knowledge development between the university classroom and the schoolroom. While institutional and political constraints often make such reciprocity difficult to achieve, there are programmatic features that can facilitate that exchange.

In many programs, coursework and classroom teaching occur during the same semester. Thus, in the program at Berry College, field experiences are coordinated with teacher education content courses and students move back and forth between the college classroom and the field experience. Students keep reflective journals throughout their two to three years in the program which are responded to following Van Manen (1977), and Zeichner and Liston's (1987) levels of reflection.[4] Because students are asked to reflect and question and are supported in this endeavor by skillful probing and questioning by their supervisors, all three sorts of knowledge, conceptual, procedural, and metacognitive, are developed.

At Mills College and UC Berkeley the simultaneity of course-work and student teaching is also a feature and, while it is temporarily messier, it allows student teachers to develop a more metacognitive stance, particularly because they are in continual disequilibrium between their ideals and beliefs, on the one hand, and making those ideals and beliefs work within the reality of urban public schools. For example, they have to juggle the pedagogical needs of individual students with the moral need to distribute their time and attention equitably across students. Thus, it is not only coordinating how to teach particular subject matter with the challenges of classroom management and instructional organization that is difficult for preservice teachers. If they consider the moral aspects of their actions in the context of the public school classroom, they are forced to reflect on and reconcile their moral beliefs with the actions they feel are forced upon them by the "system". In addition, in thinking about how they teach and what they teach, they must make sense of the different cultural, linguistic, and familial experiences of their students and themselves. Finally, teachers want not only to teach in a way that is moral, they also want to promote moral development among their students.

The seminar which accompanies student teaching placements provides additional reflective support to this learning and development process. In seminar, student teachers have the benefit not only of their journal respondents' support, but also the benefit of one another's expertise and perspectives. From the perspective of the social nature of knowledge construction, an essential aspect of learning is reflecting with one's peers. In addition, when the seminar is facilitated by a faculty member familiar with the coursework the student has either had or is currently taking and with the classrooms in which student teachers practice, then the faculty member can better support reflection on practice and connections between theory and practice. Thus, writing and talking reflectively about what one is learning and the connections one is making between coursework and fieldwork is essential for the continuing development and learning of conceptual, procedural, and metacognitive knowledge related to teaching. The preservice years are merely the beginning of this process.

Continuing Teacher Education and Professional Development

Continuing education for practicing teachers is essential to a constructivist view of teacher learning and development. As stated in the introduction to this book, one vision for education is to create life-long learners. Thus, teachers must have the opportunity for life-long learning. A constructivist way of thinking about such learning is to continue the constructivist aspects of preservice programs that, in particular, enhance and support practicing teachers' abilities to reflect on, and learn and develop from, their own practice and the work of others (e.g. from other teachers and from educational researchers). One way that this continued learning and development can occur is through teacher research, which provides teachers with the opportunity to examine their own practice in a systematic way, with colleagues, to develop more coherent views of the connection between what they are trying to do and what is actually happening in their classrooms. Classroom teachers, in contrast to preservice teachers, are peculiarly well-situated to do action research on their own practice, but such self-reflection is enhanced by participating in a research community. Some professional development programs offer such an opportunity. In the Collaborative Master's Program at Georgia State University, Atlanta, one requirement of the program is for the practicing teacher, who is also a master's student, to design and implement an action research project. Participants spend 15 months together working with faculty to design curriculum and assessment that will lead to their personal professional development. The program is organized democratically with participants and faculty working together to determine the best program for the particular group of participants. All participants earn a master's degree in early childhood education.

Similar research projects are required for the master's degree at Mills College, where graduates of the program who are teaching return to complete their master's degree. Over a one or two-year period students conduct a research study focused on either their own teaching or on the context of schooling in which they are teaching. During this program they have two opportunities to present their research; first at the beginning in the form of a research proposal colloquium and second at the end in a research conference format. A further opportunity for continuing development for graduates of the master's program at Mills occurs when they return to serve as discussants on the panels when current MA students present their research proposals (in the Fall) and their completed research (in the Spring). This process provides a structured opportunity for continued learning and development, even after the formal aspects of teacher education are complete. Thus, teacher development and learning does not end with the end of their status as a student at the College. Rather, they can continue to reflect on their own practice, while mentoring students who follow them through the research process.

Another example of further professional development is the Superbridge program offered at Mills for first year teachers. Any first year teacher graduate may come for biweekly meetings held by the teacher education coordinator. These new teachers keep journals which the coordinator responds to and use their twice-monthly meetings to provide insight and support to one another. This program fosters continued learning and reflection as they embark on their teaching careers.

In a less formal context, a faculty member at Mills, in conjunction with a professional development program sponsored by several local county boards of education, offers an ongoing seminar in teacher research. Mills graduates are among the teachers who participate in this research, reflection, and writing opportunity. In this way, communities of teachers can work together to collaborate in research about their own classrooms, or other aspects of the educational process, providing life-long learning opportunities for themselves. Similarly, Mills is sponsoring a Teacher Scholars Workshop for practicing teachers to support one another as they begin the process of research on their own teaching. Teachers are paired with one another as support partners in their research. They are released monthly from their classrooms to come to an all day conference at Mills. At the end of the year, they, too, will present their research to one another and to the greater Mills Education community. The ultimate goal of constructivist teacher education should reflect the possibility for self-generative learning and reflection. Collaborative groups such as these jointly sponsored ones can provide such a forum.

Conclusion

There seem to be five major goals in supporting both teacher learning and development that teacher education programs can pursue. One is the interdisciplinary nature of content. By viewing and experiencing the learning of content as a knowledge construction process, teachers (all of us) can come to see how content is not so easily divided into discrete categories and that it is useful to think about the integration as well as the differentiation of subject matter. (See chapter on Content and Process.) In relation to this goal, a second goal is the continual reconsideration of Big Ideas and their relationship to content knowledge. A third goal is the construction of metacognitive knowledge to monitor one's own action, learning and development. The reflective stance provided by the development of metacognition enables teachers (all of us) to be in control of what we are doing and why we are doing it (based on the coordination of multiple considerations and multiple perspectives), and to discover the limitations of our current "whats" and "whys." Such a stance is significant in all domains of learning—academic, social, and moral. (See chapter on Action and Reflection.) A fourth goal is that teachers recognize the similarities and differences between their own ongoing development and learning and their students' ongoing development and learning. Development of this recognition can contribute as well to the development of metacognitive knowledge. Finally, learning to learn from and with one's peers provides teachers with a means of continual support and opportunities to be life-long learners together. (See chapter on Autonomy and Community.)

Teacher learning and development are life-long processes. Teacher education programs that are based on a constructivist view of learning and development aim to educate teachers to be able to continue this process throughout their careers. Teachers continue their learning through structured programs, both as students, and perhaps later as instructors themselves (as, hopefully, we have continued to grow ourselves). But they also need support in developing informal networks of colleagues and community members that can foster this learning and development in an ongoing way at school sites and between classrooms and home. In this way, teachers can contribute to our vision of schools and communities as places for life-long learning and development for all.

ENDNOTES

[1]It is of more than passing interest that both Vygotsky and Piaget were quite concerned with the establishment of new and more viable social orders in eastern and western Europe, following the Russian revolution and World War I, and therefore both appreciated the need for people to think beyond conventional ways of doing things that are transmitted to them by the present social order. Any effort to reduce knowledge to that which we receive from others, either socially or biologically, seems at odds with such notions as critical pedagogy and teaching to change the world.

[2]The limitations of lower developmental levels in the pedagogical domain can also be discussed in terms of contradictions or inconsistencies internal to the current knowledge system itself, along with failures of the system to produce desired results in practice. For example, at level 1 the idea that learning aptitude is an attribute of a person contradicts the idea that learner competence can be increased through instruction. The contradiction is resolved at level 2 by the idea that learning, which results from instruction, increases aptitude for further learning. But then the level 2 knowledge system contains contradictions of its own, which are resolved at level 3, and so on.

[3]The teacher needn't do all the showing, telling, and asking herself. She can arrange situations where students do those things for each other. In fact, when students and their peers are not too far apart in their levels of understanding, then the showing, asking, and telling they do with each other seem especially likely to be productive. There is, of course, a real possibility that students might misinform and mislead one another at times. But if the emphasis is on students making sense of things, and if the teacher is monitoring and facilitating the process, then there will be opportunities to address such misunderstandings.

[4]The three levels of reflection are: technical (focus on the efficiency and effectiveness of applied means to achieve certain ends), practical (focus on alternative outcomes and questioning the assumptions upon which traditional goals are made), and critical (incorporating moral and ethical criteria into reflection).

REFERENCES

Ammon, P., & Black, A. (1998). Developmental Psychology as a Guide for Teaching and Teacher Preparation. In N. M. Lambert & B. L. McCombs (Eds.), *How Students Learn: Reforming Schools Through Learner-Centered Education* (pp. 409–448). Washington, DC: American Psychological Association.

Ammon, P., & Hutcheson, B.P. (1989). Promoting the Development of Teachers' Pedagogical Conceptions. *Genetic Epistemologist, 17*(4), 23–29.

Bijou, S. W., & Baer, D. M. (1961). *Child Development*. New York: Appleton-Century-Crofts.

Calderhead, J. (Ed.) (1987). *Exploring Teachers' Thinking*. London: Cassell.

Chang-Wells, G. M. & Wells, G. (1993). Dynamics of Discourse: Literacy and the Construction of Knowledge. In E. A. Forman, N. Minick, & C. A. Stone (Eds.) *Contexts for Learning: Sociocultural Dynamics in Children's Development* (pp. 58–90). New York: Oxford University Press

Child Development Project (1996). *Ways We Want Our Class to Be*. Oakland, CA: Developmental Studies Center.

DeVries, R., & Zan, B. (1996). *Moral Classrooms, Moral Children: Creating a Constructivist Atmosphere in Early Education*. New York: Teacher College Press.

Diamond, M., & Hopson, J. (1999). *Magic Trees of the Mind*. New York: Plume. (Original work published 1998.)

Erikson, E. (1968). *Identity: Youth and Crisis*. New York: Norton.

Fenstermacher, G. D. (1994). The Knower and the Known: The Nature of Knowledge in Research on Teaching. In L. Darling-Hammond (Ed.), *Review of Research in Education: Vol. 20* (pp. 3–56). Washington D.C.: American Educational Research Association.

Fischer, K. W. (1980). A Theory of Cognitive Development: The Control and Construction of Hierarchies of Skills. *Psychological Review, 87,* 477–531.

Fosnot, C. T. (Ed.) (1996). *Constructivism: Theory, Perspectives, and Practice*. New York: Teachers College Press.

Gessell, A. (1940). *The First Five Years of Life* (9th ed.). New York: Harper & Row.

Ginsburg, H. (1997). *Entering the Child's Mind: The Clinical Interview in Psychological Research and Practice*. Cambridge, UK: Cambridge University Press.

Hausfather, S. (1999). Unpublished Notes for ATE Monograph on Constructivist Teacher Education.

Kroll, L.R. (1980). *The Development of Consciousness and the Child's Concept of a Story*. Unpublished manuscript.

Ladson-Billings, G. (1994). *The Dreamkeepers: Successful Teachers of African American Children*. San Francisco: Jossey-Bass.

Levin, B. B., & Ammon, P. (1992). The Development of Beginning Teachers' Pedagogical Thinking: A Longitudinal Analysis of Four Case Studies. *Teacher Education Quarterly, 19*(4), 19–37.

Levin, B. B., & Ammon, P. (1996). A Longitudinal Study of the Development of Teachers' Pedagogical Conceptions: The Case of Ron. *Teacher Education Quarterly, 23*(4), 5–25.

Moll, I. (1994). Reclaiming the Natural Line in Vygotsky's Theory of Cognitive Development. *Human Development, 37*(6), 333–342.

Moshman, D. (1998). Cognitive Development Beyond Childhood. In W. Damon (Series Ed.) D. Kuhn & R. S. Siegler (Vol. Eds.), *Handbook of Child Psychology: Vol. 2. Cognition, Perception, and Language* (pp. 947–978). New York: Wiley.

Pascual-Leone, J. (1970). A Mathematical Model for the Transition Rule in Piaget's Developmental Stages. *Acta Psychologica, 32*, 301–345.

Piaget, J. (1967). *Six Psychological Studies.* New York: Random House.

Piaget, J. (1970a). Piaget's Theory. In P. H. Mussen (Ed.), *Carmichael's Manual of Child Psychology: Vol. 1* (3rd ed., pp. 703–732). New York: Wiley.

Piaget, J. (1970b). *Science of Education and the Psychology of the Child.* New York: Orion Press. (Original work published 1935, 1965.)

Piaget, J. (1971). *Biology and Knowledge.* Chicago: University of Chicago Press. (Original work published 1967.)

Piaget, J. (1976). *The Grasp of Consciousness: Action and Concept in the Young Child.* Cambridge, MA: Harvard University Press. (Original work published 1974.)

Piaget, J. (1978). *Success and Understanding.* Cambridge, MA: Harvard University Press. (Original work published 1974.)

Piaget, J. (1995). *Sociological Studies.* London: Routledge. (Original work published 1965.)

Putnam, R. T., & Borko, H. (2000). What Do New Views of Knowledge and Thinking Have to Say about Research on Teacher Learning? *Educational Researcher, 29*(1), 4–15.

Rogoff, B. (1995). Observing Sociocultural Activity on Three Planes: Participatory Appropriation, Guided Participation, and Apprenticeship. In J. V. Wertsch, P. Del Río, & A. Alvarez (Eds.), *Sociocultural Studies of Mind* (pp. 139–164). Melbourne, Australia: Cambridge University Press.

Schifter, D. and Fosnot, C.T. (1993). *Reconstructing Mathematics Education: Stories of Teachers Meeting the Challenge of Reform.* New York: Teachers College Press.

Schön, D. (1983). *The Reflective Practitioner: How Professionals Think in Action.* New York: Basic Books.

Shulman, L. S. (1986). Those Who Understand: Knowledge Growth in Teaching. *Educational Researcher, 15*(7), 4–14.

Sprinthall, N. A., Reiman, A. J., & Thies-Sprinthall, L. (1996). Teacher Professional Development. In J. Sikula, T. J. Buttery, & E. Guyton (Eds.), *Handbook of Research on Teacher Education* (2nd ed., pp. 666–703). New York: Macmillan

Van Manen, M. (1977). Linking Ways of Knowing with Ways of Being Practical. *Curriculum Inquiry, 6*, 205–228.

Von Glasersfeld, E. (1996). Introduction: Aspects of Constructivism. In C. T. Fosnot, (Ed.), *Constructivism: Theory, Perspectives, and Practice* (pp. 3–7). New York: Teachers College Press.

Vygotsky, L. S. (1978). *Mind in Society: The Development of Higher Psychological Processes* (M. Cole, V. John-Steiner, S. Scribner, & E. Souberman, Eds.). Cambridge, MA: Harvard University Press.

Vygotsky, L. S. (1987). Thinking and Speech. In R. W. Rieber & A. S. Carton (Eds.), *The Collected Works of L. S. Vygotsky: Vol. 1, Problems of General Psychology* (pp. 43–285) (N. Minnick, Trans.). New York: Plenum. (Original work published 1934.)

Zeichner, K. M., & Liston, D. P. (1987). Teaching Student Teachers to Reflect. *Harvard Educational Review, 57*, 23–47.

Concluding Thoughts

Edi Guyton, President, Association of Teacher Educators 1999–2000

I cannot teach anybody anything, I can only make them think.

—Socrates

I have one regret. Since I appointed the Commission on Constructivist Teacher Education, I have not been able to participate in the process of the commission's work. I still regret not being privy to the dialogue, struggles, intellectual stimulation, and just plain fun the members of the Commission experienced. I am privileged, though, to be the first person not on the commission to enjoy the product of their work.

CONSTRUCTIVIST TEACHER EDUCATION AS POWERFUL TEACHER EDUCATION

I chose the theme Powerful Teacher Education for my term as President of the Association of Teacher Educators. One aspect of what I defined as Powerful Teacher Education was using effective models for educating teachers. The most powerful models in teacher education today are constructivist in nature, programs that place constructivism as core content, that model constructivist practices, and that help teachers to understand and create constructivist approaches to teaching. These powerful programs include the dimensions explicated in this book.

Power is an abstract concept—it is hard to describe, to convey the "sense" of it. As a powerful way to educate teachers, the essence of constructivist teacher education also is elusive. I have spent many hours working with my friend and colleague Julie Rainer trying to find words to convey the work we do in graduate programs in the Early Childhood Department at Georgia State University. The authors of this book are clear that no single constructivist theory exists. They also are clear that teacher education is a complex process with educational, social, political, social and moral goals focused on teaching and learning, social justice and democratic ideals. And yet they accepted my challenge to define and describe constructivist teacher education, even as I myself wondered how they could do it. And yet they are bold enough to explicate a vision of constructivist teacher education and try to make it accessible to other teacher educators. The way they did this was nothing short of brilliant. They took the contradictions within constructivism that make it so difficult to understand and made them not points of confusion but the very framework of understanding constructivist teacher education. This approach effectively articulates the power of constructivist teacher education, its power to address multiple and even contradictory goals. This framework can facilitate understanding for teacher educators who are least versed in constructivist teacher education. It also can challenge and develop ideas and practices for more experienced teacher educators.

PERSONAL PERSPECTIVE

I am committed to constructivist approaches to teaching and learning. Constructivist teacher education is not easy but having tasted its power, I cannot be satisfied with the more traditional, transmission, teacher educator as expert approach. As stated in the first chapter about teachers, I would not go back. I have seen and documented transformations among teachers as they become empowered as thinkers, learners, teachers, and community participants (see Rainer and Guyton,

2001). I believe that our graduate teacher education programs affect teaching and learning in P–12 schools. Delivering courses in more traditional programs made me feel as if I was tossing a penny into a pond without having any notion of neither what ripples it caused nor what the effects of any ripples might be. Now I develop programs of teacher education in concert with teachers and have become an empowered teacher educator.

I have a lot of knowledge and experience in constructivist teacher education. Does this mean that this book is for others and not for me? Or can it reach me where I am and help me grow as a teacher educator? This book does for me what the Kroll and Ammon chapter describes as teacher development. It raised questions for me to think about in relation to specific procedures and concepts used in my practice. These questions lead me to reflect on why a particular practice in a given situation does or does not make sense—the same questions raised by constructivist teacher education for teachers. Asking and trying to answer these questions promoted broader understanding and a better ability to raise questions for myself in my journey in constructivist teacher education.

MAKING MEANING FROM THE BOOK

This book can meet teacher educators where they are and provide them with conceptual and practical ways of thinking about constructivist teacher education. A good paper, essay, book has many entry points. Where one enters into the conversation with these authors depends on one's experience, knowledge, context, and attitudes. This book is rich in entry points. The examples are real and powerful. The ideas are well developed, provocative and generative rather than conclusive.

I have read the book and the agreed upon part of my contribution was the "conclusion." It really is the beginning if one believes that knowledge is socially constructed in teacher education. Now that you have read the book, what next? Certainly systematic personal reflection and action can make the book more useful. Re-read the book and let it help you examine your knowledge and practices. Using this resource for book groups also can enhance its meaning and power. Engage in conversations with teacher educators who have diverse perspectives about and experiences with constructivist teacher education. Explore teacher education knowledge and practices at your institution in light of this book. Invite transmission proponents, behaviorists, core knowledge advocates and others from across the university or college to join the conversations.

Teaching and learning are at the heart of working in an institution of higher education. Teaching and learning are the process and content of teacher education. Teaching and learning are not static endeavors; they cannot be defined or understood "once and for all." Teaching and learning must be constantly re-visioned, must be committed to social justice and equitable educational opportunities for every person; must be exposed to critical thinking and hard questions. This book can be a catalyst for important dialogue about teaching and learning, conversations too often absent from learning communities.

THANK YOU

Julie, Linda, Paul, Margaret, Christie, Carrie, Sandra, Teresa, and Sam, you have accomplished what I wanted you to accomplish even though I did not know what that was when I conceived of the commission. You have created a vision and made it accessible through the power of ideas and examples. You have facilitated the conceptual work that must be done autonomously and in community by teacher educators. Thank you.

Program Descriptions

BERRY COLLEGE

Berry College is a small private liberal arts college nestled in the foothills of northwest Georgia, enrolling mostly white middle class students along with some rural first-generation college students. The undergraduate majors in early childhood/elementary and middle grades teaching along with the minor in secondary education have undergone significant changes as part of a BellSouth Foundation funded effort to totally redesign teacher education. Teacher education faculty, including faculty in education, psychology and the arts and sciences, collaborated to create cross-disciplinary links and diverse experiences for all preservice teachers. Graduate programs serve teachers in the area interested in attaining master's and specialist degrees.

GEORGIA STATE UNIVERSITY

The Collaborative Master's Program (CMP) is a M.Ed. program offered by the Department of Early Childhood Education at Georgia State University, a public institution located in downtown Atlanta. The CMP is a 15-month program designed for the practicing teacher who wishes to establish a learner-centered classroom. This program is based on the assumption that learning is a constructive process that builds on the knowledge and experience of the learner. Through an integrated approach that provides choices and opportunities for decision-making and dynamic group interactions, the program is designed to be constructed around academic givens so that content areas have blurred edges, and teacher participants partner with faculty to shape the paths by which content is learned. Certain beliefs characterize this program. Learning happens in a social setting where children and teachers learn together. Meaningful learning occurs in the context of the university and in classrooms. With these beliefs as the core, this program provides opportunities for teachers to reflect upon and refine their understanding about teaching and learning.

JAMES MADISON UNIVERSITY

Located in the Shenandoah Valley of Virginia, James Madison University is a public, comprehensive university, offering programs on the bachelor's, master's and doctoral levels. Originally a state Normal School, JMU's education program is the oldest on the campus. Undergraduate licensure programs and master's degrees are offered in early childhood, middle grades, secondary, special education, and ESL. Graduate level licensure programs include reading specialist and educational leadership. At this time, all initial licensure programs have undergone extensive revisions in response to state level changes in licensure standards. New programs will lead to initial certification and a master's degree.

MANSFIELD UNIVERSITY OF PENNSYLVANIA

Mansfield University of Pennsylvania is one of fourteen state universities that comprise the State System of Higher Education of Pennsylvania. Mansfield is a relatively small university (3000 fulltime undergraduate students) located in rural, north central Pennsylvania. Mansfield advertises that it is a student-centered, teaching institution that provides caring faculty-student relations in a dynamic learning environment. Mansfield has always enjoyed a close relationship with the region as the only four-year institution serving the citizens of the northern tier of Pennsylvania and the southern tier of New York. The link has been especially strong with regional school districts and their teachers, many of who are graduates of Mansfield's undergraduate and Master's programs. Undergraduate degrees and certifications that meet both Pennsylvania and NCATE standards are offered in art, early childhood, elementary, secondary, music, and special education. In addition, Master's degrees are offered in many of the same subject areas, plus certifications in school library and information technology and in reading. Mansfield University's size facilitates collaboration between education faculty and others interested in teacher education, including arts and sciences faculty and regional P–12 educators.

MILLS COLLEGE

Mills College is a small liberal arts college for women only at the undergraduate level and for men and women at the graduate level located in Oakland, California in the San Francisco Bay Area. At the undergraduate level about 25–30% of our students are women of color. Many of our undergraduate students are resuming their education and are older than traditional age college students. The Education Department includes two interdisciplinary undergraduate majors, one in child development and one in liberal studies.

At the graduate level, the Education Department is the largest on campus with about 120 students enrolled in a variety of credential, masters and doctoral programs. The programs include teacher and administrator preparation, early childhood education, child life education, early childhood special education, and educational leadership. The focus of the department is the improvement of urban education and the preparation of professionals who can contribute to this improvement in schools, hospitals and other institutions devoted to educating children and youth. In addition the department houses the oldest laboratory school on the West Coast, educating children from 0–11 years old.

All programs in the department are committed to social justice and equity and excellence in education for all children and youth. To this end, the department has identified six principles that are the foundation of what is taught and what we aim for. The principles, briefly, are as follows:

1. Teaching is a moral act based on an ethic of care.

2. Teaching is an act of inquiry and reflection.

3. Learning is a constructivist/developmental process.

4. Teaching is for the acquisition and construction of subject matter.

5. Teaching is a collegial act.

6. Teaching is a political act.

NEW JERSEY CITY UNIVERSITY

The mission of New Jersey City University (NJCU), New Jersey's only public urban college, is to provide a diverse population with access to an excellent university education and the support services necessary for success. The University is also committed to the improvement of the educational, intellectual, cultural, socio-economic, and physical environment of its surrounding urban region.

NJCU's student body is drawn from a broad base of the population and includes the high school graduate pursuing a four-year degree sequence and non-traditional students. These include the older student, the part-time student, and the working student—all of whom are able to avail themselves of flexible class scheduling. The student body, while drawn primarily from Northern New Jersey counties, also comes from the Virgin Islands and Hawaii, as well as forty foreign countries.

Although the University was founded as a teacher training institution, this multipurpose institution houses three colleges and offers more than 25 degree programs. Students in all academic areas have the opportunity through cooperative education to work in salaried positions in related fields while studying for a degree.

NJCU's College of education provides leadership in meeting the educational needs of all students. It is committed to building a learning community and too providing high quality instruction to those seeking careers within an urban, multicultural and educational environment. The goal of the College of Education is to prepare knowledgeable, capable, and reflective urban practitioners.

UNIVERSITY OF CALIFORNIA AT BERKELEY

The University of California at Berkeley is a large, research-oriented public institution in a major, highly diverse urban area. Its Developmental Teacher Education Program (DTE) offers two years of pre-service graduate study leading to a master's degree and an elementary teaching credential with special emphasis on the teaching of culturally and linguistically diverse learners. Guided by a constructivist developmental perspective, the program aims to prepare teachers who will promote learning with understanding for all students, will continue to grow professionally, and will work collaboratively for progressive change in our schools and society. The academic core of DTE is a four-semester seminar on the study of child development and its implications for education. Throughout the program, coursework and student teaching are pursued simultaneously by cohorts of 20–25 students who vary widely in age and background but have all demonstrated academic ability and promise as teachers. Students also complete original research projects on development and teaching for the master's degree. Course instructors in DTE include a mix of tenure-track and other faculty in the Graduate School of Education, and field supervisors are generally program graduates and/or doctoral students in education who have had substantial teaching experience. Additional information about the DTE program is available at *www-gse.berkeley.edu/program/dte/dte.html.*

A Selected
Annotated Bibliography
of Constructivist Education

BOOKS AND BOOK CHAPTERS

Aaronsohn, E. (1996). *Going against the Grain: Supporting the Student-Centered Teacher.* Thousand Oaks, CA: Corwin Press.

This book provides helpful evidence and support for preservice teachers as they begin to develop a constructivist understanding of instruction. Aaronsohn presents a rich case study describing the challenges that face a first year student-centered teacher. This beginning teacher learns how to handle her own uncertainties about her non-traditional practice as she struggles to overcome resistance from other teachers in her new school. Chapters help the reader to see teaching as a process, not a product, and to learn how to deal with institutional realities that may conflict with more student-centered priorities. The book also includes suggestions for how teacher educators can develop an effective mentoring relationship with their preservice teacher-students.

Bedrova, E. & Leong, D. J. (1995). *Tools of the Mind: A Vygotskian Approach to Early Childhood Education.* Columbus, OH: Prentice Hall.

The author's objective is to enable future teachers to provide young children with the mental tools necessary for learning. They view mental tools as a cycle in which ideas are learned from others, modified and changed, and passed back to others. They offer practical applications and suggestions for applying elements of social constructivist theory in the classroom. The book includes examples and activities that profile the Vygotskian approach at work in various schools in the Denver metropolitan area.

Brooks, J. G. & Brooks, M. G. (1999). *In Search of Understanding: The Case for Constructivist Classrooms* (Rev. ed.). Alexandria, VA: Association for Supervision and Curriculum Development.

The authors present a case for constructivist classrooms in which the teacher searches for students' understandings of concepts and then structures opportunities for students to refine or revise these understandings by posing contradictions, presenting new information, asking questions, encouraging research, and engaging students in inquiries designed to challenge current concepts. The book is organized around five overarching principles of constructivist classrooms: (1) teachers seek and value their students' points of view, (2) classroom activities challenge students' suppositions, (3) teachers pose problems of emerging relevance, (4) teachers build lessons around primary concepts and "big" ideas, and (5) teachers assess student learning in the context of daily teaching.

Cobb, P., Perlwitz, M. & Underwood-Gregg, D. (1998). *Individual Construction, Mathematical Acculturation, and the Classroom Community.* In M. Larochelle, N. Bednarz & J. Garrison (Eds.), *Constructivism and Education* (pp. 63–80). Cambridge, UK: University Press.

This book chapter argues that every classroom is a unique mathematics microculture that significantly affects the mathematical activities and learning of the students. The authors also discuss the theoretical and pragmatic tensions arising from viewing mathematical learning as a process of individual cognitive construction and as a process of social acculturation into conventional mathematical practice. These issues form the background of the authors' consideration of instructional activities appropriate for inquiry-based mathematics classrooms.

DeVries, R. & Zan, B. (1994). *Moral Classrooms, Moral Children: Creating a Constructivist Atmosphere in Early Education.* New York: Teachers College Press, Columbia University.

This book provides a constructivist rationale for a sociomoral atmosphere in early childhood education that optimally promotes social, moral, and affective development in children. The teacher-child relationship is conceived as one of mutual respect in which the teacher minimizes the exercise of unnecessary authority, and which aims to replace external teacher control of children with moral behavior motivated by internalized principles. In addition to several chapters explaining this approach from a theoretical standpoint, there are a number of chapters discussing the theory's practical implications in common early childhood classroom activities.

DeVries, R., Zan, B., Hilderbrandt, C., Edmiaston, R., & Sales, C. (2001). *Developing Constructivist Early Childhood Curriculum: Practical Principles and Activities.* New York: Teachers College Press.

This book clarifies a constructivist approach to early childhood education. It addresses theoretical and practical issues, for example, play in the early childhood curriculum, definitions and principles of constructivist teaching, and assessing and documenting learning. The authors include many realistic and useful examples for working in constructivist classrooms.

Dillon, D., Anderson, L., Angio, J., Kahan, N., Rumin, A., & Sherman, R. (1995). Teaching and Learning Together in Teacher Education: "Making Easter." In C. Dudley-Marling and D. Searle (Eds.), *Who Owns Learning? Questions of Autonomy, Choice, and Control* (pp. 190–212). Portsmouth, NH: Heinemann.

This book chapter gives an overview of the primary author's semester-long, graduate level course called "Language and Learning Across the

Curriculum," starting with a brief comparison of constructivist and behaviorist educational beliefs. Four key principles undergirding the course, an outline of course readings, and a brief description of assessment methods are included. Each of the five secondary authors' viewpoints as former students in the course are given in their own words, with a summary reflection by the primary author. The unusual subtitle is explained at the end of the chapter.

Duckworth, E. (1997). *Teacher to Teacher: Learning from Each Other.* New York: Teachers College Press, Columbia University.

This book describes the experiences of thirteen teachers in a one-year, graduate level Experienced Teachers Program (ETP) at the Harvard Graduate School of Education. The ETP is outlined in the introduction; and the remainder of the book is a collection of discussions, essays, and first-person descriptions of experiences of the teacher-students during their year in the program. The book relates the achievements and challenges of a democratic teacher education program from the insiders' viewpoints.

Goodman, J. (1992). *Elementary Schooling for Critical Democracy.* Albany, New York: State University of New York Press.

In this book Goodman argues for and illustrates the way in which elementary education can serve as a vehicle for critical democracy. The concept of critical democracy is drawn from Dewey's political ideologies. However, Goodman's primary source of inspiration emerged from his observations in an independent school that is actively searching for ways to create an elementary education for democracy.

Guyton, E., Rainer, J., & Wright, T. (1997). Developing a Constructivist Teacher Education Program. In D. Byrd & D. J. McIntyre (Eds.), *Research on the Education of our Nation's Teachers* (pp. 149–171). Thousand Oaks, CA: Corwin Press.

This chapter focuses on three phases of curriculum decision making for an early childhood department at a large urban state university engaged in developing a new master's degree program based on constructivist theories and principles. Authors identified a) tasks, issues, and decisions for each phase; b) foundations for change; and c) faculty struggles in making a paradigm shift in higher education.

Harlen, W. (Ed.) (1985). *Primary Science: Taking the Plunge.* **Portsmouth, NH: Heinemann.**

This book is a collection of articles outlining issues in teaching elementary and middle school students, with detailed sections on dialogue, observation, questioning, communication, and misconceptions. Brought to life with examples from classrooms and children, this collection of articles is especially useful with undergraduates or beginning teachers.

Henderson, J. G. (1996). *Reflective Teaching: The Study of Your Constructivist Practices* **(2nd ed.). Columbus, OH: Prentice Hall.**

This book reflects two emerging, interrelated educational reform trends: (1) the constructivist approach, stressing teaching for meaning making rather than for rote memorization and (2) schools as centers of inquiry, where teachers function as students of their professional work. Responding to these trends, the text is designed to help readers become career-long students of constructivist educational practices.

Hillkirk, K. (1994). Teaching for Democracy: Preparing Teachers to Teach Democracy. In J. M. Novak (Ed.), *Democratic Teacher Education: Programs, Processes, Problems, and Prospects* **(pp. 89–102). Albany, NY: State University.**

This book chapter describes the initial three years of the undergraduate Teacher Education for Civic Responsibility (TECR) Program at Ohio State University, which is "framed around the civic mission of teachers in educating their students about the rights and responsibilities of citizenship in a democracy" (p. 90). A table lists six contrasts between TECR and what the author describes as a more traditional teacher education program.

Jonassen, D. H., Peck, K. L. & Wilson, B. G. (1999). *Learning with Technology: A Constructivist Perspective.* Columbus, OH: Prentice Hall.

Approaching learning from a constructivist viewpoint, this book addresses how to use very specific types of technology and focuses on how technology can be used as a thinking tool to foster meaningful learning. Each chapter provides various activities and implementation strategies with follow-up questions. Current uses of technology such as video theater, cybermentoring, creating homepages, and hypermedia are discussed throughout the book.

Lambert, L. (Ed.). (1995). *The Constructivist Leader.* New York: Teachers College Press, Columbia University.

Beginning with an overview of the histories of learning and leadership theory, this book leads the reader toward a conceptualization of constructivist leadership that will enable significant school change. Constructivist leadership is defined by the authors as "the reciprocal process that enables participants in an educational community to construct meanings that lead toward a common purpose for schooling."

Chapters include such topics as the linguistics of leadership, the role of narrative and dialogue in constructivist leadership, and the school district as an interdependent learning community. The book concludes with a discussion on the preparation of constructivist leaders and insights into the future of schooling.

Lambert, L., Collay, M., Dietz, M. E., Kent, K., & Richert, A. E. (1996). *Who Will Save Our Schools? Teachers as Constructivist Leaders.* Thousand Oaks, CA: Corwin Press.

This book looks at systemic school reform through the lens of constructivist learning theory. The authors propose what they call "constructivist leadership" as a new way of viewing and working with the issues of power, school culture, and classroom instruction as constructivist teachers attempt to build learning communities that support radical school change. The authors advance nine design principles for reforming professional teacher education.

Larochelle, M., Bednarz, N. & Garrison, J. (Eds.). (1998). Constructivism and Education. New York: Cambridge University Press.

This international and interdisciplinary collection of chapters discusses the many issues and educational practices that are touched on by constructivism. Drawing on perspectives from a range of different fields (ethics, mathematics education, philosophy, social psychology, science education, social studies), this book invites us to reposition ourselves in relation to the major currents that have influenced education in this century, namely pragmatism, genetic epistemology, and social interactionism.

Lieber, C., Mikel, E., & Pervil, S. (1994). Radical Change in Assessment: A Catalyst for Democratic Education. In J. M. Novak (Ed.), Democratic Teacher Education: Programs, Processes, Problems, and Prospects (pp. 229–250). Albany, NY: State University of New York Press.

This book chapter presents a rationale for the authors' belief that "teachers can fundamentally reorganize the whole of their teaching by adopting a democratic paradigm of assessment" (p. 223). A four-page chart is included that contrasts democratic assessment practice with what the authors describe as traditional assessment methods. An overview of the goals, strategies, and assessment methods of a week-long graduate course in democratic education for experienced teachers is also presented.

Littledyke, M. & Huxford, L. (Eds.). (1998). Teaching the Primary Curriculum for Constructive Learning. London: David Fulton.

Providing guidance in teaching across all subjects of the primary curriculum, this text draws on extensive research in constructivist ideas in children's learning which shows that effective learning occurs when teachers understand and build on children's previous views and experience in their teaching programs. The authors provide both specialist subject knowledge and coherent cross-curriculum perspectives.

Marlowe, B. A. & Page, M. L. (1998). *Creating and Sustaining the Constructivist Classroom*. Thousand Oaks, CA: Corwin Press.

This book attempts to consolidate the theoretical foundations of constructivist education with their practical implications in the classroom. Key issues regarding the shift from a traditional to a constructivist approach are discussed; and guidelines, practical tips, and model checklists are presented to help teachers make the change an enduring one. Firsthand reports of successes and problems in classroom teachers' attempts to change paradigms are included.

Oldfather, P., West, J., White, J. & Wilmarth, J. (1999). *Learning Through Children's Eyes: Social Constructivism and the Desire to Learn*. Washington, DC: American Psychological Association.

The authors of this book show how teachers who take a social constructivist stance may enhance motivation and meaningful learning. They suggest experiences that deepen understanding of social constructivism and its relevance for multicultural, democratic classrooms. The authors analyze transcripts of in-depth conversations with children in order to better understand children's individual thought patterns, and they describe strategies for discussing carefully selected children's and young adult books to help both teachers and children understand learning through a social constructivist lens. An extensive annotated bibliography is provided.

Osborne, R. & Freyburg, P. (1985). *Learning in Science: The Implications of Children's Science*. Portsmouth, NH: Heinemann Publishers.

This is a classic book using findings on student conceptions and use of language to explore issues in learning and teaching. Many examples of classroom teaching are used to develop understanding of the challenges to bringing about deep understanding. It develops a teaching sequence based on a constructivist learning model. Implication for working with teachers are included.

Richardson, V. (1997). *Constructivist Teaching and Teacher Education: Theory and Practice.* In V. Richardson (Ed.), *Constructivist Teacher Education: Building a World of New Understandings* (pp. 3–14). Washington, D.C.: The Falmer Press.

In this chapter Richardson reviews different forms of constructivism with teacher educators in mind. She discusses issues of power, authority, and the role of formal knowledge. Richardson notes that some teacher educators are using a direct approach to teach about constructivism and others are modeling the constructivist approach to involve their students in examining of teaching and model alternatives.

Scott, P. (1987). *Children's Learning in Science Project: A Constructivist View of Learning and Teaching in Science.* Leeds, England: University of Leeds, Centre for Studies in Science and Mathematics Education.

This booklet written for teachers provides an insightful look at the justification for a constructivist view of learning. It then outlines the key parts of this view and gives general implications and examples, including a generalized model for a constructivist teaching sequence.

Selley, N. J. (1999). *The Art of Constructivist Teaching in the Primary School: A Guide for Students and Teachers.* London: David Fulton.

This book gives an overview of constructivist learning theory and the development of constructivist teachers. The author gives tips on dealing with system-wide curriculum expectations and common objections to constructivist teaching. Chapters with constructivist teaching suggestions are presented for each of the four main school subjects: science, history, language, and mathematics.

Spivey, N. N. (1996). *The Constructivist Metaphor: Reading, Writing, and the Making of Meaning.* San Diego, CA: Academic Press.

This book presents a major reconsideration of constructivist theory through an applied examination of the ways in which people create meaning for texts. The author describes major historical constructivist positions throughout the twentieth century and uses them as an essential starting point for her presentation of current approaches to the generative, organizational, and selective nature of human communication. The work illustrates an integrative conception of discourse, placing cognitive activity in relation to the text while assuming a social orientation encompassing both composition and comprehension.

Steffe, L. P. & Gale, J. (Eds.). (1995). *Constructivism in Education.* Hillsdale, NJ: Erlbaum.

This book contains manuscripts from leading constructivist thinkers about how epistemological theory impacts educational theory and practice. Major sections discuss radical and social constructivism; information-processing constructivism and cybernetic systems; social constructivism and sociocultural approaches; and alternative epistemologies in language, mathematics, and science education. Three separate analysis and synthesis articles help the reader to understand the articles in their larger context.

Tobin, K. (Ed.) (1993). *The Practice of Constructivism in Science Education.* Hillside, NJ: Lawrence Earlbaum Associates.

This book provides a thorough review of issues in constructivism, focusing on the nature of constructivism, its relationship to teaching and learning of science and mathematics, and constructivist perspectives on teacher education. It is very in depth and complex in its coverage, and is recommended for graduate students and college faculty.

Vadeboncour, J. A. (1997). Child Development and the Purpose of Education: A Historical Context for Constructivism in Teacher Education. In V. Richardson (Ed.), *Constructivist Teacher Education: Building Toward a World of New Understandings* (pp. 15–37). Washington, D.C.: Falmer Press.

This chapter builds an argument for an emancipatory approach to knowledge construction in teaching and teacher education programs. Emancipatory and socialcultural constructivists believe that knowledge is first created on the social plane through interactions with others and then is moved by individuals to the psychological plane. Students are encouraged to explore and act on their discoveries. Emancipatory knowledge construction is a commitment to social change, justice, and responsibility.

Waite-Stupiansky, S. (1997). *Building Understanding Together: A Constructivist Approach to Early Childhood Education.* Albany, NY: Delmar.

This informative theory-to-practice textbook clearly demonstrates how Piaget's constructivist theory translates into solid instructional principles to be used in preschools through primary classrooms today. Chapters are included about the following topics: understanding constructivism, children's social understandings, and guiding children's moral development. Additional chapters about constructivist implications for teaching the subject areas of reading and writing, mathematics, science, and art are also presented.

Westheimer, J. (1998). *Among School Teachers: Community, Autonomy and Ideology in Teachers' Work.* New York: Teachers College Press, Columbia University.

This book discusses the author's concept of teacher communities and what factors encourage or impede their growth in schools. Case studies of the efforts of faculty and staff at two diverse middle schools to create and sustain teacher communities are presented and compared. Lessons learned from these case studies are explored, along with their implications for administrators, researchers, and other stakeholders in education.

JOURNALS AND JOURNAL ARTICLES

Condon, M. W. F., Clyde, J. A., Kyle, D. W. & Hovda, R. A. (1993). A Constructivist Basis for Teaching and Teacher Education: A Framework for Program Development and Research on Graduates. *Journal of Teacher Education, 44,* 273–278.

This article describes the Committee for Alternative Programs in Teaching and Learning (CAPITAL) Program, formed in 1988 at the Center for the Collaborative Advancement of the Teaching Profession at the University of Louisville for non-traditional students earning a K-4 Master of Arts in Teaching. This program is a joint effort by the university's Early and Middle Childhood Education Department and the Jefferson County (Kentucky) Public Schools. In addition to discussing the CAPITAL Program's features and goals, the article presents a 15-question Developing Teacher Interview the authors used in their research of preservice teachers' changes in attitudes about teaching and learning.

Ellsworth, E. (1989). Why Doesn't This Feel Empowering? Working through the Repressive Myths of Critical Pedagogy. *Harvard Educational Review, 59,* 297–324.

Reference in M. O'Loughlin in engaging teachers in emancipatory knowledge construction," to the idea that all students possess multiple frames of reference with which to construct knowledge by virtue of their ethnic background, etc.

Kroll, L. & Black, A. (1993). Developmental Theory and Teaching Methods: A Pilot Study of a Teacher Education Program. *Elementary School Journal, 93*(4), 417–431.

An in-depth understanding of developmental theory and research, in the tradition of Piaget, is used as core knowledge for helping preservice and inservice elementary teachers restructure their conceptions of teaching and learning. The 2-year Developmental Teacher Education (DTE) program is summarized and linkages between developmental conceptions of learning and educational practices that Piagetian theory was not originally developed to encompass are proposed.

Phillips, D. C. (1995). The Good, the Bad, and the Ugly: The Many Faces of Constructivism. *Educational Researcher, 24*(7), 5–12.

This article argues that the main constructivist writers can be located along each of three different dimensions, which also serve to highlight the relationships and differences among them. The author calls the first two dimensions "individual psychology versus public discipline" (whether the theorist is more concerned with how knowledge originates within the individual or built up within society as a whole) and "humans the creators versus nature the instructor" (whether knowledge is created within the learner or if it comes from somewhere external to the learner). The third dimension is not named, but is described as whether or not the constructive activity is discussed in terms of individual cognition alone or in terms of social and political processes.

Posner, G. J., Strike, K.A., Hewson, P.W., & Gertzog, W. A. (1982). Accommodation of a Scientific Conception: Toward a Theory of Conceptual Change. *Science Education, 66*, 211–227.

This is an original study that established the role of students' prior ideas on learning and postulated a theory of conceptual change instruction. It includes a general model of conceptual change which is largely derived from current philosophy of science. Pedagogical implications are presented.

Rainer, J. (1999). Faculty Living Their Beliefs. *Journal of Teacher Education, 50*(3), pp. 192–200.

In this article, the author describes a programmatic reform based on constructivist theories, identifies how the reform changed faculty practice, and articulates faculty members' reflections on personal and professional change.

Rainer, J. & Guyton, E. (2001). Structures of Community and Democratic Practices in Graduate Teacher Education, Teacher Change, and Linkages Facilitating Change. *Action in Teacher Education, 23*(2), pp. 18–29.

In this research study, the authors describe practices in a constructivist graduate program in teacher education, document changes in teachers and their practice, and analyze connections between program practices and teacher change. The authors also develop a model for constructivist teacher education with linkages between community, democratic practices and teacher change.

Schattgen, S. F. (1997). From Piagetian Theory to Educational Practice: Developing and Supporting Constructivist Early Childhood Teachers through Project Construct. *Journal of Early Childhood Teacher Education, 18*(2), 34–42.

Project Construct, an early childhood reform initiative designed to translate Piagetian theory into educational practice, represents an expansive effort to develop and support constructivist early childhood teachers. This paper describes the Project Construct framework, its accomplishments and challenges, and continuing issues and questions.

Starver, J. R. (1998). Constructivism: Sound Theory for Explicating the Practice of Science and Science Teaching. *Journal of Research in Science Teaching, 35*(5), 501–520.

Taking on the critics of constructivism as a theory of knowledge, Starver presents a detailed explanation of the epistemological grounds for constructivism, five long-standing epistemological issues that challenge constructivism, and responses to critics' objections. A complex yet satisfying read for college faculty and graduate students.

Von Glaserfeld, E. (1989). Cognition, Construction of Knowledge, and Teaching. *Synthese, 80,* 121–140.

Von Glaserfeld's seminal article defining the radical constructivist theory of knowledge with applications to education provides a concise and influential analysis of our understandings of knowing, learning, and teaching, appropriate for college faculty and advanced graduate students.

Watson, B. & Konicek, R. (1990). Teaching for Conceptual Change: Confronting Children's Experience. Phi Delta Kappan, 71(9), 680–685.

This article provides a review of theories behind constructivist approaches to science, including micro-conceptions research, interspersed with the story of a third grade classroom. It explains the difference between children's sensible reasoning and Piagetian conceptions of concrete reasoning. Suggestions are provided for teachers. Enjoyable read.

THEMATIC JOURNAL ISSUES ON CONSTRUCTIVISM

Constructivism in Teacher Education [Thematic issue]. (1996, Summer). Action in Teacher Education, 18(2).

This thematic journal issue includes the following nine articles on constructivism in teacher education: (1) Vygotsky and Schooling: Creating a Social Context for Learning [Hausfather, S. J., pp. 1–10]; (2) Learning about Learning: An Interactive Model [Burk, D. I. & Dunn, M., pp. 11–18]; (3) Implications of a Model for Conceptualizing Change in Mathematics Teachers' Instructional Practices [Edwards, T. G., pp. 19–30]; (4) Foxfire: Constructivism for Teachers and Learners [Teets, S. T. & Starnes, B. A., pp. 31–39]; (5) Constructivist-based Experiential Learning in Teacher Education [Kaufman, D., pp. 40–50]; (6) Changing Beliefs: Teaching and Learning Mathematics in Constructivist Preservice Classrooms [Anderson, D. S. & Piazza, J. A., pp. 51–62]; (7) Practicing What We Preach: Constructivism in a Teacher Education Program [Kroll, L. R. & LaBoskey, V. K., pp. 63–72]; (8) Reflective Theory and Practice: A Constructivist Process for Curriculum and Instructional Decisions [Jadallah, E., pp. 73–85]; and (9) A Constructivist Teacher Education Program that Incorporates Community Service to Prepare Students to Work with Children Living in Poverty [DeJong, L. & Groomes, F. L., pp. 86–95].

Constructivist Approaches to Teacher Education [Thematic issue]. (1992, November–December). *Journal of Teacher Education, 43(5).*

This thematic journal issue explores the implications of constructivism for teacher education. It includes the following three thematic articles: (1) A Developmental-Constructivist Approach to Teacher Education [Black, A. & Ammon, P., pp. 323–335]; (2) Engaging Teachers in Emancipatory Knowledge Construction [O'Loughlin, M., pp. 336–346]; and (3) Constructing New Forms of Teaching: Subject Matter Knowledge in Inservice Teacher Education [Mosenthal, J. H. & Ball, D. L., pp. 347–356].

The Constructivist Classroom [Thematic Issue]. (November, 1999). *Educational Leadership, 57.*

The following articles are presented in this issue: The Many Faces of Constructivism by David Perkins;The Understanding Pathway: A Conversation with Howard Gardner by Marge Scherer; The Courage to Be Constructivist by Martin G. Brooks and Jacqueline Grennon Brooks; Getting the Discussion Started by Margaret G. McKeown and Isabel L. Beck; Problem Solved: How to Coach Cognition by Karoline Krynock and Louise Robb; Strategies for Mathematics: Teaching in Context by Michael Crawford and Mary Witte; What Is a Standards-Based Mathematics Curriculum? By Lynn T. Goldsmith and June Mark ; Art Lessons: Learning to Interpret by B. Stephen Carpenter II; When Students Create Curriculum by Marsha Grace; Does the Universe Have a Job? By Catherine Bennett, Jacqueline Grennon Brooks, and Nancy Morvillo; Helping Students Ask the Right Questions by Cynthia Richetti and James Sheerin; In New Zealand A City Site Classroom by Perry Rush; Constructing Knowledge, Reconstructing Schooling by John Abbott and Terence Ryan; To See the World in a Grain of Sand by Steven Levy; Architects of the Intellect by Robin Fogarty.

WEB SITES

Heylighen, F. (1997). Epistemological Constructivism. In
F. Heylighen, C. Joslyn & V. Turchin (Eds.), *Principia Cybernetica
Web*. Brussels: Principia Cybernetica [On-line]. Available:
http://pespmc1.vub.ac.be/CONSTRUC.html.

This web article gives a basic overview of constructivism and its philosophical background. It contains many links to related information,
including radical constructivism, social constructivism, constructivism:
from philosophy to practice, and one to other constructivist sites.

Price, B. J., McFadden, A. & Marsh, G. E. (1999). *Constructivism
and Related Sites* [On-line]. Northport, AL: Emtech.net.
Available: *http://www.emtech.net/links/construc.html*.

This website contains links to over one hundred articles and essays on
constructivism. The links are categorized into those dealing with controversial issues, major theorists, and general topics related to constructivism. The Emtech homepage itself has over fifty links to
educational topics, including constructivism and learning theories.

Riegler, A. (1999). *Radical Constructivism* [On-line]. Available:
http://www.univie.ac.at/cognition/constructivism/index.html.

This web page leads to over 400 links to constructivist organizations,
theorists, definitions, software, periodicals, and conference information. There are also links to full text archives of books and papers concerning constructivism, including documents which deal with the
application of constructivist theory to education.

Ryder, M. (1999). *Constructivism* [On-line]. Denver: University of
Colorado. Available: *http://carbon.cudenver.edu/~mryder/itc_data/
constructivism.html*.

This web page is a collection of over seventy links to other web pages
and articles on constructivism. The links are categorized into basic definitions, readings by various theorists, corollary sites, and a small section on Vygotsky.